Runway Visions

ALSO BY DAVID KIRK VAUGHAN
AND FROM McFARLAND

*Flying Adventurers: Juvenile Aviation Series Books
in America, 1909–1964* (2023)

Words to Measure a War: Nine American Poets of World War II (2009)

MiG Alley to Mu Ghia Pass: Memoirs of a Korean War Ace
by Cecil G. Foster with David K. Vaughan (2001)

*Runway Visions: An American C-130 Pilot's Memoir
of Combat Airlift Operations in Southeast Asia, 1967–1968* (1998)

Runway Visions

*An American C-130 Pilot's Memoir
of Combat Airlift Operations in
Southeast Asia, 1967–1968*

Second Edition

DAVID KIRK VAUGHAN

VOICES IN AMERICAN MILITARY AVIATION
Series Editor David Kirk Vaughan

McFarland & Company, Inc., Publishers
Jefferson, North Carolina

All photographs are from the author's collection

LIBRARY OF CONGRESS CATALOGUING-IN-PUBLICATION DATA

Names: Vaughan, David Kirk, author.
Title: Runway visions : an American C-130 pilot's memoir of combat airlift operations in Southeast Asia, 1967-1968 / David Kirk Vaughan.
Other titles: American C-130 pilot's memoir of combat airlift operations in Southeast Asia, 1967-1968
Description: Second edition. | Jefferson, North Carolina : McFarland & Company, Inc., Publishers, 2024 | Includes index.
Identifiers: LCCN 2024021199 | ISBN 9781476694689 (print) ∞
ISBN 9781476652719 (ebook)
Subjects: LCSH: Vaughan, David Kirk. | Vietnam War, 1961-1975—Personal narratives, American. | Vietnam War, 1961-1975—Aerial operations, American. | United States. Air Force—Biography. | Air pilots, Military—United States—Biography | Airlift, Military—Vietnam. | Hercules (Turboprop transports)
Classification: LCC DS559.5 .V38 2024 | DDC 959.7/04348092 [B]—dc23/eng/20240513
LC record available at https://lccn.loc.gov/2024021199

BRITISH LIBRARY CATALOGUING DATA ARE AVAILABLE

ISBN (print) 978-1-4766-9468-9
ISBN (ebook) 978-1-4766-5271-9

© 2024 David Kirk Vaughan. All rights reserved

No part of this book may be reproduced or transmitted in any form or by any means, electronic or mechanical, including photocopying or recording, or by any information storage and retrieval system, without permission in writing from the publisher.

Front cover images: C-130E taking off from the field at Dak To, South Vietnam; *inset* author standing under the wing of a C-130E on the ramp at Cam Ranh Bay, South Vietnam. Both photographs dated 1967.

Printed in the United States of America

McFarland & Company, Inc., Publishers
Box 611, Jefferson, North Carolina 28640
www.mcfarlandpub.com

Dedicated to

all those who flew, are flying, or will fly the Lockheed C-130,
one of the classic aircraft of all time, in any of its configurations

and to those who flew the C-130 in Southeast Asia,
especially to those who died in the line of duty,

and to the following individuals,
who were important to me personally in my flying career:
Al Williams, Larry Fordham, Virgis Hill, Jerry Coleman,
Irving Torchinsky, Les Fredericks, Sidney Richardson, Kirk Waldron,
Gomer Lewis, Howard Dallman, Ross Kramer, Horace "Horse" Pemberton,
Frank Passarello, Bill Knipp, Tommy Lee Butler, Edgar "Bill" Lorson,
Elmer "Dusty" Watkins, Frank Kricker, Ed Scholes, Mike Brown,
Mike Jones, Roger Wright, and Don Greenwade

and most especially to the memories of
Karl Klein and David Risher

Table of Contents

Preface	1
Introduction to the Revised Edition	5
Poem: "Visions of Runways"	7
Before	9
1. New Guy	11
2. The View from the Air	18
3. Check Out	27
4. On the Shuttle	36
5. Rubber Plantations and Banana Runs	47
6. Da Nang ABCCC	55
7. Piece of Cake	62
8. The Golf Course	70
9. Blackout Flight to Khe Sanh	77
10. Orbit City	81
11. Phan Thiet in Blue	87
12. Long Night over the South China Sea	96
13. Dancing in the Alligator House	102
14. Ground Pounder	109
15. Gear and Flaps Man	114
16. Taipei R&R	119
17. Christmas at Khe Sanh	123
18. Bao Loc in the Fog	133
19. Tet	144
20. Rising Dust at Dak To	156
21. Blind Descent to Kham Duc	164
22. Low Visibility at Quang Tri	171

23. Bangkok Shuttle	179
24. Old Head	187
After	198
Poem: "Incident at Tuy Hoa"	200
Postscript	201
Pronunciation Guide	205
Military History of David K. Vaughan	207
Index	209

Preface

When I was flying in Southeast Asia from February of 1967 until April of 1968, I did not keep notes of my airborne activities. I have often wished since then that I had. The letters I wrote home were for the most part void of the details of my specific flying tasks and experiences. My comments were typically something like this: "Just got back from flying the shuttle for sixteen days in Vietnam. Glad to be able to take a long, hot shower. Going to fly again in two days, to Naha, Clark, and Bangkok." Who had the time—or the capacity for self-analysis—to adequately describe the full range of experiences those words summarized? Sometimes, later in my time in Southeast Asia, I spoke into small reel-to-reel tapes. Talking into a microphone was easier than sitting down to write. It was also therapeutic. But the content of those tapes was superficial also. I suppose I viewed my messages home as evidence of my continued safe existence and the slow but steady passage of time until my tour of duty was up and I returned to the States.

It did occur to me in the final hectic months that detailed accounts of my experiences might provide interesting reading. But I realized that if I were to write about my experiences in Southeast Asia, it would take time, time that I did not have. I told myself that I would undertake that task, fill in the details, after I returned. However, when I returned to America, my life in Southeast Asia seemed increasingly remote, and it did not seem important to revisit those experiences. Besides, some of my experiences were not the kind that you could describe easily. About some of the more hazardous flying experiences, you could say, if you were willing to admit it, "I was nervous," but even that brief statement conveyed little of the range of sensations involved.

And how to describe the activities of your off-duty hours, when those activities, which involved relationships with women from Taiwan and Thailand, were the kinds of things you were not supposed to engage in, not if you were a responsible husband and upright son of proud, if worried parents? Some details better left unreported, perhaps? But those off-duty activities were important because they helped you maintain your emotional equilibrium. They constituted an essential part of the total account and were as important as the flying activities.

Whether you are a fighter pilot, bomber pilot, helicopter pilot, or cargo pilot, flying in combat changes you; the more intense or frightening the experience, the more profound the changes. Although the military system and social expectations try to condition you to encounter stressful experiences without internal change, change does occur, and if you are to survive in something like a state of psychic wholeness, you do what you need to do to compensate for stress. It's not a planned thing, your compensating activities, you just do them. And the things you do—your actions, reactions, and behaviors—may not be the kinds of things you have been conditioned to do or tell others about, especially if those others have not shared experiences similar to yours. Nor are you able, if you are honest, to be particularly proud of all of the things you have done, inside the aircraft or out. But if your hope to relate anything like a truthful account, you must describe all aspects of your behavior, as best as you can recall—those you would readily admit having done, and those you would rather not admit having done, those activities that make you uncomfortable, that make you squirm a little as you write about them.

To accommodate the possible discomforts of the often unpleasant truths of combat, some writers camouflage their experiences under the guise of a novel. Novels allow writers to manipulate experiences and events, to say things that might be embarrassing in an autobiographical work. But I did not want to write a novel, not about what I felt and experienced when I flew C-130s in Southeast Asia. To me that would misrepresent, trivialize, or worse, sensationalize the experience. And so I have tried to tell what life was like for me when I was on duty, when I was off duty, when I did my job pretty well, and when I screwed up. Fortunately for me and those with whom I flew, I did my job mostly successfully and my screw-ups caused minimal distress.

In telling my story, I have tried to illuminate the flying activities of the crewmembers of the C-130s who flew in Southeast Asia, the A-model men, the B-model men, and the E-model men. Most especially, however, I recall the efforts of the E-model men who flew with the 345th Tactical Airlift Squadron and the other two squadrons of the 314th Tactical Airlift Wing, the 50th TAS and the 776th TAS, at Ching Chuan Kang Air Base, Taichung, Taiwan, with whom I flew for the better part of fifteen months in the hazardous skies of Southeast Asia. The names of many of these men appear in the narrative that follows. Some names appear briefly, others appear more frequently. A few names I have changed.

Although I made no notes of my experiences in Southeast Asia, I did keep a log of missions flown, takeoff and landing times and dates, aircraft numbers, and airfields visited. I also collected other kinds of documentation that helped to jog my memory: some squadron crew lists, flight orders, duty rosters, and a few clippings from the base and division newspapers.

I have not attempted to recreate the complete account of my fifteen months of flying in Southeast Asia. The details of some missions are vague and hazy in my mind. Those flying tasks we did regularly, commonplace, unexceptional, redundant events are blurred in memory. Those events that were exceptional stand out vividly. The dialogue I include in the narrative is my best effort to reconstruct conversations as they occurred. I have not invented the occasions of those conversations. I can clearly recall the subject matter, the setting, the environment of those conversations. In some cases, I vividly remember words and phrases.

To the best of my ability to recall, the events described occurred at the time indicated. I may have remembered the sequence of events incorrectly, but all of the events occurred. There is one unique aspect of telling a story as a C-130 crewmember: at least three or four other people were present when the event occurred. Unlike some pilots, who fly alone in the cockpits of their aircraft, C-130 pilots are never alone; the co-pilots, flight engineers, navigators, and loadmasters are there too. If the pilot is inaccurate in his account, other knowing voices will soon correct him.

Preface

This account is not just about me and those individuals with whom I flew; by extension, it is the story of all C-130 crews who flew in Southeast Asia at the time. The Lockheed C-130 Hercules is one of the safest, most rugged, most reliable aircraft ever made. It has been in the Air Force inventory for forty years and may well remain in the inventory for forty more. [Note: as of the date of this revised edition, 2023, it has been in the Air Force inventory for nearly seventy years, flying with updated engines, cockpit displays, and extended fuselages.] I would be willing to bet that more people have flown the C-130 or maintained it or supported it than any other USAF aircraft. It has been adapted and modified to perform numerous specialized duties, from gunship to hurricane hunter to aerial refueling. Each one of these versions has its unique story. This book is an account of one pilot's experiences flying the C-130 E-model into normal and abnormal airfields often under normal but occasionally difficult or hazardous circumstances. That is the story this book tells.

Introduction to the Revised Edition

In the years since *Runway Visions* first appeared, many readers have communicated with me directly, in letters and e-mails, telling me that they enjoyed reading my account of those distant days. In addition to several positive reviews that appeared in a number of magazines and journals at the time of initial publication, over 260 readers have provided comments on Amazon. Some readers stated that the book helped them visualize the activities of parents or other family members who had flown or worked on the various versions of the C-130 (in addition to the E-models, the A- and B-models) that carried supplies through the skies of Southeast Asia. Now those early versions of the C-130 have been retired, replaced by the H- and J-models, with new engines, new propellers, new glass cockpits, and modernized (in some cases extended) fuselages. The C-130, now as then, has been modified to fit various missions: weather reconnaissance (WC-130J Hurricane Hunters), special operations (MC-130H Combat Talon), and gunship (AC-130U "Spooky"). It has become a much more technologically advanced aircraft than it was fifty years ago. Its evolution into ever more mission-specific tasks does not surprise me, as I fully appreciated its muscular strength and adaptability over half a century ago.

One never knows how a book will affect readers. When I was teaching my Air Force Literature class at the Air Force Institute of Technology in 1998, I included a chapter from what was then a draft of *Runway Visions* in the course readings. The chapter described my landing at the Dak To army camp, in the hills of South Vietnam, in January of 1968, shortly before the Tet Offensive of that year. While most of the students in the class were rated officers (pilots and navigators, mostly captains and a few majors) with extensive flying experience, one student was a non-rated first lieutenant who had been in an administrative position. As the class drew to a close, he told me that the course readings (especially my account of flying C-130s in Vietnam) had inspired him to apply for a pilot training slot. He was accepted into pilot training and became a C-130 pilot, eventually flying in a Special Operations C-130 squadron. I would like to think this book would similarly affect other readers.

This revised edition contains several new episodes and expanded versions of previous episodes. Some readers of the first edition complained that I had not sufficiently described the operation of the aircraft systems or the interior of the C-130 cockpit. I had in fact originally included such a description when I wrote my first draft of *Runway Visions* but decided not to include it because I thought that such information would be too technical and uninteresting. I have restored that section in this revised edition. I have added a few new episodes describing both operational and off-duty activities. Realizing that some readers today might not have been alive at the time these events occurred, I have also added a few explanatory details.

I have also taken advantage of improvements in digital technology to upgrade the quality of the original photographs and have added several new photographs which help to convey not only the challenges of operational flying, but the unusual conditions of flying in a combat zone. I have included these additional photographs to provide a larger, more complete context to help readers visualize the challenges the C-130 crew members faced on a daily basis.

It is difficult to believe that it has been twenty-five years since *Runway Visions* first appeared. The events which that book describes occurred thirty years earlier. That means that the events described occurred fifty-five years ago! To me, and I'm sure to many who were there, it does not seem possible that half a century has passed since we were engaged in that unfortunate Southeast Asian conflict.

I thank Steve Wilson, editorial director at McFarland & Company, for encouraging me to prepare this revised version. He and the editorial and production staff have consistently helped me to create books that, when published, appeared much better than I envisioned them as I worked on drafts.

Visions of Runways

Approaching the field, the old head told the story
of the South Vietnamese army guard standing high
in his foxhole at the end of the coastal runway.
One of our crews, low on short final, bounced
their main gear off his unsuspecting helmet.
New to the business, thinking it funny, I grinned.
Later, on a day blue in rain, heavy with doubt,
I landed badly on that thin, wet strip, and my legs
shook with movements of their own as I tried
to stop the heavy aircraft. Ah, those small, hard,
runways, their names a grim two-step cadence:
Phan Thiet. An Khe. An Hoa. Kham Duc.
Dak To. Khe Sanh. Their visions now, as then,
dryness in the mouth, tightness in the lip.

Before

The light was bright in the early October afternoon. It reflected off the concrete ramp at Dyess Air Force Base, located on the west side of Abilene, Texas. The ramp was filled with a number of large aircraft, B-52s and KC-135s, not surprising because Dyess was a Strategic Air Command Base. There were also a few C-130Es, the aircraft I was flying. In the distance, to the south, were the short flat mesas that typified west-central Texas. I had just come from a meeting with Colonel Sidney Richardson, the squadron commander. I had told him that I was volunteering for one of the C-130 aircrew openings at Ching Chuan Kang Air Base in Taiwan. I had been on Dyess AFB for only a little over seven months, yet I had just told Colonel Richardson that I wanted to leave Dyess so that I could fly cargo planes in the war in Southeast Asia. After asking some questions concerning my motivation for volunteering, he told me he would approve my request.

Bill Knipp didn't believe it. Bill and I had been assigned together for a long time, through a year of pilot training at Webb Air Force Base in Big Spring, Texas, and then two years as young lieutenant copilots flying obsolete KC-97s for Strategic Air Command at Selfridge Air Force Base near Detroit.

"What do you mean, you volunteered?" he asked. He was incredulous. "Haven't you learned never to volunteer? We haven't been on base a year. You don't have to go yet."

"The way I see it, it doesn't make much difference," I said. "We go now, we go a year from now. Will it be any better a year from now?"

It was late in the summer of 1966. President Johnson had announced another increase in troop strength in Vietnam. His weathered visage was a familiar sight on the television screen, as he solemnly announced the necessity for even greater numbers of American armed forces to assist the South Vietnamese in making their country and, by extension, all of Southeast Asia safe for democracy.

I remembered my pilot training tactical officer at Webb Air Force Base, Captain Scott "Press-on" Smith, gleefully rubbing his hands together three years earlier as he told us of the potential of Vietnam as an arena for aerial combat. We flying students had found it hard to believe that a shooting war might occur anywhere in the world, much less in the distant lands of Southeast Asia. The last aerial combat had taken place in Korea, several years before. In 1963 few of us had heard of Vietnam.

The latest list of assignments consisted of vacancies at a recently established C-130E wing at Ching Chuan Kang Air Base. The B models, we knew, were flying out of Mactan Air Base, in the Philippines. We'd heard less than enthusiastic reports about living conditions there. The A models were flying out of Naha Air Base in

Okinawa. A nice place, but an assignment there meant an accompanied three-year tour. The E models were the best of the C-130 cargo fleet, in my opinion, with external tanks and the latest navigation and communications gear. With their extended range and proven durability, they were given the most interesting missions.

I had been flying E models at Dyess. I liked flying E models. If I had to fly in Southeast Asia, I wanted to do it in one of the few aircraft the Air Force had that was fun to fly. And I didn't particularly want to retrain into anything else, even a fighter. I had a special fondness for the E-model of the C-130. I had been flying it for less than a year and was just beginning to feel comfortable in it. And although the base in Taiwan had just been established, we'd heard favorable comments about it.

"What does your wife think about your volunteering?"

"She's not happy about it."

"Where's she going to live?"

"Go home and live with the family, I guess." Bill and I were both from Michigan.

"When do you leave?"

"My port call is in four months—early in February."

Bill walked away shaking his head slowly. He liked it at Dyess and didn't want to leave. I liked the area, too. Abilene, Texas, was a nice place to live, and Dyess was a good place to fly out of. Lots of wide open spaces for low-level navigation missions at 500 feet, a clear and unobstructed drop zone west of the north-south runway to practice personnel and heavy equipment drops. Low altitude ground proximity extractions. Assault landings. A good place to come back to after extended missions to Europe, Africa, the Far East.

But events in Southeast Asia were happening too quickly. I thought it was a good idea to try to anticipate, at least a little, the movements of the forces that were turning us. And so, in early February 1967, I boarded a contract air carrier at McChord AFB in Spokane, Washington, for the long flight to Japan, Taipei, and finally, Taichung, Taiwan, my home for the next fourteen-and-a-half months.

Chapter 1

New Guy

We had flown all night from McChord Air Force Base, south of Seattle, a plane full of officers and enlisted men in a contract air carrier bound for the Far East. Over two-thirds of the passengers left the airplane at Tachikawa Air Base, near Tokyo, Japan, and the remainder of us milled around the flightline coffee shop waiting for the plane to refuel for the shorter flight to Taiwan. When we arrived at Taipei airport, the sun was just beginning to lighten the eastern skies. We waited in the airport at Taipei, smelly, rumpled, tired. Two hours later a C-130 from the wing at Ching Chuan Kang Air Base (CCK AB) arrived, and we carried our bags through the open cargo ramp at the rear of the aircraft. Twenty-five of us assorted aircrew, maintenance, and support personnel settled ourselves into the uncomfortable red cloth seats. After a half-hour flight to CCK, we stepped out through the C-130 crew entrance door into the bright morning light on the CCK flight line. The sun was in my eyes above the hangars to the east, and I held my hand up to shade the glare. The morning air was pleasant, warm, and fragrant, the land surrounding the base flat and fertile.

I walked along the flight line, looking for my new squadron, the 345th Troop Carrier Squadron, and found it located in a newly completed concrete block building. A couple of aircrew members walked by, said hello, and directed me to the squadron commander's office. The squadron commander, Lieutenant Colonel Robert Craig, shook my hand.

"Hello, Vaughan. Just arrived?"

"Yes, sir. Just got off the airplane."

I handed my flight records to him.

"Thanks. Where you from?" He started flipping through the pages of the package I had just handed him.

"Dyess Air Force Base, Abilene, Texas. I was in the 347th."

"How much time do you have?"

"Over thirteen hundred hours total," I said. "Four hundred in the C-130."

"Aircraft Commander qualified?"

"Yes, sir. I got checked out as aircraft commander before I left Dyess. But I wasn't there long enough to have a crew."

"Okay," he said. "We'll try to get you checked out and on the schedule as soon as possible. We've got a lot of troops who are anxious to rotate Stateside. You'll find that flying in Southeast Asia will be the toughest, most challenging flying you'll ever do. Flying in the States is nothing compared to the flying you'll do over here. Get yourself squared away and check in tomorrow. We'll try to get you out on a trip right away."

The clerk in the billeting office assigned me a room in a new officers' dorm, located five blocks from the flightline. "They're not bad," he said, "much better than the tents we used to have."

My roommate was Major Les Fredericks, an experienced navigator who had come over on the plane with me and with whom I had often flown at Dyess. We each had a small but comfortable metal frame bed, a dresser, a night stand, a desk. Next to the window was a refrigerator. Our beds were made and rooms kept clean by a Taiwanese house boy. I quickly emptied my green B-4 bag of its few belongings, wondering how long it would be before I would feel that this sparsely furnished room was home.

Three days later, I was scheduled for a late-night departure with one of the squadron's experienced instructor pilots, Captain "Duke" Williams, suave, good-looking, easy-going. Duke gave the impression of being on a continuous high, a feeling created, no doubt, by the knowledge that he was shortly to leave CCK for the States, returning to "the land of the big BX," as he was fond of saying, to be checked out in one of Military Airlift Command's new C-141 cargo aircraft.

Duke led me out of the squadron building to base operations, a large structure built by the Chinese Air Force in the days (not so long ago) before the Air Force arrived at CCK. Chinese personnel were in charge of flight clearances, while Air Force personnel ran the weather briefing station. Duke filled out the Form 175, the flight clearance form, with the dexterity of a year's practice. He helped me prepare maps with our route of flight penciled in, so that I could follow our progress while we flew.

Our route of flight would span much of the area I would be flying over in the next year: the first leg: from CCK to Clark Air Base, in the Philippine Islands. Then from Clark across the South China Sea to Bangkok, Thailand, overflying the northern portion of South Vietnam on the way. We would be given our remaining flight schedule when we arrived at Bangkok.

In the lighted aircraft, the loadmaster and flight mechanic were busy completing their preflight inspections and securing the load, mostly packaged in crates and boxes, on three pallets. A few passengers were settling in for our three-hour flight to Clark Air Base. We started engines and taxied out of the parking area. I sat in the right seat and read the checklist while Duke steered the aircraft through the darkness toward the end of the runway. The four turboprop engines generated their familiar, peculiar growling sound as we taxied. After we completed our before-takeoff checklist, we departed to the north. We turned left into the darkness of the night, swinging around to the west briefly, until we were over the Formosa Straight, the thin strip of sea separating Taiwan from mainland China. The island of Taiwan, shaped approximately like a teardrop, was separated from mainland China by less than one hundred miles.

We turned south gradually, heading for the southernmost point of the island of Taiwan. Our departure route avoided the mountains that formed the north-south backbone of the island of Taiwan; they sat like a fence on the east side of the island, rising to a height of twelve thousand feet. We climbed steadily to our en route altitude and headed south toward the Philippine Islands, across the South China Sea.

We landed at Clark Air Base, north of Manila, at 1:30 in the morning and parked near base operations, where a forklift removed our few loaded pallets and replaced them with others. After a quick tour of the airlift control center—our operations

WESTERN PACIFIC AREA, 1967-1968

Map of Western Pacific Area, 1967–1968.

center—and a visit to the flight line snack bar, we were back in the aircraft, starting engines, taxiing out. We departed to the north, turning left to climb past Mount Pinatubo in the dark. We leveled off at cruise altitude, heading west toward the coast of South Vietnam.

I sat in the right seat, surrounded by the instruments and controls of the cockpit environment. On my left hand, the four throttle and four propeller condition levers rose out of the center console that separated the pilot and copilot seats. The C-130 was powered by four turboprop powerplants; a turboprop consisted of a jet engine driving a propeller. There were two controls for engine operation instead of the standard single control—the throttle—typically found in most jet-powered aircraft. Our throttle levers worked much like the throttles of a jet engine—moving them fully forward provided full thrust. Moving them fully to the rear provided minimum in-flight thrust.

Once the throttles were fully to the rear, at the flight idle position, they could be lifted up, over a mechanical stop, and pulled farther to the rear. This position gave minimum forward thrust, used on the ground for taxiing. Pulling the throttles farther to the rear caused you to hit a detent. Beyond that detent was the reverse thrust range, provided by the action of the propeller blades moving from the forward thrust blade angle to the reverse thrust blade angle. We used reverse thrust during the final segment of landing and for backing out of tight parking areas. The application of reverse thrust was crucial for landing at short fields. Reverse thrust could be applied only after the weight of the aircraft was on the gear; reversing the propellers in flight would have catastrophic consequences.

When we landed, we moved the throttles from the forward thrust range to the reverse thrust range steadily but carefully; we wanted to avoid a situation in which one propeller blade would remain in the forward thrust area while the other three propeller blades entered the reverse thrust area. In such a situation, if full power were applied (by pulling all four throttles to the full reverse stop), three propellers would provide full reverse pitch while the propeller that remained in forward blade angle would produce full power in the opposite direction. This situation could cause loss of directional control, and resulting in a serious accident, especially if the propeller of an outboard engine were producing full thrust.

We always paused for a moment during landing when we moved the throttles from the forward thrust range into the reverse thrust range to make sure all four propeller blades had moved into the reverse thrust range. Because the pilot was fully occupied keeping the aircraft moving down the centerline of the runway, he relied on the flight engineer (and the co-pilot, and anyone else in the vicinity who cared to look) to tell him that all four propellers were safely in the reverse thrust range. This indication was shown by a fluctuation of the needles on the torquemeter gauges, located in front of the engine control console.

The throttle levers were located to the pilot's immediate right; farther to his right were the propeller condition levers. These levers, one for each propeller, were used to control propeller angle when starting the engine, when shutting the engine down, and during in-flight emergencies, when it was necessary to feather the propeller, to place the propeller blades in streamline position into the wind to reduce drag on the aircraft in flight.

When the pilot was flying the aircraft and needed to move the throttles, he merely had to move his right hand slightly to the right, off his right-hand arm rest, and grab the four throttles. When the copilot was at the controls, however, he had to reach past the propeller condition levers to the throttle controls with his left hand. This left-handed reach was a little unusual and took a little getting used to. Normally, of course, the pilot flying the aircraft was sitting in the left seat. The copilot sitting in the right seat read the checklist and assisted the pilot in command as necessary. The copilot was responsible for communicating with the ground and traffic control stations over the radio.

If there were two fully qualified pilots flying the aircraft, they would normally take turns sitting in the left seat on each leg of the flight. However, an instructor pilot checking out or giving instruction to a new pilot in the left seat normally sat in the right seat; but he had to be capable of operating the aircraft safely from the right seat. He had to be adept at handling the throttles with his left hand.

Aircraft movement on the ground was maintained through the use of nosewheel steering, which was controlled by the pilot sitting in the left seat. A small round steering wheel was located at the pilot's lower front left position, which the pilot could easily reach with his left hand. The pilot controlled the movement of the aircraft on the ground by steering it with his left hand and controlling the throttles with his right hand. While the aircraft was taxiing, the copilot held the yoke (control wheel) and control column immobile.

On takeoff, as the aircraft picked up speed, the pilot gradually released the nosewheel steering and took control of the aircraft by grasping the yoke with his left hand. On landing, the pilot controlled the aircraft with the yoke until the speed of the aircraft slowed sufficiently and then maneuvered the aircraft off the runway using the nosewheel steering.

A pilot sitting in the right seat could maintain directional control of the aircraft on the ground only through use of the rudder pedals (at higher speeds) and the brakes, also controlled through the rudder pedals. Toe pressure applied to the top of the rudder pedals would result in braking action. Pressure to the left rudder pedal caused brake pressure to be applied to the main wheels on the left side of the aircraft, and pressure on the right rudder pedal created braking on the main wheels on the right side. The aircraft could be steered from the right seat relatively easily by an experienced pilot adept at the use of differential braking and throttle manipulation.

The engines of the C-130 gave an unmistakable growl as it taxied on the ground, a sound that fairly suggested the strength and power of the aircraft. Its appearance as it taxied also suggested strength, for it resembled a large animal, an overgrown groundhog with wings, trundling down the road, with a slightly protruding nose created by the placement of the radome beneath and in front of the cockpit. Looking at it

C-130 cockpit. This photograph of an Air Force Reserve C-130 crew, taken after the conflict in Southeast Asia ended, clearly shows cockpit details. The flight engineer, on the left, is probably updating his fuel log. The photograph was taken from the navigator's position.

parked on the ramp, you might not think that it was capable of smooth and graceful flight, but when it lifted into the air, any doubts vanished.

In the center console, in addition to the engine controls, were the radio controls, one set for our standard UHF (ultra-high frequency) radio, another for our less-used VHF (very high frequency) radio, and a third for our even less-used HF (high frequency) radio, which we used only for extended overwater flights (across the Atlantic or Pacific, or the South China seas) or to contact operational control centers from remote locations. Here were also the controls for the navigation radios, the TACAN, the VOR, which combined to give us our bearing and distance from known stations, and the little-used automatic direction finding (ADF) unit.

Ahead of me, on the copilot's side of the front instrument panel, were the copilot's aircraft control instruments, the altimeter, aircraft attitude indicator, compass, and the turn and bank indicator. The pilot had a similar set of indicators in front of him. In the center of the instrument panel, easily visible to both pilots and the flight engineer who sat immediately behind us, were several sets of engine instruments: turbine inlet temperature gauges, exhaust gas temperature gauges, oil pressure gauges, and turbine RPM (revolutions per minute) indicators.

Mounted on the top center of the instrument panel was our radar scope, whose image repeated that of the radar scope located at the navigator's position. To my right rear, below my side windows, were the control switches for our airdrop indicators, my oxygen mask connector, and a panel of fuses and circuit breakers. A few feet behind my right shoulder was the navigator's position, where the navigator sat at his desk, watching his radar scope and navigation instruments, marking the progress of our flight on his map and in his flight log.

Just behind my left shoulder sat the flight engineer. His elevated seat was located immediately behind the center console; he had an unobstructed view of the engine instruments on the main instrument panel and easy access to any of the engine controls if he needed to act in a hurry. Over his head was the fuel control and air conditioning panel; he was responsible for maintaining control of the fuel as it fed from the wing and fuselage tanks into the engines. Using the controls on the air conditioning panel, he tried to maintain a comfortable temperature in the cargo compartment, an impossible and thankless task given the primitive system he had to work with.

A few steps behind the engineer and to the right of the navigator's position were two padded benches, one above the other, the equivalent of a double-deck bunk; these bunks were secured to the back wall of the crew compartment. There was room for two people to sit comfortably on the bottom bunk, three in a pinch, and if we carried only one or two passengers, we would normally invite them to sit up front with us. If we chanced to carry women passengers, a rare event, they definitely sat up front, and we spent more time looking at them sometimes than we did monitoring our progress through the air.

The upper bunk was not easily accessible but there was not enough room for anyone to sit on it, for there was only about a four-foot clearance between the top bunk and the top of the cabin. We often threw our larger B-4 bags and duffel bags onto the top bunk. Above the top bunk was a removable circular hatch which we would use to climb up on top of the fuselage while we were parked on the ground if we needed to inspect any part of the exterior surface of the fuselage or either wing. The fuel tank filler caps were located on the top of the wing, and the flight engineer often used this exit to monitor refueling activities, especially when it was necessary to refuel in remote fields.

More often than not there were no passengers, especially when we flew in-country, and our loadmaster would sit on the bunk after he completed his after-takeoff walk-around inspection. It would be one of his first tasks after takeoff to see if any of us needed coffee (we always needed coffee, especially flying at night), and he would fill our paper cups from one of the coffee jugs located at the rear left of the crew compartment, at the right side of the stairs leading down to the crew entrance door on the left front side of the aircraft fuselage, forward of the number two engine. In all, the C-130 crew compartment was a comfortable and even pleasant working environment, made even more enjoyable by the twenty-three window panels which extended across the cabin from left to right.

Chapter 2

The View from the Air

This leg of our flight lay west across the South China Sea, over the northern section of South Vietnam, the southern tip of Laos, and then across Thailand to Korat and Bangkok. It was still dark and no lights appeared below. If there were ships on the sea, I couldn't see any evidence of them. After flying west from Clark for over an hour, the distance measuring equipment (DME) portion of the TACAN navigation system showed that we were one hundred nautical miles east of Da Nang.

Above us, the sky was slowly lightening. Thin wisps of cloud moved past beneath us. Ahead, small points of light appeared, swinging, swaying slowly beneath us. Along the irregular coastline a hilly peninsula of land jutted out into the water to the east, and behind it a large circular bay with the city of Da Nang, a good-sized city, to the west, and two long north-south parallel runways extending south of the south end of the bay. Around the southern and western edges of the airfield flares appeared, suspended beneath parachutes, swaying as they descended into the fog and dark. I looked for the aircraft that was releasing them, but it was too hazy, too dark, and I saw only the flares, appearing magically at regular intervals of time and space around the perimeter of the area.

As we passed over the area, the sun's rays reached the land beneath, illuminating first the hills to the west and north, then the flat land around the bay. Slowly, as the sunlight spread, the flares diminished.

Duke reached down to the autopilot control on the console between us, turned the knob, and brought the airplane a few degrees to the left to our new course outbound from the Da Nang TACAN. Then he went back to reading the *Time* magazine he had bought at the Clark snack bar. He ignored our aerial progress over the terrain below.

"Why all the flares?" I asked.

Duke looked up and smiled. "Maybe they're scared of the dark. Keeping the bogeyman away."

He showed me the article he was reading. "Says here we're not in Laos. But we are. Not officially, of course, but we've got operations going on in there all the time. Hell, look at your map. Laos and Cambodia separate Thailand and Vietnam. How could we operate in Thailand and Vietnam and not be in Laos? We couldn't afford to fight a war with that kind of geographical split. Besides, the Ho Chi Minh Trail runs along the east side of Laos from Khe Sanh to Dak To and beyond. The fighter boys are flying interdiction along it all the time, and we've got lots of stuff going on up in the Plain of Jars—that's northern Laos—too. You can hear them talking all the time on guard channel."

Chapter 2. The View from the Air

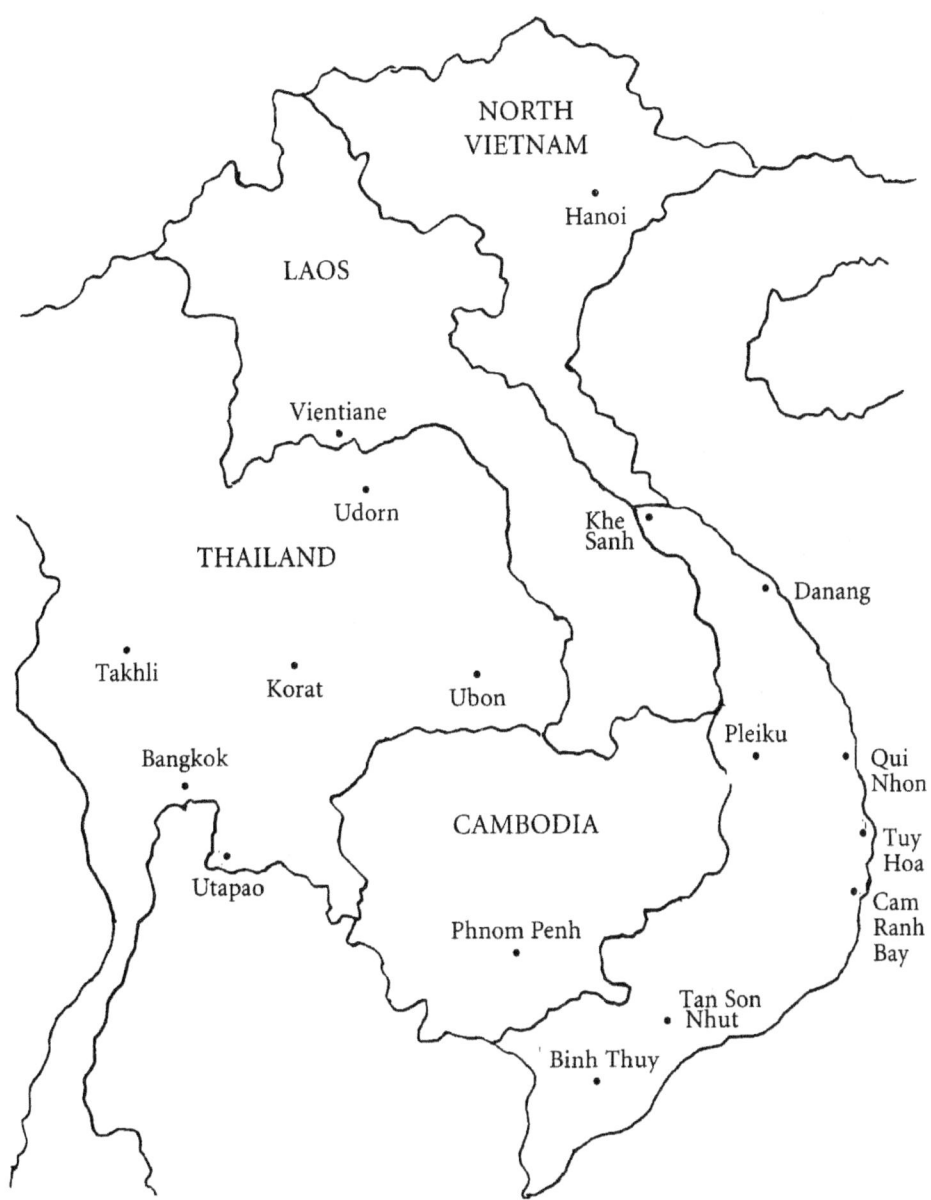

SOUTHEAST ASIA, 1967–1968

Map of Southeast Asia, 1967–1968.

"Cambodia, now, we steer clear of that place," he continued. "Or if we are in there, it's really secret, because we never overfly any part of the country. Right now we're following the main route of flight, from Da Nang to Ubon to Korat to Bangkok. If we have to fly south of Cambodia, we fly out over the Gulf of Thailand to the southern tip of Vietnam, and then up to Saigon. There are a lot of black holes around here, and Cambodia is one of the biggest. But it's no big deal flying across the southern end of Laos. Just try not to have an emergency landing down there. More than half of the natives are unfriendly."

He pointed to the chart. "You can see the minimum altitude posted for flying on this route. They figure most of the hand-held weapons can't reach any altitudes higher than that. The heavy, scary anti-aircraft guns are farther north."

The mountainous territory over which we had been flying since we passed Da Nang flattened slightly, and we passed over a large river, flowing north to south. "The Mekong," said Duke. "It makes a clear and obvious landmark along the northeast border separating Thailand and Laos. It flows through the middle of Cambodia and empties into the delta region of South Vietnam."

After we crossed the Mekong, the land beneath flattened considerably, and villages and farms appeared in the forest growth. We soon began our descent into Korat, landing to the west on its long, wide runway. Numerous F-105s were lined up in neat rows. "This base and Takhli are the two F-105 bases," said Duke. "Their pilots have the toughest mission of the war."

Korat was surrounded by lush green vegetation. The base seemed new, clean, efficient. On the large concrete ramp were Lockheed EC-121s, large, four-engine radar-carrying aircraft. There were Douglas C-47s, the twin-engine cargo aircraft built during World War II. Low, two-story buildings were laid out in an orderly fashion beyond. We off-loaded our few pallets of cargo and loaded a few passengers for the hop to Bangkok.

The flight from Korat to Bangkok was short—less than half an hour. We climbed to 5000 feet, then let down into Don Muang, the airfield that served Bangkok. The bright morning sun was reflected in the ground water, in small streams, fields, rice paddies. We lined up on the left of two long parallel runways. "We use the south runway; civilian aircraft use the right runway," Duke pointed out. "Our aerial port facilities are on the south side." A few aircraft were parked on the ramp; they apparently belonged to the Royal Thai Air Force—a few helicopters and some North American T-28s, a low-wing, single-engine prop-driven aircraft.

Don Muang airport was located ten miles northeast of the city of Bangkok, too far out to see much of the city as we landed. A Thai driver in a mini-van drove us into the city. He drove down a wide street flanked by modern-looking buildings. The Thai men were dressed in short-sleeve shirts and casual pants, and the Thai women wore longer, fashionable dresses. There were some areas of poorer housing, but in general the city presented a cheerful appearance, especially with the Thais on bicycles or carts or in automobiles filling the streets with traffic. There was a rich, humid aroma of fried food, spices, vegetation, and occasionally decaying matter. It was the smell of Bangkok.

I expected that we would be housed in something like a military compound with two-story military barracks. Instead our driver drove us up to the entrance of a small but modern hotel before which stood a tall, well-built Thai in a dark uniform. "Ah," said Mike "Brownie" Brown, our loadmaster, "here's Sinbad, waiting to welcome us to Bangkok."

"Sinbad?" I asked. "That's really his name?"

"That's what he calls himself," Brownie answered. "We've never heard him called anything else."

Chapter 2. The View from the Air

As we stopped in front of the hotel door, Sinbad stepped over to greet us, a gold tooth shining in his gleaming smile. "Welcome to Bangkok, gentlemen. You have a good flight? You ready for the pleasures of Bangkok? You want good food? Thai jewelry? Thai girls? I know where to get them. All number one."

Brownie smiled at me as he grabbed his bag. "See? Now you know how he makes his money. If you go to one of the places he recommends, he makes a fistful of baht." A baht was the fundamental unit of Thai money, worth about a nickel.

"The pleasures of Bangkok," said Brownie. "I don't know about you, Captain, but I'm going to hit the pool." On the other side of the lobby sat a circular pool with one or two palm trees overhanging it. Four women in bikinis were sipping drinks at the pool's edge. Two of them looked American.

"American women?" I asked, surprised.

"Probably officers' wives or girlfriends waiting for visits from their husbands or men friends who are stationed up-country," Brownie said. "If they're out here by the pool at this hour, you know they're lonesome. How about a swim?"

The hotel room was pleasant and airy. The windows were open, letting the morning breeze blow in before the afternoon heat and humidity increased. The bed was firm, a thin foam mattress on a wood plank. A bit of movement on the whitewashed wall caught my eye, and suddenly a small lizard zipped across the wall and paused to check me out before disappearing around the corner.

By the time I walked out to the pool, Brownie was engaged in a conversation with one of the women, an attractive brunette. The other woman, a striking blonde, was talking to a well-built guy in a military haircut. Brownie came over. "They were waiting for two friends to show up. One of them showed. The other didn't."

"No problem, Brownie. I'll just lie here in the sun and enjoy life in the combat zone."

So this was what war in Southeast Asia was like. Smoke and flares over Da Nang, beer and good-looking women, American as well as Thai, in Bangkok. I fell asleep by the pool.

Our load back to Clark the next afternoon was light: three pallets and four young men wearing hospital greens who stepped out of a bus marked with a large red cross and onto the aircraft. Two of them had obvious medical problems: a broken arm, one man on crutches. One had an escort, two air policeman wearing well-pressed fatigues sitting on each side of him. Brownie told me he was a supply clerk at one of the bases in Thailand who had used a .38 sidearm to shoot out windows and lights in his supply building, so they were sending him home. Brownie said later he smiled all the way to Clark.

The flight to Clark was the reverse of the route over: across Thailand, a little of Laos, a little of South Vietnam, the South China Sea, into Clark at dusk. Clouds billowing up from the land, from the sea, a picture book flight through the sunny skies of Southeast Asia. Autopilot on, coffee cup in hand, I studied the area maps and charts.

The Clark Officers' Club was a large, comfortable building busy with activity. The dining room was quieter than the rest of the club, but not much. After we ate we sat at the bar, which was filled with people. A band was playing and the room was noisy and vibrant. A good-looking nurse came in and Duke struck up a conversation with her. I put a few coins in the slot machines, won a little, lost more. I drank a few more beers, then walked back to our crew trailer. The night air was warm and moist and smelled of tropical flowers.

The following day we flew west again. We were stopping first at Tuy Hoa, then Bien Hoa, and finally Tan Son Nhut. I knew that Tan Son Nhut was the airfield that served Saigon and that Bien Hoa was a large supply center northeast of Saigon that lay at the heart of the American army's war effort. Tuy Hoa I had never heard of.

"Tuy Hoa is a new field," said Duke. "Right on the coast. Like Cam Ranh Bay. They're pouring a lot of concrete on a beach and calling it a runway, an airfield. We've had a lot of missions into it the last few weeks."

We were arriving about an hour before sunset. We let down through the clouds, whose colors showed a mix of gold and blue. We leveled about ten miles off the coast and could see inland for several miles below the overcast. The field at Tuy Hoa was set up on the beach in the middle of a wide flat valley that ran to the west from the sea with mountains several miles to the north and west and hills to the south. One or two large ships sat at rest in the waters offshore.

"There it is." Duke pointed. I saw something that looked like a small brown road.

"We're going to land on that?" I couldn't believe it was the runway. It was much too narrow, too short. Where was the tower, the taxiways, the parking ramp?

"It's an aluminum matting runway," said Duke, squinting into the sun, which was breaking through the cloud layers, as he turned the aircraft south onto a right downwind. "It can make a bit of noise when the weight of the aircraft settles on it. Just hope they've got it all tied together tight. One strip comes loose, a piece of it can poke a hole in your tire. But they're pretty safe normally."

Duke brought the airplane around, wings level, and rolled out on final approach. A left crosswind was blowing across the runway, but Duke handled it without trouble. We landed with a graceful thump! I tilted forward into my shoulder straps as Duke simultaneously applied reverse thrust and brakes.

"Where do we unload?" I asked, as we rolled to the end of the runway.

"Right here. They haven't got around to building a separate offloading ramp yet." We shut the engines down as a forklift came chugging around the corner of a hill of sand.

"We might as well sit in the cockpit and wait," Duke suggested. "It won't take them long to offload, and I doubt that we'll have a load for Bien Hoa." Duke pulled on the handle of his pilot's side window and slid it back to let the breeze in. I opened the window on my side.

"Is this a safe area?" I asked, apprehensively. I couldn't see any kind of perimeter, and the shadows from the hills to the west were growing longer; in a few minutes they would reach the field and our aircraft.

"So far, it is. Nothing here for anybody to attack, yet. No airplanes, no supplies, and the location is out of the way. The whole operation reminds me of a Boy Scout camp. But after it gets built up and the airplanes come in, yeah, Charlie'll be around. Another six months."

To the west, I thought I saw another aircraft. The light of the setting sun made it difficult to see clearly. "Is that another C-130 parked over there?" I asked pointing.

"Yeah, you could say that," Duke snorted. It looked like the profile of a 130, the balloon-like fuselage, the high tail. But much of the aircraft was missing, the wings, the engines.

Duke leaned back and squinted into the light of the setting sun. "It was one of the first 130s to land at Tuy Hoa. It landed long and went off into the sand. The crew tried to get it out by backing, but just got it stuck more firmly. So they asked the Army for assistance."

Duke laughed again. "The Army assisted, all right. They got a bulldozer and a chain. Tied the chain through the open parachute doors to pull it out of the sand. The bulldozer moved forward but the aircraft didn't. They succeeded in bending the parachute doors—practically sliced through the fuselage. Then they decided to move it from the other end—ran the chain around the nose wheel steering."

"What happened?"

He shrugged. "They bent the nose gear. Screwed the aircraft up real good. So there it sits. Used it for some kind of office for a while. They come and take it away a little bit at a time, piece by piece." He chuckled to himself.

The first field I land on in Vietnam, and I see an unfinished runway, no tower, no airfield facilities, no perimeter fence, no roads. And what is the one thing I do see? A shell of a C-130 parked on a sand dune. One thing I knew for sure: if I had tried to land at Tuy Hoa, I would have done the same thing—off in the sand for sure. I had never landed on a runway this short. A small metal strip by the sea. People pulling pallets out of the tail end of the aircraft and carrying them behind some sand dunes. First Da Nang, hidden underneath layers of smoke and falling flares, and now Tuy Hoa, a short strip in a world of sand.

By the time we were offloaded it was dark. We took off to the south and climbed to the southwest. With the exception of a few towns, the countryside was unlit. Soon, however, we saw flares and lights ahead. "Must be coming across An Khe," said Duke. "The Army's got a big base there, part of a supply line between Qui Nhon on the coast and Pleiku farther west."

I looked at my map. The names Duke had mentioned didn't mean anything to me. Qui Nhon. There it was, on the coast south of Tuy Hoa. An Khe. About fifty miles inland from Qui Nhon. Pleiku was even farther inland, another fifty or sixty miles to the west.

Once past An Khe darkness prevailed. Then, a glow on the horizon. More flares. Duke gestured. "The city of Saigon. Bien Hoa's this side of it, slightly to the right. See the rotating beacon?" In the darkness I saw the turning green and white lights of the rotating beacon.

Approach control cleared us to land. Duke asked for firing advisories and was given a negative. "Always check on firing advisories when you come in to Bien Hoa," he said. "The Army's got a big artillery support base here. They can fire out to the Cambodian border, which is not that far away. Our problem is avoiding the firing outbound. Their shells go up to three, four thousand feet before they begin to descend again. Five thousand is usually a safe approach altitude if they're firing. You don't want to become a casualty of friendly fire."

"The problem," Duke continued, "is that approach control's firing information is always at least a half hour to an hour old. If the Army artillery folks get a call for fire support, they fire first and tell everybody else later, especially if it's an emergency. It's pretty safe coming in at night, though, and you can see the artillery fire easily. It's like an immense flash bulb going off. Then you hear the boom. You hear a boom but don't see the flash, watch out; they're probably underneath you."

We landed to the southwest at Bien Hoa. In spite of the darkness we could see North American F-100s and Cessna AT-37s, jet-powered fighters, parked in revetments. Farther along were a number of Fairchild C-123s, twin-engine cargo aircraft. We pulled

Map of airfields in South Vietnam, 1967–1968.

into the parking area in front of base ops. To the left of base ops was a concrete platform, over which extended a metal roof supported by posts. No walls. A few Army troops were sleeping on benches and duffel bags. There were two pallets of cargo for us to take to Tan Son Nhut.

Bien Hoa departure control cleared us immediately to Tan Son Nhut approach control. "The two fields are twenty miles apart," Duke explained, "and Tan Son Nhut's the busiest airfield in Vietnam. You don't call them until you're at the designated VFR traffic entry point. Then, if it's clear to enter, you give a quick call and get off the air."

As we approached Tan Son Nhut, Duke looked out the cockpit, left and right. "Tan Son Nhut's a busy place, even at night. The problem is at night you've got lots of aircraft flying around with their position lights turned off, gunships, spookys, fast movers. They're supposed to turn their position lights on when they approach the airport area, but sometimes they forget. Or don't want to."

The city of Saigon was brightly lit in contrast to the darkness of the surrounding countryside. To the south and west parachute flares descended slowly. The dark shadow of the Saigon River wound its way up from the southeast; several ships were tied up in docks.

As we turned downwind, I noticed a firefall of tracer fire off to the west. "Spooky," said Duke. "An Army patrol must have run into some VC over that way and called in the Spook." The Spook was a C-47 gunship, a twin-engine cargo aircraft converted into a flying gun platform, with a Vulcan cannon sticking out the left side of the fuselage. It looked like a solid stream of tracer fire falling steadily to the ground beneath. I wondered aloud about the intense activity so close to the airfield.

"Cambodia's only twenty-five miles away," said Duke. "Full flaps." I lowered the flaps, more fascinated by the aerial display to our west than by the complexities of the Tan Son Nhut airport.

Tan Son Nhut featured two parallel runways which ran approximately east and west. "We use the inside runway, the one close to the ramp," he said. "The outside runway is longer; the fighter types and large cargo haulers use that one. If you are landing to the west, like we are, land long. That way you have a shorter distance to taxi to the C-130 cargo loading center. If you're landing to the east, try to land in as little room as possible and make the first turn off. It reduces time on the runways and taxiways and makes the folks in the tower happy. It also means you have to spend less time taxiing."

We parked among several other C-130s, mostly A-models, characterized by their three-bladed props and small tip tanks, and B-models, which had four-bladed props as we had but no exterior tanks. In front of us was a small two-story building with a tin roof. "That's our cargo-hauling office, the airlift command element, or ALCE for short," Duke said.

We walked the short distance across the ramp and went in. Inside, air conditioner units in the windows provided the cool, slightly mildewed smell typical of all ALCE units in country. There was a desk with a status board and an officer and a couple of NCOs working behind it. Down the hall was a crew rest room with soft drink and candy machines. A television set was tuned to the Saigon Armed Forces Network station and two or three bodies were dozing in vinyl-covered chairs.

We had arrived late in the evening, too late to find a room on base. Instead, we were instructed to stay in a contract hotel in Saigon. The first hint I got that Saigon wasn't like Bangkok was the blue Air Force bus that came to carry us into town: wire mesh screens over the windows. The windows were down to let what little breeze there was pass through the bus. We asked the driver why the mesh. "Don't you read the papers?" he asked. "A month or so ago some Vietnamese guy on a motorbike lobbed a hand grenade into an open window. Killed some Army troops."

The bus made its way slowly into the traffic moving along the half-lit streets of Saigon. The girls on their áo dài outfits, riding on the backs of the small motorcycles, hanging on to their boyfriends, seemed preoccupied, as if they had a business meeting to attend. The bus bounced us around unmercifully; the hard seats and the insufficient springs on the bus jolted us at every one of the numerous bumps in the road.

We pulled up in front of a dimly lit, nondescript structure three stories high. It was gloomy and forbidding. Even Duke seemed surprised. "This is it?" he asked. The driver nodded. "Everybody out," he said. The small lobby was ill-lit. "Where's the pool?" I asked Brownie, joking. "No pool," responded the Vietnamese clerk. "Where do we eat?" asked Duke. "No food," said the clerk. "Unless you go downtown Saigon." It was after midnight. "No thanks," we said.

Brownie saved us. He was toting a large brown box. "What is it?" I asked. "C-rations," he said. "I found it in the cargo compartment after we offloaded at Tuy Hoa." He smiled. We bought a few cans of warm beer at the desk and climbed up the steps to the top of the hotel.

The roof of the hotel was dimly lit by a light from the stairway which led to it. The lights from the city of Saigon shone fitfully through the trees scattered around the sides of the hotel. There were a couple of beat-up folding chairs; the rest of us sat on a low concrete ledge that bordered the roof. We drank our warm beer while Brownie cracked open the box of C-rations.

Duke squinted in the dark to read the labeling on the box Brownie handed him. "I can't read the writing on these boxes," he said. Someone lit a match. "I'll be goddamned," said the flight engineer. "These are Korean C-rations! Where'd you get these, Brownie?" he asked.

"They were on one of the pallets we off-loaded at Tuy Hoa," said Brownie. "Those must have been supplies for that Korean Tiger outfit that's operating in the area," Duke said. "I hear they're a mean bunch. Like to cut the ears off all the VC they kill."

"They'd have to be a mean bunch if they can eat this stuff," said the flight engineer, digging into one of the cans. I cautiously opened one. It smelled spicy. "What is it?" somebody asked. "Kimchi, probably." It tasted as spicy as it smelled. "Thank god we got beer," somebody said. "Warm beer," somebody else said.

We sat quietly, eating the spicy food, drinking the warm beer, the lights of Saigon shining upon us through the leaves of the surrounding trees, while beyond, to the west and south, the parachute flares descended with mechanical regularity, tracer fire ascended and descended sporadically, and overhead flew darkened aircraft, helicopters, jets, their noise mixed with the sounds of the city.

"This is the life," said Duke. "A ring-side seat on the night life of Vietnam." He raised his can of beer. "Vaughan," he said, "this is all yours. Welcome to the exciting life of a cargo pilot in the combat zone. May you profit from it." He drained the remainder of his beer in one gulp. "I'm going to bed."

We all followed his example, trudging downstairs to fall asleep in our ill-lit, uncomfortable rooms.

Chapter 3

Check Out

"We've got to get you ready to fly in-country on the shuttle," Lieutenant Colonel Craig said to me. "I've put you on the local schedule to practice some assault landings and air drops."

These maneuvers were practiced at the CCK auxiliary field, twenty miles south of the main field. Colonel Craig, the squadron commander and an experienced instructor pilot, was checking me out himself. We took off at nine in the morning on a bright, sunshiny day. After turning left, we approached from the west, maintaining 1500 feet of altitude, crossing over the rice fields that covered the western plains of Taiwan. The visibility was reduced by the sea haze typical of the area.

I was in the left seat. Colonel Craig, in the right seat, suggested I make a normal landing first, before attempting my first assault landing. We flew straight over the runway at 1500 feet. As we passed over the far end, I turned the aircraft to the left to enter the downwind leg. "Gear down," I said. Craig moved the handle, located in front of him, firmly down.

"Flaps fifty," I said. Craig placed his left hand on the flap lever, located to his left, and moved it to the rear. The lowering flaps caused the aircraft to lift slightly as it slowed; I adjusted for the changes in aircraft attitude with the trim button on the top left-hand portion of the pilot's yoke. The approach end of the runway began to slip under my left wing, and I made another 90-degree turn to the left to place us on base leg, simultaneously reducing power and easing the nose forward to begin my descent.

I turned to final, rolling out about a half mile from the end of the runway, 500 feet above the ground. "Full flaps," I called, and Craig lowered the flaps to the full down position. Again the aircraft lifted and then slowed, and I adjusted the elevator trim so the aircraft felt reasonably light on the controls. "Not too bad," Craig commented. "But in some of the smaller fields in Vietnam you won't want such a wide pattern." I expressed some surprise to myself, having flown what I thought was a pretty tight pattern, especially for a first landing at a field I hadn't seen before. But aloud I said nothing.

I came in over the end of the runway, pulled the throttles back to the flight idle position and flared slightly, pulling the yoke gradually back and feeding in nose up trim with my left thumb. The aircraft settled in for a relatively smooth landing. When the weight of the aircraft was clearly on the main gear, I lifted the throttles over the stop and into the detent, waited for the engineer to announce "clear to reverse."

It was the flight engineer's job to observe the engine torquemeters for appropriate indications that the blades of all four engines had gone into the reverse pitch range. If one of them hadn't, then instead of producing reverse thrust when I pulled the throttles into the reverse thrust range, the uncooperative propeller would produce forward thrust, resulting in an extremely dangerous asymmetrical thrust situation, producing severe controllability problems at a crucial moment during the landing sequence. But the props functioned properly, and I pulled all four throttles to the full reverse stop. The aircraft slowed noticeably.

I maintained directional control with the yoke, then, just before the airspeed slowed to a point that I could no longer hold the nose of the aircraft up, I said "Your yoke," released the yoke, which I had been holding all the while in my left hand and reached for the nose wheel steering. Colonel Craig immediately grabbed the yoke to prevent it from slamming forward or thrashing about. I applied the brakes and the aircraft slowed to a stop.

"Okay," Colonel Craig said. "Taxi it around for takeoff and we'll do some assault landings, unless you want to make another landing?"

"No," I said. I doubted I could make any better landing than the one I had just made.

"That landing wasn't too bad. But you'll need to speed things up when you do an assault landing, especially at the moment of touchdown. Your movements have to be accomplished much more quickly and smoothly." We taxied back to the end of the runway.

I thought that I had made a good landing, moving the aircraft controls with better than average swiftness. I wasn't sure that I could demonstrate a much more aggressive, more accurate approach and landing than the one I had just made. I checked the flaps, held the brakes, ran the engines up, then released the brakes. With no load, we moved forward quickly and were soon airborne. "We'll leave the flaps and gear down," I said. On downwind, I glanced down at the runway, which was passing rapidly out of sight under my left wing. I reduced throttles, turned base, started my descent, and, when the time seemed right, began a turn to final approach. So far so good.

"Too high," Craig said. "Remember, you're aiming for the end of the runway. That means right where the runway marking begins, not fifty or one hundred yards farther along."

Oh. Okay. In the States I never aimed for the exact end of the runway. But I wasn't in the States any longer. I pushed the nose over. Now I was aiming for the end of the runway, but something didn't feel right. Airspeed. Too high. I retarded the throttles abruptly. I should have pulled the throttles back at the same time I pushed the nose over.

"Flaps?" Craig asked.

"Full flaps," I said. Damn. Things were going to hell in a handbasket. As the flaps extended, the nose of the aircraft rose slightly. The end of the runway disappeared under the nose of the aircraft. Trim. Nose down. Now nose up. Power off, throttles to idle.

"Keep your wings level."

Lift the left wing—how did that happen? Here comes the runway. Flare! Pull back on the yoke! Too late. I had an awful feeling of not really controlling the aircraft at the moment of contact with the runway. I felt like I was aiming the aircraft at the runway and flying into it. I didn't feel as if I had much to do with the outcome of events.

The aircraft slammed into the runway with a great rattle of noise and dust. "Jesus Christ!" I heard somebody say. It might even have been me.

With my right hand I pulled the throttles back to the stop, then over and into the detent, forcing myself to wait until the engineer called out "cleared to reverse," and pulled them back to the limit of their travel in reverse range. Instantaneously the aircraft began to slow. I remembered I needed to use brakes also, and applied them much too heavily, pushing forward with the balls of my feet on the top part of the rudder pedals. The aircraft slowed in a series of jerks, as I pumped the brakes erratically.

"Nose wheel steering," called Craig. I released the yoke and grabbed the nose wheel steering with my left hand. The aircraft was moving more or less in a straight line down the runway, but the airspeed had long since dropped below the speed at which the ailerons were effective. The aircraft slowed almost to a stop, and I moved the throttles back into the forward pitch range. Finally the aircraft came to a stop. We were well past the mid-point of the runway. I wasn't sure how much runway I had used up, but I knew it was more than I should have.

Colonel Craig reached down and moved the flap lever from full flaps to half flaps. "Let's taxi around and try it again. Everybody okay in the back?" The navigator, engineer, and loadmaster appeared to have survived the impact, and not only that, were willing to ride through another one. Good sports. I imagined they had seen worse landings, but I wasn't about to ask.

We tried three more assault landings, and by the time I was through I began to feel a little more comfortable with my ability to manipulate the aircraft. At least I was

C-130E demonstrating an assault landing on a dirt strip at Fort Leonard Wood, Missouri, November 1964. Presumably the pilot moved the propeller blades into forward pitch before the aircraft was completely engulfed by the dust cloud it created on landing.

getting the aircraft stopped near the mid-field mark. "Okay," Craig said finally. "Let's call it a day." We headed back to CCK.

We shut the aircraft down and walked into the ops building. Colonel Craig talked to me briefly. "How many assault landings have you made?" he asked.

"Probably two or three, when I checked into the 347th, in February or March, and then another three or four, back in October."

"So you've done maybe five in the past year?"

"About that."

"Mmm. Well, you'll do a lot more before you're through with your tour here. Making a successful assault landing is probably the most important maneuver you can do while you're flying in-country. If you can't do it well, some people might get hurt and some airplanes might get bent. You need to practice some more, to get some more experience, before you're fully qualified.

"Our pilots are classified according to the length of runway they're capable of landing on. They're listed as normal, assault, or short-stop qualified. *Normal qualified* means you are able to land on longer runways 3500 feet in length or greater. *Assault qualified* means you can land on runways as short as 2900 feet. *Short-stop qualified* means you can land on runways as short as 2200 feet. Many of the runways in-country are 3500 feet long or longer. But some of them are in the 2000 to 3000 foot range, and those are ones you've got to be able to land safely on. Right now you're in the normal category, and if you want to fly in-country you need to be at least assault qualified. So you've got a lot of work to do.

"You're scheduled for some air drop practice tomorrow," he continued, "and I recommend you do a couple of assault landings at the end of the mission. You remember the old saying about the three most useless things to a pilot? The airspeed you used to have, the altitude above you, the runway behind you? Well, it's true about the runway behind you when you shoot an assault landing—always aim to land at the exact end of the runway. Otherwise you won't make it into—or out of—some of the small fields you'll encounter in Vietnam." He turned and walked into his office.

I stood in the hall near his door, remembering my reactions when I had made my first assault landings back at Dyess. I hadn't said anything to Colonel Craig about how bad my landings had been then. I had never gotten used to the idea that this large, four-engine aircraft was supposed to slam onto the runway like some kind of Navy aircraft trying to catch a hook on a carrier deck. The idea of plumping this high-wing cargo aircraft onto a dirt strip and making a panic stop was foreign to everything I'd learned in my previous flying experience. Landing this relatively large aircraft in a relatively short distance was one of the most bizarre departures from normalcy I had ever encountered. I hadn't gotten used to it at Dyess and I certainly wasn't used to it here. I heaved a deep sigh. How would I ever be able to execute such an unusual and demanding maneuver?

I needed some diversion. I asked some crew members lounging against the operations counter, "What's the easiest way to get into Taichung?"

"You haven't been in yet?" one of them asked, eyebrows raised. "Well, your indoctrination isn't complete until you've been to town," another one said. He was one of the navigators in the squadron. "Tell you what, I feel like going into town myself. If you want company, we can go together."

Just before ten o'clock in the evening, dressed in slacks, short-sleeved shirt, and

Chapter 3. Check Out

a light jacket, I walked down the road to the main gate. My navigator was waiting. "Ready?" he asked. I guessed I was.

We walked past the entrance gate. The first in a string of small red cars moved towards us. "It's about seven miles into town," my friend explained. "The taxi is the best way in. Some of the support troops buy bicycles or motorcycles for transportation, but for us flying troops, it's not worth the expense. We're just not here that much." We got in the back seat and closed the doors.

The Taiwanese driver didn't ask "where to?" but took off in a hurry. Once again I was venturing into new territory in the dark. The road into Taichung was roughly paved, not especially well lit, and narrow. We passed through one small community, or at least I judged it was that, because I could see one or two stores, and one or two street lights. Our speed, which seemed pretty rapid for such a small vehicle on such a small road, did not decrease.

Eventually, we saw more street lights and then businesses and houses, which I assumed were part of the city of Taichung. The town looked prosperous, though it seemed unusually dark. The combination of faint florescent lights, sparse street lights, and weak display lights from the shop windows made the crowded city streets seem mysterious, unsafe. The special aroma of the city came in through the cab window as well, the sweet-sour smell of Chinese cooking.

"Since you're new here, I'll show you the main attractions," my guide volunteered. Our first stop was a large nightclub on the north side of town. It featured a live band and was crowded with people dancing, Taiwanese women and American and Taiwanese men. We had a drink at the bar. While we were sitting there, I noticed that we were being given the visual once-over by a group of women sitting at a nearby table.

Two girls walked up to us. "Hi GI. You buy us drink?"

My escort said, "No thanks. Not this time, sweetheart. I'm just showing my friend around. We're going to be leaving soon. But tell us your names in case we decide to come back."

"My name is Mary," said one.

"My name Sally," the other one said. "Come back soon, GI." They smiled and walked away.

The nav saw my look. "What's the matter?" he asked.

"Their names," I said. "Not what I expected."

"Oh, they all adopt American names. It's easier for us to talk to them. We have trouble saying and remembering their Chinese names. When you're talking to a woman named Mary, it seems a little less like you're a thousand miles from home sitting in a dark bar trying to forget the pressures of the job."

"One other thing you need to know," he said. "When you buy a girl a drink, she drinks iced tea. The bar profits from the drinks we buy the girls; iced tea is a lot cheaper than whiskey or beer. The girls stay sober and the bar makes money. But some guys get sore if they don't know about the system. When you buy a girl a drink, the bar makes money. That's the way the system works."

Outside, he gave the taxi driver instructions, and we headed into the central part of the city. The navigator leaned over. "Each of the squadrons has its own watering hole. The place we just left, a lot of the guys from the 50th hang out there."

The taxi pulled up in front of another bar. I thought we were getting out, but the nav held my arm. "It's getting late. Let's go over to the 345th hangout. But in case you ever want to know, this is where the 776th guys like to come." He gave the taxi driver more instructions, and we headed further into town.

"Do the members from the other squadrons get upset if you go into their bar?" I asked.

"Oh, no, not at all. It's just that the guys on the crews tend to party together when we're in town. And there's never that many of us around. Seems like we're always on the road."

The taxi driver drove up a street leading away from the train station. In the middle of the block on the right-hand side was a small, nondescript building. In neon lights over the door was a sign that said, in English, CHINA NIGHTS. "This is the 345th's unofficial club."

We went through the door. There was a bar along the left rear wall, some booths along the right wall, and a few chairs and tables in front. There was a wooden dance floor and some American music was playing. Two or three long florescent lights were suspended from the ceiling at the front and over the bar.

In the back booths several women were sitting and talking, a few smoking cigarettes. There were one or two other men in the bar, which otherwise seemed deserted, at least compared to the last place we had been. The navigator and I sat at a booth towards the front.

"Do you have a regular girl here?" I asked.

"Yes. She would have come over already, but she's waiting until they decide who's going to come with her."

"What do you mean?"

"To see who drew your lucky number."

Even as he was speaking, I saw two girls detach themselves from the group and walk slowly but carefully over. One was taller than the other. "You want company?" the shorter one asked. But she wasn't looking at me. My companion grinned broadly and patted the seat beside him. "Sure," he said, sliding down the padded seat toward the wall.

I looked up at the other girl. She was tall, one of the tallest girls I had seen in Taiwan. Not that I had seen that many. "Hi," I said, sliding over to make room.

The tall one sat down beside me. She was exotically attractive in a long silk dress, her dark hair piled up on her head to accentuate her height. The smell of perfume. In a quiet voice she told me her name and then asked, "What you drink?"

"Scotch," I said. She said something to the waiter who had come over. She had a direct look when she looked at me, yet I felt she was reserved, maybe even shy. She sat straight, her hands clasped in her lap. Her companion, however, was evidently familiar with my guide, and was giving him an enthusiastic embrace.

The waiter returned with our drinks. Mine was scotch, sure enough, and hers looked a little like whiskey, a brown liquid in a glass with ice in it. She saw me looking at it. "I drink tea," she said. I nodded and smiled.

"You from CCK? What squadron?"

"The 345th. I just came in from the States." She nodded.

"You want dance?"

I hadn't seen anyone dancing. But the dance floor was there and the music was suitable. "I'm not very good," I said.

"That okay. Slow music."

Chapter 3. Check Out

We got up and went onto the dance floor. I was surprised at her height. She had heels on, and with her hairdo, she was taller than I was. Few women I had known were as tall as she. I felt awkward and uncomfortable. I wasn't sure I wanted to be there. I'm not sure I'm ready for this, I thought. I held her lightly, at a distance. She was light on her feet and graceful, and when I made a misstep she pretended not to notice.

When we returned to our booth, my navigator and his girlfriend had moved and were sitting at a more secluded booth in the back, talking, their heads close together.

"How old you?" she asked.

"I'm twenty-six," I replied. "And you?"

"I twenty-five." I studied her. It was hard to tell. Twenty-two, maybe twenty-three. Her face was smooth and from what I could see, unlined. But her brown eyes were wary and showed some unhappiness.

Abruptly, she asked, "You have wife?"

"Yes," I said, after a pause, deciding there was no point in lying.

"How long you married?"

"Almost three years." She took her time processing this information.

"You have children?"

I shook my head. "No."

I realized I hadn't heard her name when she mentioned it. "Tell me your name again. I didn't hear it when you told me before."

"Karla."

My head popped back suddenly and I gave her an astonished look. My amazement showed clearly.

She must have thought I was surprised that she had an American name. "That not real name. That American name. What's the matter? You no like name?"

"Oh, no, it's a nice name. I like it very much. It suits you well. It's nothing. I just didn't expect you to have that name." My explanation wasn't very convincing.

We talked some more, danced again, and then, as a group of men, clearly from the base, came in, she looked over at them and suddenly stood up, saying, "You excuse me now. I have customer."

I didn't know how the evening was going to end, but I didn't expect it to end like this. "Oh. Oh, sure."

She looked at me. "You come back and see me again?"

"I think so," I said. "Yes, I think so."

She smiled and walked over to one of the men, not looking back. While we had been talking, the bar had filled. I looked around for my guide, but he was not to be seen. I went outside. A little red taxi immediately pulled up and the driver asked, "Base?" I nodded and got in. As the car raced down the narrow road I kept thinking over the evening's events, shaking my head in disbelief.

How could this tall, slender, good-looking woman who lived on the opposite side of the earth from me have chosen that name? How could she have chosen the same name as my wife's name?

* * *

The next day I was scheduled for my airdrop practice with another instructor pilot, a captain I had never seen before and never saw again. "This is my last flight," he told me, as we walked out to the airplane. "Going back to Pope." Pope AFB was co-located with Fort Bragg in North Carolina.

We departed CCK to the northwest, began a low-level navigation training route, simulating an extended low-altitude run into the drop area. In Texas we had flown for hours over the sparsely populated areas of scrub and desert west of Abilene, bouncing along in the hot, dry air at 500 feet. Here, however, our available area for navigation training was limited. We turned inland, heading for our auxiliary base. As we approached the auxiliary field, we called the tower and told them we were approaching. About this time the flight engineer said, "We've got a slight problem. Number one engine has a mild RPM fluctuation."

Sure enough, the needle on number one tachometer was wobbling slightly. But if the prop were moving as the indicator showed, changing speed as rapidly as the needle was moving, we would have felt and heard the sensation. It would have been a steady irregular pulsing from the left outboard engine.

"We'll keep an eye on it," the IP said. "It's okay right now. I'd like to get this drop out of the way." We were dropping a pallet of sandbags on the dirt strip to the south of the paved runway. The navigator checked his time; simulating a realistic scenario, we were supposed to arrive at a specific time over the target. A newly arrived navigator was being checked out as were two new loadmasters in the rear of the aircraft. On an airdrop the procedures were much more challenging for the navigators and loadmasters than they were for the pilots.

The navigator alerted us at the one-minute point prior to arrival at the pop-up point. When the pop-up point arrived, I reduced power, pulled the nose up, ascending from our en route altitude of 500 feet to 1000 feet, dropped half flaps, and held our airspeed constant at 125 knots. When we had slowed, we gave the loadmaster the red light, the signal to open the cargo doors. At this signal, he deployed the preliminary parachute, a small parachute that immediately filled with air and extended behind the tail of the aircraft. At the set time, the navigator gave the call and the instructor pilot, sitting in the copilot's seat, turned on the green light on a side panel at his right elbow.

When the green light came on, the loadmaster released the main parachute. Once it deployed, he released the locks holding the pallet to the aircraft. The fully deployed parachute pulled the load along the rollers on the cargo deck floor. When the load moved out, the aircraft nose pitched up as the load rolled off the tail. In extreme situations, when a heavy load exited too slowly, the combined efforts of both pilots could be required to push forward on the yoke, to force the nose of the aircraft down before the high pitch angle caused the aircraft to stall. But on this run everything worked smoothly, and the load left the aircraft without a problem.

I was anticipating the opportunity to attempt some more assault landings. After my previous showing with Colonel Craig, it was clear that I needed more work. But it was not to be.

"Let's call it a day," the IP said. "That RPM indicator is still fluctuating."

The engine in question appeared to me to be operating acceptably, but the IP had decided it was time to quit. I judged the mildly fluctuating RPM indication to be a malfunction in the gauge, but it was nothing to treat lightly, for it could also indicate an imminent loss of controllability of the propeller, whose stability was controlled by the prop oil supply. Though the problem was probably not serious, it was probably wise not to ignore it, especially now that the main purpose of the flight had been accomplished. So we landed at CCK after a two-hour flight, and no practice assault landings.

"You'll get plenty of practice in-country," the IP assured me. He seemed preoccupied with thoughts of returning to the States. A few days later I walked into the squadron and saw that I had been scheduled for my first in-country shuttle.

Chapter 4

On the Shuttle

The flight to Vietnam began with a short, two-hour run over to Naha, an air base located on the southernmost point on the island of Okinawa, the scene of intense combat during World War II. The southern part of the island was a major American logistics facility, with harbors and airfields at Naha and Kadena, a larger base about ten miles northwest of Naha. Five other airfields and installations were located along the coasts of the southern part of the island; these belonged to the Army, the Navy, and the Marines.

Our route of flight brought us in from the southwest. We flew over little of Okinawa itself, landing and departing over the clear blue waters of the ocean west of Naha. As we descended on a right downwind, I marveled at the variety of colors and textures of the sea: numerous small rock islands protruded from the water, waves breaking over them. The main island was a rugged outcropping of rock, with the dark blue of the ocean waters lightening in color to aquamarine as we approached the shoreline.

After onloading palletized cargo for Vietnam, we departed Naha shortly before noon and flew an uneventful six-hour flight straight to Nha Trang. The weather was usually clear when we approached the coast of Vietnam from the east in the morning, the mountainous terrain rising out of the sea. We let down through layer after layer of clouds, until finally, under a broken ceiling of clouds at about 2000 feet, we saw the coast ahead. We flew over the south end of the island that sat to the east of the shoreline; our final approach placed us over a ship that was anchored just off-shore.

The airfield at Nha Trang was located at the south side of a wide valley that ran east and west with a river meandering through its center. Farther to the southwest, a long, high hill overlooked the field. The city of Nha Trang, north of the field, lay spread out behind a coastline where the green sea washed gently onto a bright white beach. West of the city a large white Buddha rested on a low hill, looking east over the city to the sea.

We taxied in and shut down the aircraft; there were two or three other C-130s and C-123s parked on the ramp as well. The parking area extended to the south of the runway; beyond that, a large collection of two-story dormitories and administrative buildings ran in rows.

We walked over to the operations building up the outside steps to the second floor. Inside the briefing room were rows of lockers for storing flight gear. Behind a glassed-in window the duty crew monitored aircraft readiness and flight progress of the crews flying missions. Six or seven crew members were lounging around in

Chapter 4. On the Shuttle

Approaching Nha Trang from the east, March 1967. Nha Trang Buddha visible as a small white dot on the right.

Nha Trang ramp, March 1967. C-130 B-model in foreground, three C-123s in background.

various combinations of uniforms and civvies—flight suits, tan summer uniforms, t-shirts, cutoffs.

The crew with which I was receiving my checkout had just departed on an afternoon mission. I was told to walk over to one of the crew buildings and find a bed. The building to which I had been directed was one of several two-story, concrete buildings. Over the windows were thin bamboo mats, rolled down, to keep out the light for the sleeping crewmembers who were scheduled to fly at night. The mats reduced the noise, supposedly, but there was little noise reduction, with aircraft taxiing, taking off and landing. There were two floors of beds and vertical lockers. The beds were Army green metal double-decker bunk beds, draped in mosquito netting. I found what looked like an empty bottom bunk and spread my sheets on it.

Immediately outside was the base movie theater, an outdoor theater where I sat on a green wooden bench and watched a film which had first appeared in the States six months earlier. The film began just as the sun set, and as I watched I could see the flashes in the hills beyond the tall wooden screen. When I heard the noise of the firing, I thought it was thunder and looked for the clouds. I asked the sergeant sitting next to me what the noise was. Firing, he said. Artillery fire. Who? I said. Us, he said. At whom? I asked. Them, he said. "Them?" I asked. He shrugged his shoulders and said, better us firing out than them firing in.

The next morning I rode the bus to the beach recreation area. The sand was white, and the waves of light green water gently broke along the shore, the hills north of the bay dark green. Army helicopters kept moving past overhead, patrolling, I assumed, until I was told they were love-starved helicopter troops eyeballing the American nurses sunbathing farther up the beach. A steady flow of aircraft departed from the base, heading east over the water, camouflaged C-7 Caribou, C-123 Providers, C-47 Gooney Birds, even a shiny metallic and white Australian C-130. I spread my blanket and lay down on the sand.

The following morning I met my instructor pilot, Lieutenant Colonel Frank Passarello, a slender, good-looking, slightly nervous man, whose hair was graying prematurely, probably due to the pressures of the job. I guessed he was the kind of individual who would not tolerate mistakes. The other members of his crew included Lieutenant Mike Jones, navigator; Sergeant Floyd Cupp, flight mechanic; and Airman Mike "Brownie" Brown, loadmaster. I didn't know it then, but we would eventually spend many hours flying together.

Our mission that first morning was the standard in-country passenger shuttle, the pax run, which took us to fields in central South Vietnam, where we picked up Army troops in their tan uniforms and took them out of country on their rest and relaxation (R&R) trips, or back to their units as they returned from R&R. The pax run aircraft was rigged with stanchions in the center of the aircraft with uncomfortable webbed seats attached. The seat backs were formed of red webbing attached to a bar over the passenger's head. The seats ran down both sides of the interior of the fuselage, and two rows ran down the center of the aircraft supported by the stanchions. The passengers sat facing the sides of the aircraft, an uncomfortable position on takeoff and landing, when the leaps and bounces of the aircraft caused the passengers to lurch from side to side.

The pax run was a simple and usually uneventful mission: land, offload passengers, onload passengers, takeoff, fly to the next field, offload, onload. Our route of flight took us over to Cam Ranh Bay, up the coast to Qui Nhon, west to An Khe and Pleiku, back to Cam Ranh Bay, then back along the same route in reverse order: Pleiku, An Khe, Qui Nhon, Cam Ranh, and Nha Trang. Cam Ranh was the pivot point of the shuttle, for its long runway accommodated the commercial jets which brought new troops into and out of Vietnam and which also took them away for their R&R trips, to Australia, to Hawaii, to Hong Kong. The C-130s, and in some cases, the

C-123s, carried the troops from Cam Ranh—and Tan Son Nhut, Bien Hoa, and Da Nang—into the smaller fields around Vietnam. Of the fields we were visiting, I had not yet been to Cam Ranh or An Khe.

The flight from Nha Trang to Cam Ranh was short—about fifteen minutes—straight east and then a short dog leg to the south. Cam Ranh was major port facility for ships and aircraft and was rapidly developing into a major logistics center. The Bay was an inlet on the coast protected by a peninsula of land that came out into the sea and then hooked south. The airfield was located on the north end, and the Army and Navy occupied most of the area to the south. The harbor facility was usually loaded with ships offloading provisions, supplies and ammunition, which was trucked up to the airfield for distribution by air. Many of the supplies were shipped by truck, but the roads from Cam Ranh wound through hilly terrain, which made the Army drivers understandably nervous.

I was flying the aircraft from the left seat. Approach control positioned us on a right downwind for a landing to the north. The runway at Cam Ranh ran north and south, a long slab of aluminum in the narrow sandy neck of the peninsula. Our position on right downwind placed us just off the coast, and through the copilot's window across the cockpit I could see an elevated ridge next to the sea, and behind that a shallow depression filled with buildings of various sizes. This area, I later learned, was the administrative and billeting area of the base. We turned crosswind and then onto a short final.

We landed to the north and taxied to the northwest side of the field, where the C-130 ramp was located. The fighter aircraft, mostly F-4s, were located on a ramp on the east side of the field. The F-4 wing at Cam Ranh was tasked with support for ground operations in the central areas of Vietnam, and whenever the alert birds

On short final for runway 02 right, Cam Ranh Bay, March 1967. Vehicles on perimeter road; F-4s on right waiting to take off.

received a call to assist the Army troops, all other traffic on the field came to a halt while the alert aircraft launched, afterburners roaring, exhausts smoking. An F-4 could be immediately identified by the long dark smoke trail it left behind as it moved through the sky.

We taxied from the north end of the runway into the C-130 loading ramp, located on the northeast corner of the field. There we parked nose-to-nose with another C-130 waiting for its load.

"How do we move out when we are loaded?" I asked Colonel Passarello.

"We back out," he responded. This was a new concept to me. In all my (admittedly limited) C-130 experience, I had never used reverse thrust to move out of a loading area. After our passengers and pallets were loaded, he coached me in the fine art of backing out of a parking spot.

First, the rear loading ramp remained open so that the loadmaster could see out the rear to guide us in our maneuvering. Then, I released the brakes and moved the throttles of the inboard engines into the minimum reverse thrust range. I pulled the throttles back a little more to increase reverse thrust to start the aircraft rolling backwards, but not too much; we did not want to be moving backwards too quickly. And we wanted to avoid overheating our engines while in reverse thrust; no air cooling could occur in reverse thrust, especially in hot weather.

Once we were rolling slowly backwards, I turned the nose wheel steering wheel to the right so that we would begin a gradual backing turn to our right. After the aircraft continued its turn until we were pointed in the direction of the taxiway, I gradually centered the nose wheel steering. Then, once we were correctly aligned with the taxiway, I moved the throttles into the forward thrust position to stop our backwards movement. Passarello provided one crucial piece of information: never, ever,

C-130 Loading ramp. Can Ranh Bay, March 1967. Looking north from the Can Ranh Bay Tower.

Chapter 4. On the Shuttle

step on the brakes to stop the aircraft when it was rolling backwards! Depending on the load distribution, the aircraft could rock back, lifting the nose gear off the ground and causing the protective tail skid on the bottom of the ramp door to make contact with the surface of the ramp. Hitting the ramp with the tail skid was not the major problem; the major problem occurred next, when the aircraft rocked forward, slamming the nose gear into the ground. If that happened, serious damage would result to the nose gear. It was difficult to force myself not to hit the brakes when we were rolling backwards.

We taxied out of the ramp area and took off to the north, straight up the coast to Qui Nhon. We checked in with the ground radar station located on the island north of Cam Ranh and told them we were going north just off the coast (or "feet wet") at 3500 feet. The flight from Can Ranh to Qui Nhon was a half hour long, about the average length of in-country flights. We followed the coastline, and as we flew I admired the rugged, beautiful shoreline, a combination of blue seas, white beaches, and rocky hills. We landed to the north at Qui Nhon, over several ships parked in the small bay to the south.

While we waited for passengers to file out at Qui Nhon I walked around the ramp, amazed to find a couple of operational C-46s, relics of World War II, the first I had ever seen outside a museum. One wore the bright orange and white design of South Vietnam's commercial air carrier, and the other was painted in camouflage colors of the South Vietnamese Air Force.

An extended string of Army Huey helicopters lifted off from the ramp and snaked their way west. I asked Colonel Passarello where they were going. "An Khe,"

C-46, Qui Nhon, March 1967. Many of these World War II–era aircraft were operational in South Vietnam.

he said. "You'd better let me fly the aircraft on this next leg," he said. "The runway at An Khe is a little tricky." Uh-oh, I thought.

We departed Qui Nhon to the north and turned west when we cleared the hill. It was a twenty-minute flight to An Khe. "You need to take time to position yourself for an approach because of the hilly terrain, and you need to look out for helicopters," Passarello instructed. "This place is one of the Army's most active areas; they've got helicopters flying in and out of here on special operations all the time."

The morning air was clear and the visibility was good, and I soon saw helicopters maneuvering just above the trees. The An Khe camp area sat just to the west of a saddle between ridges of higher hills to the south and lower hills to the north. There didn't seem to be much flat ground for a runway. The tower operator was providing a continuing flow of instructions to the helicopters. "They must have some kind of operation going on," Passarello said.

He pointed ahead and to the right. "The field is just ahead. An Khe Golf Course, they call it. I'm going to circle over so you can get a good look at it." He flew to the west for a minute or so, and then banked the aircraft to the right. "There it is. Right down below us."

I peered out my copilot's window looking for the distinctive signs of an airfield: runway, taxiways, parking ramp, hangars, something like a tower. I couldn't see anything resembling an airfield. "I can't see it," I said.

"Right there. Right below us," Passarello said, pointing past my nose and banking the aircraft even more. I saw many buildings, clearly part of an Army camp. But I couldn't see anything I'd call an airfield. "See it?" he asked. I saw something short, narrow, and brown. My god, I thought. Are we landing on that?

"I think so," I said. My heart was sinking. It wasn't a runway, it was a short brown line in the middle of an Army camp. It wasn't a runway, it was a terrazzo, a boardwalk, a promenade. I saw a loading ramp area off the west side at about the midpoint of the runway with two narrow taxiways leading from the runway.

Passarello banked the aircraft to the right again, to the east, setting us up on a short crosswind. The more I looked at the field, the more nervous I became. Passarello turned to the right once more, retarding the throttles, descending. "Gear down," he called. I moved the gear handle down. "Gear down," I said.

"Half flaps," called Passarello. "Half flaps," I responded, moving the flap lever to the 50 percent flap position. "Take a good look at the runway," Passarello said. "You can see it's fairly long, over 3000 feet, but it's narrow. You'll notice also that we have to continue to the end when we land and then use the turn-around area down there to maneuver the aircraft so that we can taxi back up to the ramp, where the offloading facilities are."

"One other problem," he added; "landing to the north, the far end of the runway drops off significantly. As we touch down, the far end of the runway seems to disappear, and it will look as if we only have about a thousand feet of runway remaining. But we really have enough runway; you just have to remind yourself that it's there and not worry about it. Just make a good landing and everything will work out okay." He turned the aircraft from downwind to the base leg, retarding power and lowering the nose.

"Oh" he added, "watch out for those helicopters. You never know what they'll do. Full flaps." As he turned onto final approach, I could see rows and rows of helicopters, some Hueys, and some of the banana-shaped types, twin-rotor Chinooks, off to our right, parked to the east of the north-south runway. But my attention was drawn much more strongly to the amazing phenomenon of the disappearing runway.

Sure enough, just as Passarello had said it would, the runway was disappearing. The lower we descended, the shorter the runway seemed to be. It appeared we were about to land on a runway that was clearly much too short for us to be able to stop safely, and I began to anticipate bouncing off into the rough ground which bordered the field. Passarello was concentrating fully on the landing. I could see he was aiming at the near end of the runway. My attention was riveted at the point where the runway seemed to end.

At just the right moment, he pulled the power off and the aircraft thumped onto the runway. Quickly he began applying brakes, and then, after the flight engineer called "cleared to reverse," he pulled the throttles into the reverse pitch range. The aircraft slowed noticeably. But I was still looking at the point where the runway disappeared. Sure enough, just as we got to the point where I thought we would run out of runway, we came to a slight rise, and we could see more of the runway extending in front of us. We were fully slowed long before we got to the turn-around area.

"It's a no-sweat landing as long as you don't waste any runway," he said, mopping his brow. "Also, you won't want to delay slowing the aircraft." I nodded mutely.

"Well," he said. "I wanted to show you what it looked like the first time. On our return trip you can make the landing." My heart fell into my lower intestine. Holy shit, I thought. I'm not ready for this. I tried to smile. "I'm a tiger," I wanted to say; "I can hack it." But I couldn't bring myself to say anything.

We backed briefly, then Passarello swung the nose to the left and we started back up the runway to the ramp. The aircraft rocked and rattled along as we bounced up toward the far end of the runway. We taxied onto the ramp. From my window I could see the empty shell of another C-130 fuselage sitting on a small rise to the west, forlorn and abandoned. Oh god. I had no idea how it had gotten there. I didn't want to know how it had gotten there. We positioned ourselves on the pierced steel planking ramp and shut our engines down.

Several Army soldiers were boarding our aircraft, leaving their area of operations for a brief R&R. While they carried their bags out to our aircraft, I walked around the ramp, mentally trying to process the unpleasant events of our landing at the Golf Course.

The flight to Pleiku was another short trip, twenty minutes, and, sitting in the left seat again, I was relieved to see the lovely long concrete runway that came into view. The weather and visibility were still good at eleven in the morning, and I marveled at the lush green rolling hills that surrounded the field. We landed to the northwest. I called for the gear and flaps and made a decent landing. Perhaps if I hadn't just seen An Khe Golf Course, I might have thought Pleiku a bit short, but after the Golf Course anything would look like a world-class airfield.

At Pleiku the same routine, offload some troops, onload some. Start engines for the longer hop southeast, back to Cam Ranh. The direct flight back to Cam Ranh took us about 45 minutes across the central Vietnam hill country. We stopped at Cam Ranh for an hour, to offload our passengers and to take on fuel. Then another 50-minute flight back to Pleiku. By now it was early afternoon, and the calm clear air of the morning had given way to rising masses of cumulonimbus clouds, trying to turn into thunderstorms, complicating our navigational tasks. At Pleiku there were

Loading army soldiers, An Khe Golf Course, March 1967.

few passengers to offload; we kept our engines running and were airborne to An Khe. The moment I had been trying not to think about was at hand.

"I recommend you stay high and set yourself up on a right hand downwind as I did this morning," advised Passarello. I nodded. Helicopters were again maneuvering in and out of the ramp to the east of the runway, but the activity was not as heavy as it had been in the morning. That was good. But what was not so good was that I was going to have to fly a right-hand pattern into a field I did not know well, a short, narrow field, where the runway disappeared as you landed.

Flying a right-hand pattern from the left seat, I had to look across the cockpit, out the copilot's side windows, to see the field. Passarello was blocking my view of the field. I was too concerned about positioning on the downwind leg to dare to dip the right wing for a better view. That was what I should have done, of course.

"You're too tight. Move it left," said Passarello. I followed his instructions. "Gear down. Flaps half," I said, in a voice that seemed unusually uncertain.

"You're high. Better start your descent," Passarello advised. I retarded the throttles and lowered the nose. With every instruction I was feeling less and less in control of the aircraft. I was operating under remote control.

When it looked to me like it was time, I began a turn to base leg. I hadn't wanted Passarello to tell me when to make the turn. But I had misjudged again. "Looks like you're a bit close. You might want to angle out a bit," he said.

I banked the aircraft to the left a little more. At least now, after the turn to base leg, I could see the field more clearly. But this was as bad as it was good, for now I could see clearly the impossibility of my task. The runway was preposterously small. It appeared as the same brown strip surrounded by huts and helicopters. Knowing that it was going to disappear as we settled in to land was not reassuring. Even knowing that it was possible for a C-130 to land at the Golf Course—which is what we had done that morning—was not reassuring. After all, it was Passarello, the old head, who had made the landing, not I.

As I rolled the wings level on final approach, I began to feel something like panic rising in me. I felt as if I had no control. It was the aircraft that was heading in to land, not me. It knew what had to happen next; I didn't. I remembered flaps. "Full flaps," I called. Passarello set full flaps, and the aircraft rose slightly, as the increased flaps added to the lift while the airspeed slowed. My reaction was slow; instead of pushing the nose forward and adjusting with nose up trim, I did nothing. As a result, we simultaneously rose and lost airspeed.

"Get the nose down!" Passarello demanded. I complied. The edge of the runway was directly in front of us, the point at which we should be trying to touch our wheels down. But because I had not reduced throttles, our airspeed was now increasing. "Too fast! Too much airspeed!" Passarello yelled.

I pulled the throttles back, then seeing it was time to land, retarded them completely to the throttle stops. I aimed for the runway and then, just as the aircraft was about to hit the runway, pulled back on the yoke to keep the nose wheel from hitting. The aircraft main gear slammed into the runway and I lowered the nose gear, much too quickly, but I knew we couldn't afford the luxury of floating on down the runway. By having the wheels on the ground, I could apply brakes. I yanked the throttles into the reverse pitch range.

The aircraft was bouncing and careening down the runway, but at least it was on the runway. My heart was pounding. I wondered if I was hyperventilating. The landing was bad. And it was not over yet. I looked at the end of the runway. It was fast approaching. There was no way we could stop in time. I was mesmerized by the sight. Just as I thought we were about to run out of runway, we bounced over the rise, and I could see the true end of the runway, some 1000 feet further on. Then I realized Passarello was trying to get my attention.

"Slow it down! Slow it down! Get on the brakes!" I thought I was. But I was pushing on the tops of the rudder pedals half-heartedly, mechanically, the way I would do if I were landing on a long runway back in the States. Obviously, more brake pressure was needed. I pushed harder with the balls of my feet. It seemed futile; what good would it do, stopping this great huge airplane with the balls of my feet. The idea was ridiculous.

"Get on the brakes! Slow it down!" Passarello was yelling, beating the palms of his hands on the top of the dash overhanging the copilot's panel. Suddenly I felt his feet on the brakes with me, depressing the tops of the brakes more intensely and rapidly than I had been.

"Stop this god-damned airplane!" I knew he was upset now; although I had not known him long, I had never heard him use profanity. Between the two of us, we managed to slow the aircraft as we reached the turn-around area at the end of the runway. I sat there, sweating profusely, totally appalled at the landing I had made. I backed the aircraft slowly, carefully, under Brownie's directions. As we taxied onto the off-loading ramp at An Khe I tried not to think how badly I had done.

We flew to Qui Nhon and from there returned to Nha Trang. Passarello said little during the rest of the day. I knew I had screwed up; there was no way he could overlook the awfulness of that landing, the near-catastrophe it might have become.

And although I could claim many extenuating circumstances, some of them perhaps valid, I knew in my heart that I had screwed up royally. I wondered whether I might not have earned for myself the unenviable position of permanent copilot. I really wanted more than that out of my tour in Southeast Asia. But I could not, in all honesty, say that I had demonstrated the capability to be anything more.

Chapter 5

Rubber Plantations and Banana Runs

The next morning another new pilot was scheduled to fly with Colonel Passarello. I was going along to observe. I was told that was the way it had been scheduled, but I couldn't help feeling my displacement was due to my poor performance the preceding day. I strapped myself onto the padded bench seat at the rear of the cockpit, resigned to watching others fly the airplane.

We flew first to Tan Son Nhut, where we learned we were to carry troops and equipment between two small fields west of Saigon, Quan Loi and Minh Thanh, near the Cambodian border. Minh Thanh was literally a wide spot in the road. Located in the middle of a rubber plantation, the field had been made by widening a small dirt road that ran straight through a forest of rubber trees. The dirt surface had been treated with oil to reduce the dust and to keep the surface from washing away in the rain. The field was long enough. The problem was the approaches to the field: tall rubber trees lined not only the sides of the dirt strip, but also the approach edges at both ends. In landing, Passarello had to carry just enough power to hold us above the trees, then when the tree line passed, cut the power, and just before slamming into the ground, add power to check the descent, then retard power to land. This he did with practiced skill, bringing us in to a smooth landing.

Quan Loi was a fifteen-minute flight north. One end of the runway was cut through a stand of trees, but the other end of the runway ended in the back yard of a rubber plantation. The plantation, which was owned by a French family, was used as a headquarters for Army operations in the area. It was a picture-book setup, with a large, elegant-looking main house and several other buildings nearby, white and glistening in the sun.

Army Huey helicopters moved in and out of the central area at the end of the runway, refueling with their engines running, their blades stirring up clouds of fine, red dust. The skin of the ground troops was painted a dull red, the color of the dirt in the area. One Huey refueled while other helicopters hovered in the fringe area, waiting their turn to come in and refuel. Each Huey crew chief ran over to the central area, picked up a refueling hose, and brought it over to the helicopter. The refueling hoses were connected by a pump system to a series of large, heavy rubber bladders filled with JP-4. The fuel bladders were brought in by C-123 and C-130 aircraft. I asked the ground crewman if all this activity was usual. He shook his head. "Nope. Big operation going on a few miles to the west, near the Cambodian border." I could

Quan Loi, March 1967. The landing strip was cut through a French rubber plantation; original plantation buildings visible at bottom. The French name for the plantation was "Terre Rouge" (red earth).

Army UH-1 "Huey" helicopters refueling at Quan Loi, March 1967. The army was conducting a special operation along the Cambodian border.

Chapter 5. Rubber Plantations and Banana Runs

F-100, Bien Hoa, March 1967.

believe it, for as fast as one helicopter refueled, it rapidly departed low and to the west, and another took its place.

I sat on the rear seat again as we took off for the short ride to Bien Hoa, carrying a few troops back to their home area. Unlike Tan Son Nhut, which was Saigon's main airport, and which served civilian as well as military aircraft, Bien Hoa was exclusively a military base, home for many American and South Vietnamese Air Force

C-123 "Ranch Hands" in formation during engine run-up prior to departing on a defoliation mission. Bien Hoa, March 1967.

flying units. To the south, a wide river snaked its way across the horizon—the Saigon River, the natural line that separated Tan Son Nhut air traffic from that of Bien Hoa. The land around was completely flat. The extensive ramp area at Bien Hoa provided space for several units, including an F-100 unit, the 90th Fighter Squadron.

One of the more unusual units based at Bien Hoa was the 12th Special Operations Squadron, better known as the "Ranch Hands." The men in this unit flew specially configured C-123s, with interior tanks for holding a chemical defoliant, called Agent Orange, and wide spray bars which extended out the rear of the aircraft. These aircraft sprayed the defoliant across the tops of jungles and grasslands to remove top cover and reveal VC hiding places. When I talked with one of the crew members in base ops, he told me that they all wore oxygen masks to avoid breathing in the fumes, which permeated the interior of the aircraft, including the cockpit, whenever the spray operation began. These aircraft flew in close formation when they sprayed the forest; they also taxied, performed engine run-up, and took off in close formation. Years later almost all airmen associated with the spraying activity suffered from some form of physical ailment.

Also located at Bien Hoa were the aircraft used to transport high-ranking military officers on inspection trips to locations across South Vietnam. The most prominent, and certainly the most eye-catching, was the "White Whale," the C-123 assigned to Army General Westmoreland and his staff. Certainly no other C-123 in

The "White Whale," Bien Hoa, March 1967. This specially fitted C-123 was assigned to General Westmoreland and his staff. I had never seen a C-123 aircraft this clean and shiny. On this particular day, a one-star general is using this aircraft. I'm not sure that General Westmoreland fully appreciated the symbolism of flying in an aircraft with this symbol on its nose. Had he never read Melville's *Moby Dick*?

Chapter 5. Rubber Plantations and Banana Runs

the Air Force inventory was as well-maintained or as highly polished. At the time Westmoreland was the top Army general in Vietnam.

After a quick offload, we headed back to Nha Trang, landing just as the sun set behind the hills to the southwest. When we walked into the Nha Trang ALCE, I noticed one of the men behind the desk pulling out a series of paper cups and pouring something into them from a large bottle.

"What's this?" I asked.

"That's your combat ration—a shot of whisky. A tradition that goes back to World War II. After every combat mission, you get a shot of whisky. Here you are." And he handed me a small paper cup filled with strong-smelling brown liquid.

I took a small sip. When I swallowed, it felt like it was stripping the skin off my throat.

"Agh!" I said. "It's terrible!"

"You think so now," someone said, "but after a few weeks on the shuttle you'll change your mind." It didn't seem likely.

The following day I was once again the only pilot flying with Colonel Passarello. When I walked through the crew entrance door, I saw that the cargo compartment was filled with what looked like large, inflated balloon tires lying on their sides tied down on the aluminum cargo pallets. I placed my hand on the closest sample. It gave when I pushed on it.

Brownie saw me examining the cargo. "Seen those before? They're fuel bladders full of fuel. Remember those Army helicopters refueling at Quan Loi? Well, that's what these are."

"For Quan Loi?" I asked.

"Nope. Ban Me Thuot."

Ban Me Thuot was a decent-sized east-west landing strip in the middle of a large, flat plain about 75 miles west of Nha Trang. The town of Ban Me Thuot, located five miles to the southwest of the airfield, sat on the main north-south road between Pleiku and Saigon.

At Ban Me Thuot a forklift slowly and carefully removed the bladder-laden pallets from the aircraft. The thought of twenty of these bladders full of fuel in the cargo compartment made me nervous. I had visions of fuel leaking out into the floor of the cargo compartment. All it would take was one spark, a short in an electrical system somewhere, or ground fire hitting us in the right spot, and we would have an instant explosion.

Our next hop was a flight straight south to Phan Thiet, another new field. The terrain between Ban Me Thuot and Phan Thiet was rugged and mountainous. Phan Thiet was located on a slight rise overlooking the South China Sea, halfway between Cam Ranh and Vung Tau. This was another new, challenging field for me, and Passarello flew the aircraft from the left seat. The field was located on the edge of the land-sea border, another short brown line running more or less parallel to the shoreline—the same kind of runway as at An Khe Golf Course, aluminum matting, and about the same length. Unlike the Golf Course, however, this runway didn't disappear as you descended. In fact, it was slightly bowed in the middle, like a shallow dish.

The far end of the field, the end nearest the sea, widened into a parking area where many aircraft were parked randomly. Unlike the field at Quon Loi, where the parking area at the end was large, this parking area was small. Passarello observed that landing from the sea to the southwest, you often flew over parked aircraft before touching down. You had to be careful not to let too much runway pass beneath you before touching down. But most of the time, because of the onshore breezes caused by the close proximity of the sea, we landed as we were now, to the northeast, towards the parking area.

From Phan Thiet we picked up a load for Tuy Hoa, where we landed on the aluminum matting runway. The field was dry and dusty, as the construction equipment was working at an intense pace to complete the concrete runway. I made the landing there with reasonable success. Tuy Hoa any day over the Golf Course. From Tuy Hoa we flew south down the coast line to Cam Ranh, then the short hop to Nha Trang.

* * *

The next day Colonel Passarello was involved in a check ride, and I flew with another pilot, Major Aubrey Milstead. Our mission that day took us to two more fields I hadn't seen before, Phan Rang and Dalat. Major Milstead flew most of the legs in the left seat, while I played copilot. I was happy to sit and watch.

Our first leg took us from Nha Trang to Phan Rang, home of an F-100 unit and a B-57 unit as well. Phan Rang, a short distance south of Cam Ranh Bay, had a long concrete runway, necessary for jet aircraft operations. Directed to make a right-hand pattern and land to the north, we flew a normal approach. A lovely, wide river wound its way past just south of the field. On either side of the river there was rich forest growth, and beyond, to the west, a ridge of hills. As we taxied in, the tower operator asked if we were all right.

"What do you mean, all right?" we asked.

"There was some ground fire coming up at you on final. You took it out a little too far in your turn. Always turn inside the river when you land to the north. We don't own the real estate south of the river."

At Phan Rang we loaded elements of the South Vietnam Army to carry to Phan Thiet. I had envisioned ranks of troops marching in single file into the aircraft and sitting down smartly on our seats. My mistake. What happened instead was an operation called "combat loading." We put empty aluminum pallets down on the cargo bay floor and extended webbed straps across the compartment from one side to the other. It seemed a rather casual manner in which to accommodate infantry troops, especially compared to the way we handled American Army troops. But I soon saw why.

When the South Vietnamese Army moved, it took everything it needed, including baggage, wives, children, and the more portable livestock, chickens, pigs, and an occasional cow. The loadmasters were not pleased about the livestock. We couldn't blame them. Animals did not take well to flying, especially in a confined, noisy environment like that provided by the inside of a C-130. Moving elements of the South Vietnamese army presented a much different logistical problem than moving elements of the American army.

After landing at Phan Thiet we flew a short, fifteen-minute flight inland to Dalat, another new field. The flight to Dalat was over some scenic hills and mountains. As we neared Dalat, the hills began to smooth out slightly. A small city spread out along the edges of a large lake. There were smaller lakes, then houses, large, luxurious houses, extravagant for Vietnam. It looked like a resort area.

Chapter 5. Rubber Plantations and Banana Runs

"There has been almost no fighting here," Milstead said. "Dalat is a summer resort area for the wealthier citizens of Saigon. The climate is relatively cool and pleasant. It rains regularly, which combined with the cooler climate, results in an area that produces a phenomenal amount of produce. This area is South Vietnam's vegetable garden. We come in here frequently and our load is almost always fruits and vegetables."

The runway tilted uphill slightly to the west; as we landed I looked to my right into a large, apparently abandoned house that sat abeam the east end of the runway. Milstead landed the aircraft easily and taxied into the ramp area. We parked close behind another C-130 on the small ramp. In addition to the two C-130s, there was an Army Beech Baron, and Air America Turbo Porter, a South Vietnamese C-47, and a couple of O-1 aircraft fitted snugly around us. The base operations building, if that's what it could be called, was a house with a small porch on the west side, overlooking the ramp. Forklifts loaded us with pallets of bananas, pineapples, lettuce, and tomatoes while we sat on the shaded porch and drank Cokes out of a Coke machine.

This was an amazing war. Gorgeous countryside. The threat of mortars. A lovely resort area. Ground fire on short final. Coke machines. Bananas and pineapples.

We flew our load of fruit and vegetables to Tan Son Nhut, and turned around and came back for more. On our second run to Tan Son Nhut, we saw a formation of two A-1Es speeding in towards Bien Hoa. "Probably with the South Vietnamese Air Force," Milstead said.

Then, as we approached the level jungle area that stretched northeast of Saigon, we saw three F-100s diving towards some indistinct area in the jungle, a spotter plane banking to the side. As each F-100 pulled out, dark objects fell towards the ground. Then a burst of fire and dark smoke. By the time we arrived, all the excitement had ended; the F-100s had left, and so had the spotter plane, apparently. We circled over the site briefly, but all we could see was a thin wisp of smoke curling out of the trees near a bend in a small river. No activity on the ground, no aircraft in the area. By the

Crowded ramp at Dalat, March 1967. Six aircraft parked in close proximity. Clockwise from our C-130 E-model in the rear: an A-model C-130; a Beech Model 18; a South Vietnamese Air Force O-1; a U.S. Army Beech Baron; and a C-47.

time we turned on course for Saigon, even the smoke was gone. It was difficult to believe anything had happened to disturb the green jungle beneath us.

The next day Passarello's shuttle schedule was complete. We flew out just before six o'clock the following morning, taking off into the misty dawn of the South China Sea. Back in my quarters at CCK, I stood in the shower for an hour, luxuriating in the hot water and the quiet. I bought a map of Southeast Asia and tacked it to the wall by the head of my bed. The countries were defined by colors somehow symbolic: the Philippines green; South Vietnam yellow; North Vietnam pink; Laos brown; Cambodia orange; Thailand beige. It seemed important to mark places where I had landed, and I stuck pins in the places I had flown into: Clark Field, Bangkok, Tan Son Nhut, Cam Ranh, Nha Trang, Pleiku, Tuy Hoa, Qui Nhon, Bien Hoa, Da Nang, An Khe.

Chapter 6

Da Nang ABCCC

After a short run to Okinawa, I was scheduled for another flight, something new this time: the airborne communication mission at Da Nang. My aircraft commander on this flight was Lieutenant Colonel James Marable. We flew the usual route to Da Nang: CCK to Naha, Okinawa, where we picked up a load of supplies for Vietnam. Our load from Naha was to be delivered to Qui Nhon this time, and we arrived as usual in the small hours of the morning. From Qui Nhon it was a 45-minute flight up the coast to Da Nang, where we landed just before three in the morning. But you wouldn't know it was night as a result of the amount of illumination flares descending over the airfield. The west perimeter of the base was lit up like a playing field.

Approach control steered us onto a left-hand downwind heading north, parallel to the coastline, then turned us west onto a base leg that bought us north of Monkey Mountain, a high hill on a peninsula several clicks northeast of the field, where a radar station was located. The lights on the radio masts on the hill were on our left as we flew past. When we were over the bay north of the field, approach control turned us onto a southerly heading for our final approach to landing and directed us to contact the tower for landing instructions. Tower cleared us to land on the left runway. The water of the bay was dark below us, but we could see the runways and taxiways of Da Nang Air Base, lit up clearly ahead of us.

Several weeks after I had first seen it, and frequently flying over it en route from Thailand to the Philippines, I was finally landing at Da Nang. Da Nang and the other bases in the northern area of South Vietnam I had scarcely seen, yet by now I knew the larger airfields in the mid-section of Vietnam, and the territory between them, between Qui Nhon and Saigon, like the back of my hand.

The follow-me truck led us to the C-130 ramp on the east side of the field. The night was warm and humid when we exited the aircraft. Da Nang smelled pretty much like Tan Son Nhut—a little more of the sea, perhaps, mixed in with the sweet-sour aroma that drifted down from the city to the north. We would be flying only two missions, one the next day, and one the day after that, and then we would return to CCK. The crew truck took us to our crew quarters, a small air-conditioned trailer that was intended to insulate us from the heat and noise of the base.

Da Nang was a busy, noisy base; in addition to the Air Force F-4 fighter units and our own cargo operations, there was a Marine fighter unit on the west side of the field and some Army flying operations as well. It was the largest airfield in the northern part of South Vietnam. Like Tan Son Nhut and Bien Hoa in the south and Can Ranh Bay in the coastal midsection, it provided logistics support and air assistance of every variety for the numerous ground operations in Vietnam. The Viet Cong presence was also large, and the activities of the Viet Cong were brought to our attention on a regular basis. The field often experienced mortar attacks at night, and slit trenches, bunkers, and other safe havens were situated at various locations around the field. It was a common sight to see Army UH-1 Hueys and Marine helicopters hovering above some portion of the perimeter or of the open fields beyond, engaged in an exchange of gunfire with unknown and unseen (by me) persons in the vegetation on the south and west sides of the field.

Early the next morning the crew truck carried us to the operations building, where we received our mission information. The airborne command post mission, or A-B-triple-C mission, as we called it, was simple. The ABCCC bird was a specially fitted C-130 with a communications capsule inserted into the cargo compartment. Once fitted with the communication capsule, the aircraft was flown exclusively on that mission. The aircraft carried its normal crew, except for the loadmaster, whose presence was unnecessary, for the only load we had was the communications capsule, the men who manned the capsule, and a full load of fuel. The job of the aircrew was to get the aircraft safely airborne, climb as high as it could go with a full fuel load, and orbit over a predetermined location, climbing higher as we used fuel.

While we were orbiting and climbing, the communications men in the back did their work, which was to communicate with the aircraft and command posts in their area of operations. There were about ten of these individuals on board, some of them Air Force officers in uniforms and some were Vietnamese or other local nationalities; many of these were in civilian clothes. These men provided the communication linkups between spotter aircraft, like the O-1 Bird Dog, or the occasional F-100 spotter aircraft, and the strike aircraft called in to assist the Army, ARVN, or Marine Corps troops on the ground. When a ground unit needed assistance, the unit called for a spotter aircraft. When the spotter aircraft identified the ground target, the pilot called ABCCC requesting assistance from a strike aircraft. The capsule folks in the

C-130 loading ramp, Da Nang. Photograph was taken early in 1966, before permanent buildings were erected.

Chapter 6. Da Nang ABCCC

back relayed the request for strike assistance to the appropriate agencies at Da Nang (usually a flight of F-4s), or if needed, Chu Lai, Cam Ranh Bay, or other units at sea or farther south.

When the strike aircraft arrived in the target area, they checked in with the capsule folks, who coordinated their communication hand-off to the spotter aircraft flying at treetop level somewhere below. If the strike area was in questionable territory (like somewhere in southern Laos), the locals in civilian dress had the authority to approve or disapprove the air strike. As far as I know they never disapproved of a strike; but they were the first to know if an unusual operation was taking place on the ground. One ABCCC aircraft was airborne over the northern operating area at all times. The call sign of the daylight aircraft was Hillsboro and the call sign of the night aircraft was Alley Cat.

We were assigned the Hillsboro portion of the mission, which called for us to be airborne, on station over the northern section of South Vietnam, for twelve hours. Flying time to and from the orbit area added an additional hour. We arrived in the orbit area about seven o'clock in the morning. The weather on our first day's flight was generally good and visibility was excellent. Our orbit area was west and north of Da Nang, over an area of lush green hills. The navigator established orbit points by radial and distance fixes from the Da Nang TACAN. We flew over Laos as much as we flew over Vietnam.

Our initial altitude was low, about sixteen thousand feet. As we burned fuel and lightened our load, we climbed a thousand feet at a time, peaking out about 24,000 feet by the time our orbit activities ended. We flew the aircraft on autopilot all the time; to fly the aircraft by hand for that length of time would have become a mind-bending and arm-numbing experience. For most of the flight, we flew in one direction, turned when the navigator said turn, and flew back in the opposite direction. After a while we could tell when to turn by visual reference to the ground features. But when the weather was bad or clouds reduced our visibility, only the navigator knew where we were, usually by relying on the radar set.

While we were in orbit, only one pilot was required to be in the seat at a time. The other pilot could walk around the aircraft, hobnob with the communications crew, eat, catch a short nap. The other pilot's seat had to be occupied by another crew member. Often the flight engineer would sit in one of the pilot's seats, keeping his eye on the gauges and dials above his flight engineer's position as well as on the engine instruments on the front instrument panel. Occasionally the flight engineer would be able to grab a little stick time. We would take the aircraft off autopilot control and let the flight engineer try to hold it steady on course and on altitude.

Occasionally we would even let him wrestle the aircraft around one of the turns. Holding the aircraft at altitude in a turn was a bit of a challenge, especially when the aircraft was full of fuel. When the nose of the aircraft started to drop too much in the turn, the pilot in other seat would help the flight engineer get the aircraft back up to the desired altitude by pulling back pressure on the yoke. We hoped that the sudden increase of back pressure on the yoke would not distress the folks back in the communication capsule, pulling the extra Gs to get the aircraft back up to its assigned altitude.

Occasionally, however, we would pull a little too much back pressure, and one of the troops in the back, usually the senior ranking officer, would suddenly appear in the cockpit, yelling, "What the hell's going on! You're about to make us puke back there!" And we'd make up some weak excuse about rough air.

When it was my turn to stretch for the first time, I got up out of the co-pilot's seat while Lieutenant Colonel Marable settled into his pilot's seat. I made my way back to the communications capsule through the door from the crew compartment. I was impressed when I saw the elaborate setup. The communications crew seats were spaced down the left-hand side of the cargo compartment as I walked toward the rear; each set had a complete set of radio controls on the side. Each member could dial in any frequency he wanted, in the VHF, UHF, and HF ranges. The crew members wore headsets with long cords so that they could walk around and still be tuned in to any conversations that were occurring. There were also some FM radios, which were used by Army units. Across the aisle, on my right, was a large board holding a variety of maps of the area, covered with a solid sheet of thick, clear plastic. If there was a mission in progress, the names of the aircraft were written on the board with grease pencil, with target areas circled, lines showing routes of flight, radio frequencies, call signs, and any other relevant information.

Farther back were banks of radio sets and communications gear. There was also an in-flight kitchen, where hot lunches were prepared and a row of coffee and water jugs. It looked like a pretty good setup. The only disconcerting aspect was the fact that the normal attitude of the aircraft in flight at our most fuel-efficient cruising speed resulted in a slightly tail-low attitude, which meant that those sitting in the seats tended to lean to the left. Usually, however, we dropped a few degrees of flaps, which helped to bring the cargo compartment to a more even keel.

As the day progressed, our fuel load lightened, and our altitude increased. We had to continually alter our flight path, however, for the afternoon thunderclouds were beginning to build, especially over the more rugged hills to the west. We orbited closer and closer to the Da Nang TACAN, eventually holding practically on top of it, and when we received word that the evening bird was launched, we began our letdown over the field, descending in wide circles and landing to the south in the dark. We landed at seven-thirty at night, exhausted after flying in circles for nearly thirteen hours.

Two days later we were airborne again. The weather was once again clear and smooth, at least before the clouds began to build. We were once again orbiting to the northwest of Da Nang, east of the border between South Vietnam and Laos. Shortly before noon, I was flying the aircraft while Colonel Marable was out of the pilot's seat stretching his legs. Someone came up front from the capsule and stuck his head over my right shoulder to look at the scenery below. He started to talk to me, so I removed my headset to hear what he was saying. He said that we were flying over something called the A Shau Valley. I nodded and said it was very pretty. He gave me a pained look and snorted. Only much later did I learn that the A Shau Valley was owned by the Viet Cong.

Soon afterward, I was looking out, admiring the rugged terrain below. The visibility was exceptional. As we approached the northwest end of our orbit I looked down and saw a pattern on the ground below. It looked like some kind of construction work, a regular pattern of earth turned over as if some engineering company were laying down a housing development, with long lines indicating streets and excavated areas suggesting building foundations. I was confused by what I saw. Who could be doing construction work out here, in the middle of the jungle?

Chapter 6. Da Nang ABCCC

As the aircraft flew closer to the site, I could see more clearly that it was a parallel series of holes in the ground, a long series of deep holes. They had to be deep if I could see them clearly from eighteen thousand feet, our altitude at the time. They looked now like a pattern stitched in brown and white on a green blanket of jungle. And then I could see another pattern of holes crossing the first pattern at an angle. Then it dawned on me what I was looking at: patterns of bomb craters caused by flights of B-52s.

The bombs had really cratered this portion of the valley. I tried to imagine what it must have been like, to be on the ground as the string of bombs erupted along the valley floor, detonating in a long continuous series of uninterrupted explosions, the smoke and noise if the raid had occurred during daylight hours, the blinding light

B-52 bombers dropping bombs over the A Shau Valley, South Vietnam, October 1966.

and concussion if it had been at night. Even from eighteen thousand feet, the sight was impressive: long lines of bomb craters in a never-ending green jungle. The pattern started to pass underneath the nose of the aircraft.

Then my concentration was abruptly broken as a large shadow passed slowly over the aircraft, blocking out the light of the sun that had been shining down through the cockpit windows. My heart stopped. What could have caused such a large shadow to pass over us at this altitude? No birds flew this high. There was only one kind of aircraft that could be above us and cast such a large shadow: a B-52. And no B-52 ever flew alone. This must be a formation of B-52s, come to drop another load of bombs over the A Shau Valley. And here we were, directly underneath their route of flight.

Instantly in a panic, I grabbed the yoke, about to turn off the autopilot and make a sharp banking turn to the right. I knew such a move would profoundly upset all those back in the communications console, but I thought that my hard turn to the right would be preferable to being blown out of the sky by a rain of B-52 bombs. Then I paused, remembering that the sun wasn't directly overhead. Where was the sun? I twisted frantically around in my seat, looking through the copilot's windows on my side of the aircraft for the sun. There it was, off to our right, to the south. As I looked for the sun, another shadow passed between the sun and our aircraft, and I saw clearly the outline of one B-52, the high sharp tail fin first and then the bullet-like nose moving steadily through the sun. And then beyond it, another, and then another, an entire

B-52 bomb patterns, A Shau Valley, April 1967. Photograph taken from 16,000 feet.

formation, turning slowly, gracefully, impressively, onto a northerly heading towards North Vietnam. I watched until they disappeared in the haze and high clouds that rose in the north.

My heart was beating rapidly and I wanted to tell someone what I had seen, how close to death I was sure we had come, what an amazing sight, what a strange and preposterous sequence of events had unfolded in a matter of seconds, but there was no one in the other seat at the moment, and it was too late (and, I now realized, unnecessary) to call out over the intercom, because the bombers were now far to the north and out of sight.

Just then the navigator called out, "time to turn back to the east; we're moving beyond our assigned orbit area." I relaxed my grip on the yoke, reached down with my left hand, and turned the autopilot control to the right, causing the aircraft to begin a gentle turn to the right, steadying at a mild bank angle of fifteen degrees, and the aircraft came gradually around to a southeasterly heading.

I never saw bomb craters in the A Shau Valley again, never saw another B-52 in the skies of Vietnam during the rest of the time I flew in South Vietnam, but the vision of those B-52s in formation, of their elegance in flight and their impersonal awesome potential power has remained in my mind as vividly as it did at that moment. I knew fear in many forms during the time I flew in Vietnam, but I was never more instantaneously and completely frightened than I was under the shadow of those B-52s that day while we were orbiting over the A Shau Valley.

I realized later that there was no way the men in the back of our aircraft, a flying communications command center, would not have known of the movements of all aircraft, even B-52s, in the area, but at the time all I knew was extensive bomb patterns on the ground, B-52s above us, and us flying along complacently in between. I was beginning to develop an awareness that accidents could happen quickly and for the most bizarre and unexpected of reasons in the skies of Vietnam, where aircraft operations could occur in ways never imaginable in the more rigidly controlled skies of the United States of America.

The next day we flew directly back to CCK, a four-hour flight. My first ABCCC mission was over.

Chapter 7

Piece of Cake

In my mailbox at the squadron I found what I thought was an April Fool's Day joke the squadron was playing on me: orders assigning me to Colonel Passarello's crew. I imagined that Passarello had specifically requested I be placed on his crew with the idea that he would give me the special attention I needed if I ever hoped to be checked out. I was neither fish nor foul, too competent for a new guy copilot, not experienced enough to be an aircraft commander. To make matters worse, Passarello's crew went in-country without me, checking out another new pilot. So I wandered around the base, killing time, waiting for the schedule to give definition to my life.

On my next trip I flew to Bangkok and back with Captain Giles Gray. I was happy to be flying with a captain instead of a major or lieutenant colonel. Nothing against field grade types, but you could relax with another captain. Didn't have to worry about being the bright young officer and efficient aircrew member, just do your job and fly the aircraft. Once again, I was flying copilot. But I didn't mind. On the way back from Bangkok we flew into Nakhon Phanom, "Naked Fanny," as we called it, a new field for me. I saw it for the first time in the night, as usual. It sat in the northeast corner of Thailand, on a bend of the Mekong River, across the river from Laos. Giles banked the aircraft expertly over the river in the moonlight, skimming to a smooth landing on the aluminum matting runway. "Jolly Green" rescue helicopters and A-1Es, single-engine propeller-powered aircraft, sat quietly on the ramp in the darkness.

My next mission was a surprise—no flight to Okinawa or Vietnam, but to Guam, a small island in the Mariana archipelago in the middle of the western Pacific. A U.S. Territory, its strategic importance is suggested by the fact that an air base on the northern end of the island, Andersen AFB, was home to many B-52 bombers and KC-135 tankers. We were flying directly from CCK to Anderson AFB, and distance of nearly 1700 miles on an east-southeast heading to pick up some B-52 parts and carry them to Clark AB. One of the island's B-52s had had a mechanical problem on its bomb run over North Vietnam and made a precautionary landing there. The aircraft commander on this flight was Jim Douglas, a captain like myself. This was the first and only time I flew with him.

As we sat in the cockpit, I thought that it was amazing that two twenty-something young men were responsible for flying a large four-engine aircraft across the vastness of the Western Pacific Ocean to find an island only thirty miles long and five to ten miles wide, depending on where you measured its width. Of course, our success depended heavily on the navigational skills of our navigator, who, once we were out of range of any land-based radio signals, had to rely on sun shots with his sextant to track our course and keep us on the correct heading. He would also need to read the wave heights and direction of movement on the surface of the ocean beneath us to estimate the effects of the wind (at the surface, of course; the winds at our altitude would not be the same).

We departed CCK at six in the morning and spotted the island of Guam about five hours later, arriving in good weather. We turned final over the harbor at Agana, where I spotted a sunken ship in the water listing to the right at about 45 degrees. We were amazed to see so many B-52 bombers and KC-135 refueling tankers lined up on the ramp to our right as we landed to the north on the outside runway. It took over three hours for the loading crew to strap the B-52 parts to our pallets. Jim and I enjoyed our lunch in the flight line snack bar while the ground crew loaded the B-52 parts. Three and a half hours later we departed Andersen, heading due west to Clark.

As Jim had flown the leg down, it was my turn to fly the leg to Clark. While we had been waiting at Andersen, a low-pressure system had moved across our intended flight path, and I found myself flying through clouds most of the way. Occasionally the sun, moving gradually lower ahead of us, shown through, illuminating the layers with varying shades of orange, red, and finally violet. I always enjoyed the experience of flying through cloud layers, especially when we would move up or down through a thin layer, the cloud wisps flowing over our wings, the slight bump of turbulence that accompanied passage through a cloud. It was dark when we landed at Clark. Our B-52 parts offloaded, we returned to CCK.

When we returned to CCK, the men in the squadron were milling around in groups, concern evident in their voices. What was up? I asked. One of our aircraft had had an accident at An Khe Golf Course, they said. How did it happen? I asked. I envisioned someone doing what I feared doing, landing long, out of control, smashing into the rocks and bushes at the end of the runway. No, this accident occurred on takeoff. On takeoff? How could an accident happen on takeoff?

It seemed that at the same time that one of our C-130s had been cleared for takeoff with a load of passengers on board, one of the army's banana-shaped helicopters,

Andersen Field, Guam, March 1967. Landing to the northeast. Many B-52s and KC-135s parked at various locations around the field.

a CH-47 Chinook, had also been cleared to move out of the helicopter area next to the runway. The paths of the departing 130 and the hovering helicopter were parallel, and the downwash of the helicopter rotors adversely affected the controls of the 130. The pilot of the C-130 had initially applied takeoff power, and then, as the aircraft encountered rotor wash, he had reduced power. When the 130 slipped back out of the effects of the rotor wash, the pilot decided to continue with the takeoff. But when he advanced the power again, the 130 came back into the rotor wash effects. By the time the 130 pilot saw that the takeoff could not be continued successfully, there was too little runway left to stop the aircraft, and the aircraft careened out into the rough ground beyond the end of the runway. The aircraft caught fire as it skidded to a stop. All the passengers and crew members survived, but at least one passenger had suffered a broken leg, and others had suffered minor burns.

My god. I could easily envision a catastrophe occurring at An Khe Golf Course for any number of reasons, but an accident on takeoff had not entered my mind. The wing promptly generated a safety memo about not taking off while helicopters were near the runway. I had to admit that I had not fully appreciated how severely helicopter rotor wash could affect the controllability of a C-130. I had always known landing at the Golf Course was a major challenge. Now I needed to worry about takeoffs at An Khe too.

Then, once again, I was on the schedule to go in-country on the shuttle. First, however, it was time for a little relaxation. When I entered the China Nights, Karla was not around. One of the girls said to wait, she would be in soon. When Karla came

Burning C-130, Tail number 63-7772, An Khe Golf Course, March 12, 1967. The aircraft ran off the runway after rotor wash from a hovering CH-47 Chinook helicopter interfered with its controllability on take-off.

Chapter 7. Piece of Cake

in, she looked more striking than I remembered. She walked over to where I was sitting slowly, determinedly. Not rushing. Detached. She looked directly at me as she approached. If she had hurried over on my account, I couldn't tell.

"Hi, GI," she said, with a bit of a smile. "How come you stay away so long?"

"I've been flying. Fly to Vietnam, Thailand."

"You fly again?"

I nodded. "Tomorrow morning. Back to Vietnam for two weeks."

"You hungry?"

As a matter of fact, I was. I looked around the room; I hadn't noticed anyone eating.

"Wait," she said, standing up. She said something to the group sitting at a table in the rear. "I say we come back later. We go now."

"Where are we going?" I asked.

"We go to MAAG club."

The MAAG club was a club for the military assistance advisory group, as it was called. We got into a cab, and she gave brief and explicit instructions to the driver.

The MAAG club was a short distance north of the center of town. The driver followed a main paved road north; then he turned onto a narrow dirt road which he followed briefly before we reached an entryway where a guard stood on duty. The guard looked at my ID card and waved us through. The cab pulled up in front of a well-groomed brick building flanked by shrubs and trees. When we got out, the night air smelled of vegetation and the odor of food cooking.

The main room inside was comfortable. There were wooden booths, a wood floor obviously intended for dancing. Along the wall was a bar. A few people were talking and eating. We sat in a booth facing each other. The Chinese waiter came over and handed us menus. Karla seemed to know exactly what she wanted. There was a pause.

"Tell me where you fly."

I told her where I had been since I last saw her. It didn't occur to me that she had heard my story—or a story like it—numerous times before. But she didn't seem bored. She watched my face while I talked.

"How you like to fly in Vietnam?" she asked when I paused.

"I think that is the most important flying I can do. But I'm not doing it very well yet. I have to have more experience."

"Are you afraid?" She asked the question as if it was a question that could be answered like a question about the weather or about what to order for dinner. But it was asked in a spirit of concern, and it was a fair question. It was not a question I had thought to ask myself, certainly not that directly.

"No, I don't think so. Not afraid. Worried, maybe. Worried that I'll screw up. It's a lot of responsibility to steer that big airplane into some of the small runways we land on."

Dinner arrived. I had ordered my steak on the rare side. Hers was well done. The food was good. When we finished, Karla said, "Give me quarter."

I handed it to her, and she walked around one of the booths to a juke box. She punched some buttons. A slow dance tune began. She walked back. "You want dance?"

I held her awkwardly as we moved around the dance floor. It seemed that she was standing closer than she had the first time we danced. I felt clumsy and stiff, but she was moving easily, in spite of my clumsiness.

"I think you dance better than I do," I said.

She didn't disagree. "You no like to dance?"

"I've never been very good at dancing."

"When you come back we come here again and dance more. On weekend they have band, play all good songs."

Finally we called for a cab. While we waited outside she stood next to me, holding her arms across her chest. "Cold?" I asked, putting my arm around her. She leaned into me. Her perfume came to me through the night air.

When we returned to the China Nights, she asked, "You come in for drink?"

I shook my head. "No. This is just right. I'll come to see you when I get back."

She put her hand on the door handle as if to get out, and then suddenly turned back to me, closing her eyes and pursing her lips. I felt like I did when I was a freshman in high school on my first date. I kissed her quickly on the lips. Then she opened the door and was out.

* * *

By nine-thirty the next morning we were airborne for Vietnam by way of Naha. I was flying with another aircraft commander, Major William Potter, who had been with the squadron almost a year. Passarello's crew was somewhere else, I wasn't sure where. Maybe it was in-country already. I would be flying with Major Potter the entire time.

Our first mission out of Nha Trang was the passenger run to Pleiku via Qui Nhon and An Khe. The one challenging aspect of the mission would be the landing at An Khe. I was relieved that Potter would be flying the mission; he, not I, had to make the landing at An Khe Golf Course. It had been some time—not quite a month—since my last, awful, botched-up landing there. And since then the accident had occurred. I was not looking forward to seeing the Golf Course again.

We left Nha Trang at eight in the morning and flew the short hop over to Cam Ranh Bay. From Cam Ranh we had a half-hour flight up the coast to Qui Nhon. The weather was perfect, a few low clouds but no restrictions to visibility. After a short stop at Qui Nhon we turned west, to the interior, and An Khe.

I could feel my stomach tighten as we approached An Khe, and I wondered how Potter was going to deal with the challenge of landing. I looked ahead to locate the runway, that ugly brown scar among the hills of An Khe, but the morning haze had increased, reducing visibility. Potter seemed to know where we were going, though. Suddenly I thought I saw the Golf Course area passing off our right wing. Potter looked steadily ahead. I thought for a minute that he was doing what I might well have done, forget about landing at An Khe and proceed directly to Pleiku, making up some sad story about poor visibility to excuse our overflight.

Then he announced, "Before landing checklist. Flaps fifty."

I began to read the checklist and set the flaps, but I was thoroughly confused. "Where are we landing?" I asked.

"An Khe," he said. "See, there it is." He pointed straight ahead. I saw something like a real runway, a silver stripe in the dirt, but it wasn't the Golf Course. I knew we had passed it.

"That's not An Khe Golf Course," I said, still in disbelief.

"Of course not," Potter responded. "Didn't you look at the briefing folder? That's

Chapter 7. Piece of Cake

the new runway, An Khe Main. They just opened it. We're using it now instead of the Golf Course. Gear down."

"New runway?"

"Yes, a new runway. Eventually it will be lighted, with all-weather capability. I guess they decided the Golf Course was too dangerous."

Too dangerous. No kidding.

As we flew closer, I looked in disbelief. Ahead of us was a long, flat, level runway. A huge runway, a perfect runway. A no-sweat runway. The runway was not finished; dirt was piled up along the sides, and the surface was aluminum matting, but that didn't matter. The runway was long and wide; you could see all of it as you landed. No helicopters near by to worry about. It was a piece of cake. I was angry and I was relieved. Angry because I hadn't read the briefing folder, but relieved because my worst fears were over. I would, in fact, be able to land an airplane at An Khe without worrying about stopping it in time. As Potter set the aircraft down on the runway, I could feel the tension drain out of me.

We flew to Pleiku, then down to Cam Ranh, where we reversed course. I was smiling the whole distance. When we came back to An Khe from Pleiku I found myself in a state of disbelief, expecting to see that we had to land at the Golf Course again, that the first time through had been some kind of hallucination. But no, once again, we landed on that long, level runway. It was too easy. We might have been landing at Cam Ranh.

As we departed An Khe, turning toward Qui Nhon, we crossed the north end of the old runway, Golf Course. There, about a hundred yards into the scrub and dirt, rested the bent and charred remains of a C-130, clear evidence of the unfortunate

An Khe Golf Course, March 1967. Burned C-130 visible in center of photograph.

accident I had heard about the previous week. The fuselage was mostly intact, but there was a charred, black area where the left wing should have been. As I looked down at the disturbing sight, I saw the results of a situation any pilot could have found himself in. Certainly, I could easily visualize the whole episode happening to me. And I stopped smiling. I knew I didn't want to land at the Golf Course, ever, and I was truly thankful that the new runway was open.

When we returned to Nha Trang we found out that we would have a day off, and then Potter would fly with another crew while I flew as first pilot and received my in-country check ride from one of the wing check pilots. I would be flying the same passenger shuttle mission we had flown the previous day. An Khe held no horrors for me now. My check ride would be a piece of cake.

During my off day, I studied briefly, then took the written examination in the ALCE building. The next day, Captain Hennessy, a wing check pilot, evaluated my flying technique and crew coordination discipline. During the stops on the ground, he asked me the standard questions about aircraft configuration and emergency procedures. I was filled with confidence, for I had just flown the route two days earlier and had landed at all the fields several times, except for the new runway at An Khe. I knew I would have no trouble landing there. And I didn't. The weather was fine, the visibility was good, and there were no delays or unusual incidents. It was a piece of cake.

When we returned to Nha Trang, Hennessy told me I had passed the check ride. He told me that I was not yet qualified to fly into some of the shorter fields, as that would require satisfactory demonstration of my skills in the presence of a qualified instructor pilot. But I was now normal-field qualified and could fly as an aircraft commander, providing, of course, that the squadron assigned me to fly missions in that position. He guessed that they probably would have me fly a few of the squadron's regular missions—missions other than the in-country shuttle—soon, so that I could gain more experience in the left seat. He shook my hand and congratulated me. It was a standard kind of closure to a check ride, but I was pleased.

I began to think of myself as a real C-130 pilot. Then I remembered my poor showing at An Khe Golf Course, and I had to acknowledge to myself that I was scarcely an ace pilot. As I seemed to do in everything I attempted, mastery of the necessary skills came slowly. I had had the same experience in pilot training. Meanwhile, it was back to playing copilot for Major Potter.

The following day we departed Nha Trang early in the evening, carrying three pallets loaded with ammunition to Bin Thuy, a field in the delta area south of Saigon. Descending toward the field, we could see the wide, flat surface of the Mekong River running from west to east ahead of us. We landed just as it began to grow dark, the red and blue lights of the runway and taxiways illuminating the boundaries of the field in the otherwise dark terrain.

After we shut our engines down, we waited for the Army troops to arrive with the load they wanted transported to our next destination, Bien Hoa. As we waited, we noticed the men around the aircraft looking nervously towards the western perimeter.

"What's the matter?" we asked.

"The guys in the listening post heard some noises out there just before you landed. They think the perimeter's going to be probed tonight."

"Let's get out of here," Potter said, after our last pallet was removed. "This place is making me nervous." We departed to the east, then turned left toward Saigon. As we turned north, we could see a steady stream of parachute flares falling along the west side of the perimeter.

When we landed at Tan Son Nhut, we walked into the Airlift Control hut to see what our next load was.

"You guys okay?" the dispatcher asked.

"Yeah. Why?" we answered.

"There's a big firefight going on down at Bin Thuy. Thought you might have been a part of it." We shook our heads slowly, grabbed a cold Coke out of the pop machine, and went outside in the humid night air to await the arrival of our load.

I sat in the copilot's seat in the cockpit, windows open, reading my current paperback novel. When I looked out, I saw one of the strangest convoys I had ever seen. A 463L loader was moving up with three pallets of well-wrapped cargo, accompanied by a staff car and an MP vehicle, complete with armed guards.

"What is this?" I asked Major Potter, who was walking out from the ALCE building.

"High-priority load," he said. "Crucial cargo for the troops. We're even going to be carrying an MP with us to Cam Ranh."

I had never before seen cargo so important that armed guards had to accompany the load, except once in Europe, but I doubted we were carrying the same kind of cargo. "What is it?"

"Essential supplies for the war effort," he said. "Booze for the clubs at Cam Ranh."

I walked around to the back of the aircraft. Through the plastic wrapping and webbed netting I could see cases marked Gilbey's and Smirnoff and Johnny Walker. The loadmaster was helping to push the loaded pallets onto the rollers on the aircraft ramp. Armed guards stood around watching us work.

When he was done, I asked, "Don't they trust us?" He shrugged helplessly and shook his head slowly.

"They don't want to lose any of their precious cargo due to pilferage. So, they send along an armed guard for escort."

When we landed at Cam Ranh, we found another armed escort ready to transfer the load from the aircraft to the safe confinement of the club storage area.

We flew empty to Nha Trang, arriving as the eastern sky was starting to lighten. "Well, we've just hauled two of the most crucial loads we can haul in wartime," Potter said wearily, as he undid his seat belt and shoulder straps after we had shut the engines down. "Bullets and booze. And you saw which load received the most attention."

Chapter 8

The Golf Course

"She not here," one of the other girls told me, when I asked for Karla. "She go Taipei. Come back tomorrow."

"Taipei?" I said, with a puzzled look. "Why Taipei?"

"She from Taipei, have family Taipei."

Oh. Of course. I don't know why I was surprised at the idea that she might be a part of a family, might have a life of her own beyond the dimly lit environment of the China Nights.

The next night I went into town again. When I entered, Karla immediately walked over. She seemed happy to see me but a little wary. As usual, she looked lovely. I knew what she was going to say; it had been a month since I had been in.

"Hi, GI. How come you gone so long?"

"I hear you've been gone too?"

"Yes, I go Taipei. See family. I born Taipei. Family live Taipei long time."

"Do you visit your family often?"

"Yes. Every two-three weeks." She paused again. "I go see my boy."

"How old is he?"

"He two years old. Very big boy. Very heavy." She held her hands far apart, raised them as if picking up a heavy load, smiling at the thought.

"You want see picture?"

She reached down into her purse and pulled out a wallet. She released the clasp, and flipped through the plastic partitions until she found the one she wanted. She held it forward. The little boy was sitting on his mother's lap. The picture had been cropped to fit into the wallet. I could just see enough of the woman to see that it was Karla. Her hair looked different, plainer, straighter, but the face and profile were hers. The boy was chunky with a thick head of straight black hair, looking intently at whoever was taking the picture. Karla was looking at the boy with pride and affection.

I nodded and smiled. I was moved by what the picture said about Karla. Taipei wasn't far away, an hour's ride on the train, but the separation must have been hard for her.

"You have more pictures?" I asked.

She showed me pictures of her mother and father, stiff in a formal pose, taken many years ago.

"Wedding picture?" I asked. She nodded.

"Now you show me pictures," she said. I pulled out my wallet and handed my pictures over one at a time.

Chapter 8. The Golf Course

"This your wife?" Karla studied the photo of the woman who shared her name. "She pretty lady. This your mother. She pretty lady too. Where picture your father?"

"He died."

"How long?"

"Seven years."

"Too soon die." I nodded. "Why you no have father picture? Should honor dead." She seemed clear on that point. "What your father do?"

"He was a teacher in our local school."

"You have teacher for father?" She nodded, as if she thought that was a good idea. "What mother do now?"

"She's the postmaster." Karla gave me a puzzled look.

"She works for the government. Delivers the mail." Karla nodded, doubtful.

"This your brother. Look like you. Ai-yo! He in Army? He in Vietnam?"

"Soon," I said. She shook her head, as if it was a bad idea.

"When you give me your picture?" she asked.

"Do you want my picture?"

"Yes. You my boyfriend, yes?"

"Am I?" I said, and I pulled out a small official photo I had made when I first arrived at CCK and handed it to her.

She held up the tiny photograph and made a face. "Best photo you have?"

"I'm afraid so," I shrugged. She placed the small photo in the recesses of her purse.

"So now I'm your boyfriend?" I asked. "Is that all there is to it?"

"What you mean?"

"How about spending the night together?" I asked finally. She didn't answer.

I sat back, not willing to turn the conversation into a confrontation. I hadn't come into town to proposition Karla. I didn't think I had, anyway. She looked across the room, lost in thought, as if weighing factors prior to making a decision. Finally she turned to me and spoke slowly and carefully with a serious face.

"If we make love, I no see you again."

"What? Of course not!" The thought struck me as preposterous. What a strange thing for her to say! But the look in her face was unmistakable; it was the most serious, the saddest face she had ever shown me.

We danced once or twice, I awkwardly as usual, which I tried to joke about, but the mood of intimacy which we shared over family pictures was gone. Eventually I made some excuse about having to fly early in the morning and left. As I walked out the door, she walked slowly back to the table in the rear where one or two girls were sitting.

At five o'clock in the morning the squadron driver came around to wake me. "Time to get up, Captain Vaughan. Takeoff time oh-eight-hundred. Airplane's okay."

Down at the squadron operations building, Passarello was waiting for me. It had been over a month since we had flown together, on my first in-country shuttle. My performance then had not been good. I wondered what the outcome of this trip would be.

At the aircraft I did a walk-around inspection, studying my checklist against the various aircraft components: the engines, the wings, the gear. Into the seats, strap in. Check for all crew members plugged into their intercom sets, I in the pilot's seat,

Passarello in the copilot's seat, Mike Jones behind him at the navigator's desk, Floyd Cupp at the flight mechanic's station just behind Passarello and me, and "Brownie" Brown on the long cord outside in front of #2 engine.

"Clear to start #2 engine?" I asked.

"Two clear," Brownie responded.

"Turning two." I reached up with my left hand and punched the start button, simultaneously moving the #2 condition level forward with my right hand. Looking out my side window, I could see the large four-bladed prop began to turn, slowly at first, then more rapidly, quickly dissolving into a blur.

After all four engines were started, Brownie climbed back on board and closed the crew entrance door behind him. Our departure route took us due north, to the north tip of the island, then northeast across the ocean for our hour and a half flight to Naha. Into Naha just before eleven, departing about two hours later. Into Nha Trang by five o'clock local time, then the quick flight back out to Cam Ranh Bay, our shuttle base.

At Cam Ranh we landed to the north, turned left towards the C-130 ramp at the northwest corner of the field, taxied into our parking spot, and shut the engines down. A crew van took us on the long ride around the south perimeter road to the main part of the base. We checked in at the VOQ office, where we found we had been assigned to an air-conditioned trailer. Or at least the officers had; the enlisted men were assigned a couple of bunks at a dormitory.

Instead of the usual passenger run, our first mission involved hauling some troops and equipment in and out of Bien Hoa. I was in the left seat, the pilot's seat, once again. The first leg, a straight shot from Cam Ranh across the hills to the flat lands of Bien Hoa, was uneventful.

At Bien Hoa we loaded some Air Force supplies and flew them north to Phu Cat, a new base, just opened, located just in from the coast, north of Qui Nhon. Hills framed it to the north and west. It was home to an F-100 wing and other miscellaneous Air Force aircraft. It had a nice long runway, and landing on it presented no challenges. Thank God. I was beginning to worry about which field would provide the test of my short-field landing ability. I knew Passarello would need to have some clear evidence of my competence, or he would never approve me to fly in-country and I would be limited to flying the long haul missions between CCK and Okinawa, the Philippines, Thailand.

From Phu Cat we flew back to Bien Hoa, where we picked up a load of fuel bladders for the Army troops at Quan Loi. Landing at Quan Loi would be a bit more challenging. But I was not worried about landing at Quan Loi. I had been there before and knew what to expect. It was a pleasure to land at Quan Loi, even though it was a dirt strip of medium length. Its approaches were clear, and it was not bounded by hazardous natural or artificial constraints. As usual, we landed toward the French colonial buildings that were the headquarters of the rubber plantation. Once again, men with red dust-coated faces helped us offload. From Quan Loi we went back to Cam Ranh. Our first day in-country was short and uneventful.

The next day Passarello was scheduled to fly with another pilot, and I filled in as copilot for Lieutenant Colonel Louis McAdory, another old-timer in the squadron. Our scheduled mission that day took us first to Duc Pho, another new (to me) strip up the coast. It was a short but manageable dirt strip north of Qui Nhon. We were the

Chapter 8. The Golf Course

only C-130 among two or three twin-engine C-7 Caribous. Caribous had been flown by the Army until the Air Force claimed that the Army was infringing on Air Force operational responsibilities. So the Army had to give up flying the aircraft, and now the Air Force was flying them.

From Duc Pho we flew back down the coast to Phan Rang, with its nice long runway. From Phan Rang we went back up to Phu Cat and from Phu Cat we went to Cam Ranh. Another short day with minimum challenges. This wasn't the kind of activity I associated with in-country flying. None of the missions so far had brought with it the same kind of heart-pounding, sweat-producing responses that I recalled from my first flights in-country.

The next day, still flying copilot for Colonel McAdory, we were finally assigned to fly the standard passenger run, Cam Ranh to Qui Nhon to An Khe to Pleiku, back to Cam Ranh, and then reverse course. Now that landing at An Khe wasn't a problem, I actually looked forward to flying the route; although it involved a series of short hops, I saw it as one of the more useful, productive runs, hauling Army troops into and out of their jungle camps.

As we looked over the crew folders in the Can Ranh operations building that morning, McAdory said, "Well, I'll be damned. We're using the Golf Course at An Khe."

My heart stopped. I asked, "Why, for god's sake?"

"They're installing lights on the new runway and taxiways. It'll be closed for a couple of weeks."

The one field I had worried about the most, the field I had thought would no longer create a pucker factor, was back to confront me. Thank god McAdory was flying the airplane. I didn't have the nerve to ask him how he felt about landing there.

The trip up the coast to Qui Nhon was, as usual, lovely. We flew low to avoid a thin cloud layer, and we could see the coastline clearly. After a short stop at Qui Nhon to pick up a handful of passengers, we were on our way inland to An Khe.

The weather was clear. The new field at An Khe stood out like a beacon, with the freshly turned dirt and glistening white concrete. But that runway was not available to us. We called An Khe tower and were told to land to the north on the Golf Course.

McAdory called for flaps and gear down as he flew over the field from south to north on a high initial. He then began to descend, turning to the right, first on a crosswind, then to downwind. I didn't envy him, having to judge his distance to the field by looking across the copilot's seat at the field that was quickly passing below and behind. But I made it a point to note the geographical features that marked his turning points. He turned right onto a base leg, and I could see that he had set himself up well in terms of altitude and airspeed.

We turned onto final approach. McAdory was aiming the aircraft right at the end of the runway, knowing the ideal landing would require touching down as soon as possible. As we approached the end, he pulled back on the throttles. He was moving the yoke quickly and vigorously, working hard to keep exactly the approach picture he wanted.

He retarded the throttles to idle, pulled the yoke back, and we slammed into the runway, firmly but safely. The flight mechanic called clear to reverse, and McAdory pulled the throttles rapidly into the reverse thrust range. He vigorously applied the brakes, and the combination of brakes and reverse thrust slowed the aircraft noticeably.

As we approached the point where the runway seemed to end, we had slowed significantly, and as we came over the top of the rise, we could see that we had plenty of runway left. "So that's how it's done," I thought. When I tried to remember how Passarello had handled the landing two months earlier, my mind was a blank. The main impression that stayed with me when Passarello had landed was one of impossibility, that no C-130 could ever land successfully on a runway this short, this narrow, and this ugly.

I had learned two important lessons from watching Colonel McAdory land at the Golf Course. The first was the identification of the geographical features of the terrain that marked turning points in the pattern. The second, more important lesson was: Take charge. Fly the aircraft all the way in. I hoped I could hold those thoughts for the next few days. I was certain I would be seeing the Golf Course again.

* * *

Our next mission was an evening mission; I would be able to relax as we carried cargo from one field to another. I knew that when we flew night missions, we would be flying into long, well-lighted runways. I was back in the left seat, with Passarello playing copilot for me. We left Cam Ranh shortly before eight at night and flew to Phan Rang. From Phan Rang we flew to Bien Hoa and became involved in a series of shuttle flights between Bien Hoa and Plieku. Apparently the Army needed troops and equipment moved to the central highlands in a hurry. We flew three trips to Pleiku, offloading there with engines running. I stood outside to help the loadmaster make sure that no one walked into one of our spinning props in the dark.

We landed at Cam Ranh just as the sun was beginning to lighten the skies to the east. It had been a long, hard night, the most flying we had done this trip. We were scheduled to fly the following day, on the mission I knew would eventually come to me: the 850 pax run to Pleiku and back. So I would have to play the Golf Course two more times. I felt sure I knew what Passarello must be thinking, that this would be the true test. I needed to land the aircraft competently and confidently at An Khe. If I couldn't do it, I might not have another chance to prove myself capable of flying as an aircraft commander in-country.

I had one day to reflect on the importance of the mission. Then, at 8:25 the next morning, we were on our way up the coast to Qui Nhon. We landed straight in, over the harbor to the north, at Qui Nhon. Twenty minutes later we were airborne again, on a westerly heading to An Khe.

I decided to follow Colonel McAdory's example, to fly an overhead approach, to give myself time to set up for landing at the Golf Course. I was increasingly thankful I had had the opportunity to see how McAdory had set himself up for landing.

I turned onto a high overhead, observing that helicopter traffic was light. I called for the flaps and gear down on initial, as McAdory had. Two less things to worry about later, two less adjustments to make at a time when I didn't want to be making any more adjustments to the aircraft configuration than I had to. As the field disappeared beneath my nose, I waited a few seconds, then began a turn to the right, to the crosswind leg, pulling power off and descending. Then a turn to downwind. Steady at just under a thousand feet of altitude. Thank god the Army owned the real estate around here. I wanted to be as low as I safely could be before I turned final.

I could see the field through Passarello's side windows. I seemed to be in a decent position. I tried not to think about the fact that the field I was about to land on was one of the shortest fields in Vietnam and certainly one of the narrowest. A brown scar in some really bad real estate. One good sign so far, Passarello's comments were mostly informational, not directive. Another right turn to base leg, again pulling some power off, descending. Roll out a little under five hundred feet up.

Once the wings were level, I called, "full flaps." As the flaps came down, I could feel the aircraft tilt forward, try to rise. Nose down trim, then as the speed slowed, nose up trim. I reduced power, pulling back slightly on the throttles with my right hand. One hundred twenty. One hundred fifteen. I concentrated on the end of the runway. I was aware that I was over-controlling, making larger movements with my left hand on the yoke than I probably needed to. But I had the aircraft in what seemed like a good approach attitude, and I didn't want to lose it. When I detected the slightest change in the approach picture, I immediately corrected for it, if a little too aggressively.

I focused on the end of the runway, the point at which dirt ended and the aluminum began. I blocked out the thought of the illusion of the disappearing runway and concentrated exclusively on those interlocking aluminum panels about fifty feet from the end of the runway. Airspeed one-oh-five. Here we are.

Power off. Pause. Flare; bring the yoke back, holding the aircraft as it settles. Wings straight. Nose straight. There goes the lift. Full back into the lap with yoke.

Wham! On the runway. Directional control looks good. Easy on the rudders. Power to idle. Throttles back, over the stops. Has the flight mechanic, Floyd Cupp, called cleared to reverse?

There he goes. Full reverse. Feel the aircraft decelerate. On the brakes. The aircraft jerks from the effects of the brakes. I'm too clumsy on the brakes. Ease off a little. Now back on.

"Nose wheel steering," Passarello says.

"Your yoke," I call, as I release it from the grip of my left hand and reach for the steering wheel to my lower left. The wheel is shimmying in my hand as I try to hold it steady, keep it from wiggling around. The aircraft is on the runway, heading straight, slowing. Just when the dust and dirt from the reversed props are about to catch up with us, I pull the throttles forward out of the reverse pitch range, and the noise and tumult of the landing subside slightly into the growl of the turboprops as they stabilize in their idle setting. We slow noticeably, and as I look up, I can see that we are just cresting the rise of the runway, with several hundred feet of runway ahead. I slowly begin to relax. The sweat drips off my forehead, and I wipe it off with the sleeve of my shirt.

"Not too bad," Passarello observes.

As we offload the passengers, he critiques my performance, telling me about things I knew I had done wrong, a little too low on base leg, over-controlling on final. But I know, and I'm pretty sure he does, that, however imperfectly it was done, I landed the aircraft successfully. Certainly not a perfect landing, maybe not even a good landing. But an acceptable landing, and one that was a marked improvement over my previous effort.

From An Khe to Pleiku, and from there to Cam Ranh. In the afternoon we reversed the course. By the time we returned to An Khe, about four hours after my first landing, the winds had picked up a little, but now there was a bit of a headwind to help slow our landing speed. I brought the aircraft down and slammed in to another acceptable, if rough, landing. I took Passarello's relative silence as praise.

When we got back to Cam Ranh, he said, "Well, it wasn't pretty, but at least you didn't scare me. When I sign you off as assault qualified, I have to be confident that you can take this airplane into and out of tricky fields, like the Golf Course, without causing harm to your crew, your passengers, or your aircraft. That's no small responsibility, considering some of the airfields we have to fly into and some of the conditions we encounter while we fly into them. And I have to tell you that the first time you landed at An Khe, on our first shuttle, I had my doubts. But I'm going to sign you off as assault qualified. However, you've got to keep working on your short-field landing technique."

So I had played the Golf Course and survived. I was drained.

Chapter 9

Blackout Flight to Khe Sanh

Our next mission was another night mission. Thank god. We should be landing on long runways, well-lighted, easy to land on. But instead of flying to fields in the center of South Vietnam, we headed north to Da Nang. From there we took a load up to Dong Ha, just south of the DMZ, the dividing line between North and South Vietnam. We offloaded with engines running, then returned to Da Nang at 11:00 p.m. We shut our engines down and walked to the snack bar for something to eat while the ground crew loaded the aircraft. They were still loading the aircraft when we returned. The load we were carrying was not the usual load, three or four pallets of supplies or mail. There were pallets of lumber and metal sheeting.

"What are we carrying?" I asked Colonel Passarello.

"Construction supplies," he said. "For a new airfield."

I had heard nothing about a new airfield being constructed. I imagined some new base located somewhere along the coastline. And if it was new, how could we possibly land in the middle of the night? I remembered landing at Tuy Hoa with Duke Williams when it was under construction, but we landed in daylight, when we could see the field and the surrounding area. How could we possibly land at an unfinished field at night?

"What new airfield? Where?"

"A place called Khe Sanh," Passarello replied. "It's a new camp under construction in the northwest corner of South Vietnam, next to the borders with Laos and North Vietnam. Located on an upland plateau. It will be a Marine base. It's supposed to be a secret."

I struggled to process this information. How were we going to deliver this load to an unfinished field in the darkness? We were standing on the Da Nang C-130 loading ramp at midnight, where ramp lighting provided minimal illumination for onloading and offloading activities. All the fields north of Da Nang were close to the coast of the South China Sea. I knew of no field located that far inland. I was confused and becoming increasingly anxious. Passarello, however, appeared calm and composed.

"You'll be playing copilot on this flight," he said, as if to ease my concerns.

We departed to the south, then circled to the left, heading north, climbing to 6500 feet off the coast. Abeam Hue, we turned west, inland. As the lights of Hue city passed beneath us, I looked ahead. All was darkness.

"Give the controller a call," Passarello said, handing me a piece of paper with the radio frequency written on it. I dialed in the frequency and gave a call.

A voice answered: "Roger. Turn right to a heading of two eight five and descend to 4000 feet."

Who was I talking to? Whoever it was, he was expecting us.

"Turn our anti-collision and navigation lights off," Passarello said.

Normally when we approached any field at night, we turned all our lights on, including landing lights.

The controller gave us further instructions to descend, with small heading adjustments. We descended in the darkness. No lights were visible anywhere in front of us. I knew from looking at maps that this corner of South Vietnam was lined with tall hills. This unknown voice is going to lead us right into a hillside, I thought.

"Flaps down. Gear down," Passarello said.

"Landing lights on?" I asked.

"Not yet. I'll tell you when."

I could not believe it. Landing without landing lights? At an unlit field? In the middle of the night? Our descent into blackness continued.

"Take over visually and land," said the controller. You've got to be kidding me, I thought.

"Landing lights on," said Passarello.

I flipped on the landing lights. Suddenly the area in front of us lit up. Two features immediately caught my attention, one good, one bad. The good part was a runway. We were aiming directly for the end of a dirt runway, in perfect position to land. The bad part was that the end of the runway sat on the edge of a cliff, whose steep side dropping away beneath us was clearly illuminated. Holy crap! I thought. But I had little time to reflect on what I was seeing as Passarello brought the aircraft in for a perfect landing.

The landing lights showed that we had what looked like lots of runway left. Passarello retarded the throttles to idle but did not go into reverse. We slowed gradually until finally, as the end of the runway came into sight, I could see a ramp off to the left. Several men were standing there. One was standing by a forklift. But there were no ramp lights. Our landing lights were the only lights shining in the darkness.

Passarello turned the aircraft left, onto the ramp, then right and set the parking brakes. We left our engines running but turned our landing lights off. The loadmaster opened the cargo doors, and the interior lights from the aircraft fuselage provided the necessary light for offloading to begin. The forklift maneuvered behind the aircraft and several men walked into the fuselage to help shove the construction materials onto the extended prongs of the forklift, one pallet at a time. The forklift driver placed the pallets in a neat row off our left wing tip.

When the pallets were off, the loadmaster called out "Ramp closed. Clear to taxi."

Passarello taxied the aircraft forward to another ramp entrance, next to the west end of the runway. We positioned ourselves for takeoff, heading out in the opposite direction from the direction we had landed. The landing lights illuminated the runway. Passarello brought the throttles forward and we began to roll. I looked out my side windows towards the ramp on which we had just deposited four pallets of construction materials but could see nothing. All was in darkness.

The aircraft accelerated and Passarello pulled back on the yoke. We lifted into the dark night sky. I could not see it, but I knew we had just flown past the end of the runway, over the steep cliff face on which it sat.

"Gear up. Landing lights off," Passarello said. "Flaps up."

Chapter 9. Blackout Flight to Khe Sanh

I was still in a state of shock as we flew back to Cam Ranh, whose bright lights comforted me as we descended for landing. I had come to respect Passarello's flying skills, but tonight's adventure had shown me that he was a really good pilot, calm and confident in the face of a truly hazardous situation. I could not imagine that I could ever do what he had done. I hoped I would not see Khe Sanh again any time soon. And never on a black-out night mission. It turned out that both of my wishes came true. I returned to Khe Sanh several times, but never at night.

We flew one more easy night mission before we left. On the first of June, we flew back to CCK by way of Bien Hoa. In the month of May I had spent a total of six days in Taiwan, and twenty-five days on the road. My flying time for the month amounted to over ninety-six hours. I was beginning to feel like not quite so much of a new guy.

As if to make up for asking Colonel Passarello to fly the hazardous night flight to Khe Sanh, three days later the CCK schedulers sent him (and his crew, including me) to Bangkok, with interim stops at Clark and Korat. The Bangkok shuttle missions

The Floating Market, Bangkok. The canal system was the primary means of transferring fruit and other goods throughout the city of Bangkok. Today the canals have been replaced by concrete highways. Photograph dated 1967.

were similar to the Vietnam shuttle missions, carrying mail, passengers, and baggage, except that on the Bangkok shuttle, we flew to fields in Thailand, and not (normally) in Vietnam. Because of the schedule timing, we had one free day in Bangkok, and the crew agreed to take a Bangkok canal tour.

At that time, one of the main means of travel across the city of Bangkok was the canal system. Canals crisscrossed most of the city. Merchants, especially farmers, brought their goods, vegetables and fruit into the city and sold their wares at market sites along the canals. The canals, linked to the Chao Phraya River, which flowed through Bangkok, were laid out in a regular geometric pattern, typically about twenty to thirty feet wide, wide enough to allow two small boats to pass. Some sections were wider, especially near central market areas.

Some enterprising Thais had established canal boat tours, in which visitors (like we Americans) would hire a boat and guide for a tour of the canals. We had been told that a canal boat tour was the best way to see the real Bangkok. We hired a boat for the five of us. Our guide was an attractive Thai girl who spoke English very well. She sat in the front of the small boat, facing us as we sat on benches in the middle. A Thai boatman sat in the rear, operating the motor. The boat, covered with a canvas top to protect us from the sun, was powered by a small outboard motor. The motor was not especially powerful, but then it didn't need to be, as the top speed in the narrower canals was only five miles an hour.

We started out in the smaller canals, which bordered mostly living areas, where we could see the morning wash hung out to dry on clotheslines. At one of the smaller markets, we stopped while our guide handed us bananas and other fruit samples as well as bottled Thai fruit juices. We eventually made our way out to the Chao Phraya River, where we saw naked Thai boys diving into the muddy stream. We pulled up to the dock of the Royal Barge Museum, where the Royal Thai ceremonial boats were kept, long, ornately decorated boats used by the king and queen of Thailand to tour the river on special holidays. We all agreed that it was the best way to see Bangkok.

Two days after returning to CCK we again flew to Bangkok but left almost immediately, flying to Takhli this time, then to Nakhon Phanom, then to Clark before returning to CCK. In the days following, we flew a hodge-podge of missions—north to Tachikawa, south to Naha, over to Thailand, back to CCK. I hoped my schedule would ease, but it didn't. I was scheduled out again that night, flying with another crew to Bangkok and back.

In the last sixteen days I had been on the road on nine different trips and had flown a total of about seventy hours. I had spent only three nights in my bed at CCK. I barely had time to wash clothes between flights. I was beginning to feel more than a little road-weary. So when I walked though squadron operations building after returning from a Thailand mission, flying as co-pilot with another crew, I hoped I would have a break in my schedule. But as usual, I was scheduled out again, two days later. But what was not so usual about the mission was that I was on the board as aircraft commander—flying a mission as head of my own crew.

Chapter 10

Orbit City

Our destination was Udorn, in northeast Thailand, where we were to fly the airborne radio command post, officially known as the Airborne Command and Communications Capsule. ABCCC operations had been moved to Udorn from Da Nang, where I flew my first ABCCC missions. The other members of Passarello's crew were flying with me; my copilot for this trip was Lieutenant Ernie Miller. When we landed at Udorn we were assigned to the ABCCC quarters, a pleasant air-conditioned one-floor wooden hooch.

The primary aircraft stationed at Udorn were F-4s, parked along the ramp in tight, neat rows, and the noise of their engines being tested or afterburners being lit for takeoff rolled across the base. The F-4s were used for MIG suppression missions over the north and ground attack in Laos and portions of North Vietnam. The base itself was neatly laid out, with regular streets and numerous wooden hooches. There was a more relaxed atmosphere here than in Vietnam. Udorn, or any of the other Thai bases, just didn't have the same tight, nervous feel of places like Tan Son Nhut or Da Nang.

When I walked into the Udorn officer's club, I was pleasantly surprised to see an old friend from cadet days at the Academy, Richard O. "Zero" Troy. Zero was flying RF-4s. It was his job to fly his RF-4 over selected sites in Laos and North Vietnam and take pictures. He flew most of his photo missions early in the morning, so that the aircraft whose job it was to strike targets in North Vietnam, the F-105s, would have the latest visual information. And then it was his job again, after the F-105 strikes had been flown, to fly over and see what damage had been done. An occasional easier mission was to see what the weather was like, if it were clear enough for strikes, or if the clouds and haze were too thick for effective operations.

He couldn't tell me much about what he did, but I knew that his job was as hazardous as that of the F-105 aircrew members, because the planners at headquarters Seventh Air Force, at Tan Son Nhut, liked to have their pilots fly on a regular schedule. The anti-aircraft defenders around Hanoi had a pretty good idea when the reconnaissance as well as the bombing aircraft would be flying over.

Zero seemed a little more subdued and a little less spontaneous than he was when he had lived down the hall from me at the Academy. We drank beer while he told me about life at Udorn.

"The duty here is pretty nice, if you can avoid thinking about your next flight north. The weather is reasonably pleasant, and the food is good."

"It's much nicer fighting the war here than in Vietnam," I agreed. "Do you get into Vietnam much?"

Zero nodded. "Occasionally I fly to Tan Son Nhut and Da Nang. I avoid staying overnight if I can help it." He paused, then continued. "But when you come back from flying at Da Nang or Tan Son Nhut you know you're still in a war zone. You can't forget it because they mortar you at night and a trip into town can be risky. Here, when you come back from a mission, you can drink beer that's cold, not warm, take a hot shower, go on a trip into town, spend the night with a good-looking woman, eat good food. A lot of guys have girl friends in town. Some of the guys rent hotel rooms on a long-term lease; the most serious ones rent bungalows or houses. They set up a regular home-away-from-home."

"But you get spoiled living the good life. Life in Thailand reminds you of life in the States. In some ways it's even better than life in the States. But there's too much of a contrast between down here, living well, and up there, flying over the North. It can get to you. In some ways, living the good life in Thailand takes its toll as well. When you live in Vietnam, you never forget you're in the war."

I nodded in agreement. "So when are you asking for a transfer to Saigon?" I asked.

Zero gave me a broad smile. "D.K., old buddy, let's have another cold beer."

Mike, Ernie, Floyd and I arrived at the aircraft for our first flight late on the afternoon following our arrival, completed our preflight, and waited for the capsule crew to arrive. The air was warm and sweet, a perfect early summer afternoon. Finally a blue Air Force bus pulled up at the rear of the aircraft and the capsule crew filed out. Half were in flying suits, and half weren't. Only one or two wore rank, at least that I could see. There were two or three young men whom I took to be Laotian nationals. They seemed much too young to be involved in the war, even as tame an aspect of it as operating radio equipment.

When all were safely on board, we climbed up into the cockpit and started engines. We took off to the west, into the setting sun, and turned back to the east in a gentle left climbing turn. As we climbed into the growing darkness over the Mekong River below, we saw the day bird descending below us, anti-collision lights flashing brightly, taking a straight-in approach to Udorn.

We started our orbit just east of Nakhon Phanom. As we burned fuel and lightened our load, we moved our orbit north and gained altitude. We had been warned about the possibility of surface-to-air missiles. "So far, they've kept them along the northern part of the Ho Chi Minh Trail," the briefing officer told us. "Besides, they can't hit anything flying above 20,000 feet with any kind of accuracy. So once you get over 20,000, you can move it up towards the north a little. If you do get a launch, pinpoint it as well as you can, and we'll send somebody in after the site right away. They keep moving those damn things around."

We reached our first orbit area over the south central section of Laos as it grew dark. After we leveled at 16,000 feet, I left Ernie in charge and walked into the back of the aircraft to say hello and to see what was going on. Mike Jones got into my seat to help Ernie keep track of the aircraft. I studied the maps carefully, but it appeared to be a quiet evening. A few aircraft were operating, but no major activity was occurring.

After a while it was my turn to get back in the seat; Floyd Cupp sat in the copilot's seat and kept me company while Ernie and Mike relaxed. After a while, I began to play with the HF radio controls, dialing in frequencies on the radio set to discover what I might find coming across the airwaves from far away. Mostly I received various forms of static, strange tones, buzzing noises. Then I caught the strains of

Dixieland music. After a few minutes the music ended, and the announcer informed me that I was listening to a jazz program on Radio Australia. What a treat! Orbiting at 16,000 feet in the darkness over Laos, radio controllers talking to combat aircraft in the rear, while I listened to jazz on Radio Australia. I tilted the pilot's chair full to the rear and drank hot coffee, beating time with my feet to the Muskrat Ramble.

After a few hours, I crawled up on the top bunk above the crew seat at the rear of the flight deck. I had never before had a reason to curl up in it. The steady hum of the engines and the mild movements of the autopilot put me to sleep almost instantly. My first major mission as an aircraft commander, and here I was sound asleep on a crew bunk. An hour and a half later Mike woke me up. We were 2,000 feet higher and fifty miles farther to the north than we had been when I fell asleep.

Finally, we began to see the signs of morning: a slowly lightening sky to the east, showing the layers of clouds dissipating over the South China Sea; increasing chatter on the UHF radio frequency, as the radar controllers responded to aircraft coming up from Takhli and Korat, heading north, to the northwest of our orbit. Finally, a call from the head controller in the rear: we were cleared to descend; the day bird had just departed Udorn. My landing could have been smoother, but then it was the first time I had landed after flying for thirteen hours.

That night we went to the Udorn O-club, where we watched the F-4 pilots in their sky blue flight suits drink beer, flirt with the Thai waitresses, and sing rowdy songs as loudly as possible.

The next night we flew another Alley Cat mission. We departed earlier than usual because the day bird had a maintenance problem and needed to land. Otherwise, the mission went about the same as before. There were a few thunderstorms in the area, and we watched our airborne radar sets carefully to avoid the heavy return signals. Outside we could see the lightning flashes in the distance, mostly hidden in the billowing masses of cloud that were illuminated by the lightning. As morning approached, we cheated in our orbit, edging slowly closer to Udorn so we wouldn't have far to go to land. After I gave a position report to the ground radar controller at Udorn, another voice came on frequency to report inbound to Udorn, then said, "Hi, D. K."

I recognized the voice. "Welcome back, Zero. See you in the club."

* * *

After we returned from Thailand, the crew members I had been flying with returned to their leader, Colonel Passarello, and promptly went in-country on another shuttle. A new crew roster issued after our return listed me as a copilot on another crew. As a result of flying three ABCCC missions, I was high on flying time and wasn't scheduled to fly. I was sitting in my room when Les Fredericks, my roommate, walked in, back from a trip. It was a rare event for both of us to be at CCK at the same time; we had spent less than five nights together in our room in the last five months.

"Want to go into town, Les?" I asked.

"No thanks. It won't be long before I see my wife again."

Well, I'll be damned, I thought. But Les was that kind of person—straightforward, loving, caring, faithful. A really nice guy. What was he doing flying C-130s? I wondered.

The cab driver deposited me at the entrance to the China Nights about ten o'clock. I sat down at the usual table and ordered a drink. Eventually one of the girls came over.

"Where is Karla?" I asked.

"She not here. Have big party."

"Will she come in tonight?"

She shrugged. "Have big party." I nodded and she went back to her group.

I couldn't blame Karla for not being there every time I walked through the door. I hadn't come to see her for over a month. I could have come in if I had wanted, even if for one night. As I sat there drinking my scotch, I reflected that I was a lousy prospect as a male acquaintance. The girl walked over again.

"Karla say she come over soon. Not stay long."

Someone must have called her. I didn't know exactly what kind of party she was involved in, but imagined she must be escorting some VIPs from out of town, and I was certain her participation in it was helping to pay the rent. For her to leave, even if for a short time, was a sign of some interest.

After another half-hour, she came through the door, wearing a long wrap, hair stylishly done up, looking elegant. She sat down with a bit of a thump, as if glad to be off her feet. She looked at me intently with her dark brown eyes, made more striking by eyeliner and mascara. "How you, GI?"

I nodded my head. "Good. Busy. As usual."

"You in town for while?"

I shrugged my shoulders. "Two or three days. I don't know when I'll be scheduled for another flight. You busy?"

She nodded, took a sip of her tea. "Have big party. Many officers from base."

"Dance?"

She hesitated, then stood up. "One dance."

The music was soft and slow. Again, I felt awkward taking her in my arms, but I held her close, hardly moving, just swaying with the music, smelling her perfume, which was there in spite of the smell of liquor and cigarette smoke. She seemed stiff, tense. When the music ended we sat down.

"Thanks," I said. "It was good to hold you, to be close. I forget how good that is."

She looked at me warily, studying me with those eyes. "I have to go back."

I nodded.

"You come tomorrow night?"

"Yes," I said. I paused. "I want to spend the night with you."

She studied me for a few moments, then looked away. "Okay," she said, matter-of-factly. "You come here at closing time, one o'clock, tomorrow night. You bring money to pay for night." She told me how much the night would cost. She stood up briskly, all business. She walked quickly to the door, went out, and stepped into a taxicab, which sped off into the night.

The next day, I busied myself with small chores in my room, visiting squadron ops to see if I was on the schedule, reading, sleeping. In the afternoon I wandered into the O-club bar for a few drinks. I drank slowly, but when I walked to the gate several hours later, I could feel the effects. The short, half-mile walk helped to clear my head. The air was warm and humid, full of the aromas of the night.

I walked into the China Nights a little after midnight. Men and women were dancing, talking loudly, laughing. I walked over to the bar and wedged my way in.

I knew Karla was in the room. With this much activity, she had to be here. But I didn't have the nerve to go looking for her. Suddenly I felt a hand on my arm. It was Karla, calm and composed in the middle of the noise and motion. "Have customer now. When club close you wait here." I nodded.

I sat at the bar and watched the festivities. I recognized some of the crew members from the squadron along the bar and at the tables, raising their glasses, telling jokes, laughing, unwinding from the hours of boredom and pressure spent above the lands of Southeast Asia and the waters of the South China Sea. The music was slow, and on the hardwood dance floor couples were locked in tight embraces.

Eventually the men started to leave, some hand-in-hand with women. Karla was talking to a group at one of the tables. I tried not to stare in their direction, but whenever I glanced over, Karla gave me a quick nervous look. Finally the bar emptied, and the group at the table began to leave. Karla walked to the door with one of the men. He gave her a squeeze and attempted to kiss her, but she dodged the effort neatly.

When they left she came over. "You wait. I go talk to Mama-san." She went to a table at the rear, said a few words, picked up her purse, and walked back to me. "We go now."

We walked out into the night. The street was suddenly quiet. Most of the cabs were gone. When she saw me looking for a cab, she pulled me down the sidewalk. "I live near. We walk."

We walked down the street towards the center of town, in the general direction of the railroad station. The last few merchants were closing their shops. We crossed a street and turned down what looked like an alley lit in a kind of blue half-light. We paused in front of a three-story building while Karla looked through her purse for her keys. We went up a few steps through the front door, then walked up a long narrow flight of stairs to the second floor. At the top of the stairs we turned right and paused again before a door. Karla unlocked it, opened it. I followed her inside.

She walked into the room and turned on a light on a table. On the far wall was her bed, a metal double bed with a decorative metal headboard. To the right was a large iron clothes rack, bulging with dresses and coats. A large decorated cloth was thrown over it. Against the wall behind the clothes rack was a dresser filled with powders and perfumes. Photographs were stuck along the edge of the mirror.

"You want bathroom?" she asked. She gestured to the far end of the room, where there was a kind of doorway through a partition that ran parallel to the far wall but stood out about four feet from it. It was not a complete wall and was open at the top. Behind it were the bathroom features—the tub with shower, toilet, and sink. At the near end of the partitioned area was a small stove. There was a smell of fried rice in the air. I walked back out into the bedroom.

The light of her table lamp shed a hard illumination on the features of the room. The room suddenly seemed bleak and uninviting. I had a strong urge to leave. Karla took off her wrap and hung it on a hanger on her clothes rack. She went behind the clothes rack to undress. I removed my shirt and pants and placed them on a chair along the wall and sat on the bed in my underwear. The springs of the uneven mattress squeaked when I sat on the bed. Karla came around the corner of her clothes rack wearing a plain white cotton shift.

I looked at her and, suddenly, she was no longer Karla. She was a thin Chinese girl with straight black hair and no makeup. Her long, luxurious-looking hair was gone; it was a wig that was perched on top of her dresser. She was someone I had never seen before. She pulled back the covers and got into bed. I followed her example. She reached over and turned out the light.

We made love silently, efficiently, unemotionally. I felt as awkward as I did when I had danced with her the first time. I half expected her to say "What's matter? You no know how to dance?" I finished, sweating, and lay across her arm. After a few moments, she tactfully urged me over to the other side of the bed, saying, "More comfortable you lie over there."

I awoke to see the half-light of early morning through a window beside the bed. I gathered my clothes and went into the bathroom. The faint odor of cooked rice and vegetables made my stomach feel uneasy. I dressed quickly without looking at the bed. But after I dressed, I knew I had to say something; I couldn't leave without speaking. I stopped at the door and tried to think of something. But all I could say was "I'll see you later."

She was looking at me with the cover pulled up to her chin, the bedding tight as we both felt. Her eyes were big and sad in her face. I turned the doorknob and started to leave. She said something and I turned back. "What?" I said.

"Money. You leave money." She was still holding the covers tight to her chin.

For Christ's sake. I couldn't even go out the door without screwing up. I fumbled through my wallet, looking for the right amount. I folded it and placed it on the dresser. I smiled weakly and went out, closing the door softly behind me. The stairway leading down looked like a tunnel that was closing in on me. I stumbled down the stairs, struggling for breath. As I went out the door to the street, the smells of Taichung cooking breakfast hit me like a wave, and I was suddenly hot and dizzy. My stomach heaved suddenly. I staggered down the street. I had visions of walking all the way to CCK in the hot morning light. But there came a cab, a lovely red cab. When I returned to my BOQ I stood in the shower and let the hot water run.

Chapter 11

Phan Thiet in Blue

Returning early in the morning from a flight to Clark, I saw that I was scheduled to depart later that night, going into Cam Ranh Bay to fly the shuttle. The duty officer told me I was taking over the crew of my old aircraft commander, Colonel Passarello, who was being pulled off the shuttle for emergency leave. I was dead-heading in with another crew.

Several hours later I was on board an aircraft taking me into Vietnam for my first in-country shuttle mission as an aircraft commander. Here was the big test already, only a little over two weeks since I had been officially approved to fly as an aircraft commander. I had the familiar tight feeling of not being fully ready to deal with the challenges of the shuttle.

After an all-night flight by way of Naha, we landed at Cam Ranh in the morning. I checked through the ops desk at the C-130 ramp and found that my crew was scheduled to fly early the next morning. Passarello would be on the next plane back to CCK, probably later in the day. I was told I could probably find the navigator, Mike Jones, and the new pilot, Major Hartwig, hanging around the O-Club.

I caught the crew shuttle van around the south perimeter road and checked into the housing office. They couldn't put me in with the crew because Passarello hadn't checked out yet, so I was placed temporarily in a transient crewmember building. I carried my bag over to a big two-story dormitory with rows of beds down both sides of the walls. Between the beds were metal lockers. The windows of the building were covered with screens and large wooden flaps which opened to let the breeze blow through. I threw my bag on an empty bed on the first floor, took a shower, changed into civvies, and walked into the O-club bar.

When I arrived, just after noon, the O-club was quiet. I had a sandwich and was working on my second warm beer when Mike walked in. We started to tell stories and shake the dice, playing "Horse" for beers. Major Hartwig, the new pilot, showed up. He got into the dice game too, and before we knew it, it was dark and the band was starting to play. We had established owner's rights to the left end of the bar, and newcomers had to reach past us for their beer.

The band was playing louder and louder, and as the bar grew more crowded, the volume of talk, laughter, and singing grew. By the time the band was into its second set, the local F-4 crew members were dancing with the few American nurses assigned to the base, and we turned to watch the action on the dance floor. The nurses seldom had a chance to sit down.

I couldn't seem to lose at the dice game, and I was drinking can after can of free beer. The room was growing warmer. By the time the band got into its last set, the noise was deafening. The dance floor was crowded with nurses and their dancing partners. Some of the more athletic and motivated members of the club were doing gymnastics on the rafters, hanging upside down by their knees, shaking their beer cans and squirting the contents at the dancers and spectators moving below.

After the band stopped, the noise gradually subsided and the club began to empty. I felt warm and sweaty and thought it would be a good idea to lie down. Somewhere close and soon, if possible. The other members of the crew had long since departed to their air-conditioned trailer, and I was left to find my way to the transient barracks. For some reason my normally reliable sense of direction failed me, and I wandered around in the ill-lit darkness. Suddenly I was very sick. I staggered against the side of a building and then decided the safest position would be on my hands and knees. I promptly threw up. After a few minutes I felt well enough to stand again.

I turned the corner of the building and was surprised to see that it was the transient barracks. I stumbled in, trying to avoid the sleeping forms lying motionless on the small single beds. I vaguely remember undressing before collapsing on the bed. Then all was blank.

An unreasonably short time later, I attempted to focus on the face that owned a pair of hands that seemed to be shaking me with more than the necessary amount of force, and a voice that said, once I forced myself to understand the words it was speaking, "Captain Vaughan, Captain Vaughan, wake up, Captain Vaughan!" When I questioned the need for wakefulness, the face said, "Your crew is waiting for you at the airplane. They sent me to find you. Takeoff time is in ten minutes."

Holy shit. My god. I attempted to stand up. Everything started spinning. My head felt unbelievably bad. I had the hangover of hangovers. Very likely I was still a little drunk. The face and the hands finally became part of a recognizable pattern: the ALCE duty driver, dispatched to find me.

As I stood unsteadily in the early morning light, three awful truths dawned on me. One: I needed a shave and a shower. Bad. My breath smelled awful. Really foul. And I wasn't going to have time to do either. Two: I was totally, completely stark naked. In my concern to sleep in as relaxed a state as possible the night before, I had taken every stitch of clothing off, underwear included. I glanced around the dormitory to see if anyone else could notice my shame and was at first relieved to see it was totally empty. Then it dawned on me that Three: everyone had seen me. While I lay unconscious and probably snoring violently, the entire contingent of transient aircrew members had been able to observe my noisy, naked repose.

I was too stupefied by my hangover and by the pressure of time to indulge in the luxury of embarrassment. The squadron driver was determined to deliver me to the flight line as promptly as possible and was lending me every assistance in my clumsy efforts to dress. I threw on my old underwear, conveniently close by on the floor, put on my smelly old flight suit of the day before, pulled on my flight boots, grabbed my flying gear, and declared that I was ready to fly.

The driver led the way out to the blue Air Force bread van, and while it sped west around the perimeter road, I tried to clear my head and focus my thoughts. I wasn't able to think clearly; if I were, I would have discovered many other reasons to feel totally and completely humiliated. Sent in-country to replace one of the most reliable and proficient squadron pilots, I couldn't even manage to make it to the plane for takeoff.

Chapter 11. Phan Thiet in Blue

When we pulled up to the ops building near the C-130 ramp, the rest of the crew was sitting casually on the bench in front of the building, as if it were part of the normal procedure: wait for the aircraft commander to make his last-minute entrance, looking scruffy and grungy. They all got on the van without much comment, looking at me with mild curiosity. I tried not to breathe in their direction. Surprisingly, they said little, not asking where I had been or why I was late. They knew I had been assigned to another building and assumed I had overslept. Or at least that's what I assumed they assumed. I didn't ask.

The preflight had been completed and Major Hartwig had the information about our schedule. We were flying out empty to Dalat, where we would pick up a load of vegetables. But the weather at Dalat was iffy: fog and low clouds. We might not be able to land. If we couldn't make it in, we were to return to Cam Ranh. We started engines. The noise and vibration in the cockpit seemed to have a soothing effect on my condition. After a quick engine run-up, we were cleared onto the active runway, 02 Left, and took off at 0715. Fifteen minutes late. A little over a half-hour from the time I had been sound asleep.

We turned right, flying south along the coast before turning inland, toward Dalat. I began mentally to prepare for the approach and landing at Dalat. I wasn't sure how well I would cope; I wasn't at all sure. As it turned out, I didn't need to worry. The clouds billowed up increasingly the nearer we flew to Dalat. Here and there we could see patches of green hills, but no clear passageways into the Dalat area. The tower operators at Dalat made our choice for us when they said visibility at the field was poor. I wasn't pleased with myself when I announced that we were returning to Cam Ranh Bay. I thought that if I had been more familiar with the territory, had been more proficient, more alert, I could have at least made an attempt to approach the field. But—back to Cam Ranh. One hour's worth of early morning pleasure cruising.

At Cam Ranh we took on a load for Phan Rang, close to the coast, this side of the hills that led to Dalat. I could handle Phan Rang. A big long runway. Stay north of the river when turning final. The clouds were still billowing over the hills to the west as we landed. From Phan Rang we flew back to Cam Ranh. At Cam Ranh we were given a load for Phan Thiet.

I had been to Phan Thiet before. A runway by the sea. The field was relatively long, the approaches clear. No hills to avoid. A straight-in approach either way you came in, from the southwest over the level land, or from the northeast over the sea.

We flew down from the north, out over the water. We were low, about 2500 feet. The clouds that had been billowing up over Dalat were part of a mass of cloud that extended all the way down the coast to Vung Tau and west to Saigon. We were below a cloud deck that extended to the hills twenty miles inland. The tower at Phan Thiet told us to land to the southwest. We were set up on an extended straight-in approach. As we came nearer to the field, I began to hope for some reason to prevent our landing, to cause us to have to return to Cam Ranh.

As we approached, a light rain began to blur my forward visibility, and drops of water rolled back on the side windows. I turned on the windshield wipers, but their jerky back-and-forth motion distracted me. The runway was dark and wet; a few small pools of water sat in the middle of the runway, where it sagged to its lowest point. The layers of clouds overhead cast a blue, filtered light over the field. The field and hills beyond were blue, everything was blue. I looked down at the sea through my side windows; the tops of waves were breaking white over the blue water. I didn't like seeing Phan Thiet in blue; I was used to dryness, to dust, to browns and oranges in the bright afternoon sun.

Numerous aircraft were parked at the northeast end of the ramp, aircraft I would have to fly over just prior to touching down. There were too many aircraft in the parking area. We would have to land long, and the runway was too short for us to land long. I searched the area ahead, trying to see a hopeful sign. But I saw nothing hopeful. All was rain, and the dark runway, dark and wet and slick and blue. At our flat approach angle, the runway appeared foreshortened and wet, and too many aircraft were parked on the overrun over which we would have to land, and the sea was below, full of rough water, the waves washing towards the cliffs that formed the shore.

I forced myself to call for the before landing checklist. I didn't want to do this. I didn't want to land. But I had to. It was my job to land the aircraft. Flaps half. Gear down. The aircraft slowed. I pulled the throttles back slowly. We didn't want to stall out into the aircraft that were parked there, a C-123, a C-47, O-1s, helicopters, an Air America C-45, and even two C-130s parked at the far end of the runway. For god's sake! It wasn't hills or Viet Cong snipers I had to worry about! It was Americans! It was us with too many aircraft hemming in my landing on a field that couldn't accommodate all of us! I looked for the wind sock. What was the wind doing? The wind sock was hanging slack, then moving back and forth in the feeble winds. Normally, this time of the day the wind was off the ocean. I probably was picking up a tail wind!

Everything was happening too quickly for me to do much else but react by instinct. Suddenly the sea was gone; we were over the cliff. Full flaps. We were approaching the field boundary, the runway was ahead. Slow the airspeed. Throttles back. Still too fast. Hold the nose up. Get across those damned airplanes parked so carelessly underneath our whistling arrival. Get the plane down now. Throttles to idle. Pull them back. Back. They were up against the stops, back as far as they would go. I was tempted to reverse them while we were still in the air.

Too much runway going by. Down now! Slam onto the runway, throttles up over the stop into the ground idle range. Step on the brakes right away as the flight mechanic hesitates, then announces clear to reverse. Yank the throttles into full reverse right now. Step on those brakes hard, hard. Directional control seems okay. Still hanging on to the yoke. "Your yoke," I yell to Major Hartwig, grabbing the nosewheel steering. Runway going by. More brakes.

As I step on the brakes I see a small yellow light, low on the front instrument panel, to the right of my yoke, blinking at me, on, off, on, off. I feel the brake pedals moving against my feet. The light keeps blinking, the pressure on the pedals increasing, decreasing. I take a quick look at Major Hartwig. "You don't need to get on the brakes!" I yell. "Don't step on the brakes!"

He gives me a strange bemused look. "I'm not on the brakes," he says. Oh. I look up. The aircraft is slowing. We haven't hit anything, nor are we about to. I look at the blinking yellow light again. I focus on the writing beneath it. "Anti-skid Light" it says. Well, I'll be damned. I have read about it in the pilot's manual but have never seen it operate. Until now.

The C-130 anti-skid system is designed to automatically release and then apply the brakes if the pilot stands on the brake pedals too severely. The on-off brake application process prevents the tires from locking up and skidding, keeps the tires from

Chapter 11. Phan Thiet in Blue

blowing, yet continues the braking process within predetermined limits of safety. Which it was doing even as I watched.

I released my leg pressure against the brakes. My legs began to shake. I hoped nobody could see my right leg jumping. The combined effect of full reverse thrust, which I was still applying, and my super-rigorous braking efforts was causing us to come to a rapid and complete stop. We stopped. I could see, when I looked up the runway, that we had almost a thousand feet of runway left. We had stopped with runway to spare. We would have to add power to taxi to the end of the runway.

"I don't think we need reverse thrust any more," Floyd Cupp suggested, as water droplets from the ground and sky engulfed the outside of the cockpit in a fine white spray.

"Right." I pulled the throttles out of the reverse pitch range, back into the ground idle range. I noticed that my right arm ached a little. I wondered why that was. So we had made it.

Before I could devote much time to comprehending the idea, I saw that we were faced with another, troublesome, but much smaller, challenge. The C-130s up ahead had taken up all the parking space that was there, which wasn't much. The tower suggested we should taxi back to the east end of the runway, the end we had just careened past. It was a good idea, except for the fact that there was no taxiway, just the runway itself, and it was not much wider than our wingtips.

We might back up all the way, except that we carried a load, the runway was uphill towards either end from the center, and we would drown ourselves with water if we tried. So what to do? Turn around on the runway. It was the only time I ever tried that particular maneuver. It was a hideous, awful experience.

First, move forward, turn to the right and then to the left, ending up on the left side of the runway, turned about 20 degrees to the left. Then back up, loadmaster looking out the open ramp door. Turn the nosewheel steering full to the right so that the aircraft swings to the left as it moves backwards. Move backwards until wham! the right rear main gear steps off the lip of the runway. Now full forward, especially with the right outboard engine and full left nosewheel steering until wham! the nose gear steps off the runway. Then into reverse again, full right nosewheel and wham! off goes the left rear main gear. Then full forward, especially with the right outboard engine, full left on the nosewheel, and maybe a little reverse on the left outboard engine. And now we were taxiing towards the northeast end of the runway. We turned into the left side of the ramp, moved our nose gear as close to the edge of the parking area as we could, and shut down the engines.

I unstrapped from the seat, made my way out of the flight deck, and down the steps of the crew door. The air outside was cool and moist, and the rain was falling in a fine, light drizzle. I tilted my head back and let the water soak my face. It felt good, the shower I never had in the morning, the shower I badly needed.

We checked the gear for damage, cuts we might have gotten when the tires went over the raised edge of the runway, in our bizarre turn-around dance. We found no damage. A few scuff marks, but nothing dangerous. While we were being offloaded, the two C-130s at the far end of the runway took off over us, one after the other. They cleared us with room to spare. It gradually occurred to me that we might have waited for a few minutes to let one of the other aircraft depart; then there would have been more room.

We returned to Cam Ranh. No more flights. Time to call it a day. As we walked into the ops building I realized that my hangover was gone. If possible, I smelled even worse than I had that morning.

The crew bus dropped me off at the transient barracks. I went inside, stripped off my smelly clothes and stood in the shower for a long time. I felt better, but I couldn't get rid of the vision of the runway at Phan Thiet extending in front of me, wet and black, and the cliff on which it sat, and the sea below, all of it bathed in a strange blue light.

* * *

The next morning we were scheduled for the standard passenger run: around the route from Cam Ranh to Qui Nhon to An Khe to Pleiku and then to Tan Son Nhut, now, not back to Cam Ranh, and then reverse course back to Cam Ranh. I had flown the route often, and was not concerned about any of the fields, especially now that the new runway at An Khe was fully operational; there would be no more landings at An Khe Golf Course. So the mission would be a piece of cake.

Our first leg, from Cam Ranh up the coast to Qui Nhon, proceeded normally. Once we arrived in the Qui Nhon area, we were directed to land to the south instead of landing to the north. Though I had landed often at Qui Nhon, I had never landed to the south. We circled around to the east, over the coastline, in a leisurely left turn, turning on final about two miles out. As we turned in, I studied the large hill that rose just northwest of the airfield.

I called for flaps and gear while turning on final, and then called for full flaps after we rolled out on final. I set up a normal descent, not too shallow, not too steep.

Qui Nhon, March 1967. Descending to land to the south. Large hill to the right created irregular winds affecting aircraft controllability on landing.

Chapter 11. Phan Thiet in Blue

The hill passed off to our right. The aircraft seemed to be flying itself toward a landing. I reduced power slightly in anticipation of a normal landing.

We were about ten feet in the air when the aircraft fell out of the sky and slammed onto the runway. We were thrown against our seat belts, our heads rolling as if we were rag dolls. I had never been in a more violent touchdown. And I was the pilot.

The aircraft, which had been flying normally, suddenly dropped. I tried to catch the descent by pulling back hard on the yoke, but that effort was too little too late. I thought to add power, but by the time the thought occurred to me, it was too late. The aircraft had stalled completely out, ten feet above the runway.

"How is everyone back there?" I asked Brownie over the intercom after we had turned off the runway.

"Some of the folks are shaken up. It was a hard jolt. One of the Army guys cut his head on one of the metal hooks on the center stanchion."

"Is it bad?"

"Bad enough. He's holding his handkerchief on his head."

Oh my Christ. I felt terrible. It was one thing to have a bad landing under poor conditions, but it was inexcusable when conditions were good. I tried to rationalize the event: there had been a wind gust; no, the wind had suddenly changed; the wind must have eddied around the hill, causing a dramatic change in wind direction and velocity. But the truth was that I had let the aircraft get away from me. I had not responded appropriately: full power on the throttles, go around if necessary. I had not done what I had to do to keep control of the airplane.

We taxied off the runway and into the parking area. After we shut down, I hurried out of the seat and down the crew door steps to stand outside. I couldn't sit in the seat and pretend that that landing had been business as usual. I wanted to see for myself how badly the passengers had been shaken up. I stood stupidly with a limp grin on my face as they straggled off the aircraft through the crew entrance door. No one appeared too badly shaken, though they were all talking about the landing. Then an Army troop walked down the steps, holding his handkerchief to the left side of his head. I was too ashamed to ask if he was all right. From what I could see he wasn't bleeding too badly. But his handkerchief was bloody, no doubt about that. And I could see blood on his uniform.

As he walked by, I heard him say to his companion, "Six months in-country without a scratch. And now the fucking Air Force wounds me coming back from R&R. Can you get the purple heart for something like this?" At least he had his sense of humor.

After everyone was off the aircraft I paced the ramp. Floyd Cupp inspected the gear for damage. We'd have to put a write-up in the Form 781 about a hard landing. I couldn't pretend the landing had been just a little hard. It had been a catastrophe, a real failure of piloting. Yesterday I would have expected I'd do something like this, but not today. Today, this was supposed to be a no-sweat mission. No screw-ups.

After we loaded the few passengers who were going with us, we started engines and taxied out for takeoff. For some reason we took off to the north, the opposite direction from our landing direction. We turned left towards An Khe. I was relieved that no one had been hurt, but my gut hurt from anguish. The new runway at An Khe was long and wide, as I remembered it from before. I landed the aircraft without incident. From An Khe we flew west to Pleiku, where we picked up a large number of Army troops, all bound for their R&R trips.

As we approached Saigon, we could see towering cumulus rising overhead and dark skies to the south. The rain storms of the preceding day were still in the area. As we flew closer to the city of Saigon, we could see a black wall of rain blocking off the east edge of the field. It was impossible to enter the pattern for normal VFR traffic and landing. I asked Major Hartwig to contact Saigon Approach Control for an instrument clearance to land. But when we tuned in Saigon Approach, we heard a clamor of voices making the same request, and a short-tempered controller giving instructions to various aircraft to enter orbits over the coastal beacon at Vung Tau, many miles east, and hold at assorted altitudes. Apparently the Saigon approach control radar had gone out temporarily, which often happened in heavy rain.

There we were, milling around northwest of Saigon, watching the rain move steadily towards us, watching as parts of Saigon and the airfield at Tan Son Nhut gradually disappeared from view. It occurred to me that landing at Tan Son Nhut was not only a bad idea, it was impossible. I looked to the left. "Where's Bien Hoa?" I hollered. "Anybody see Bien Hoa?"

There it was, off to our left, about ten miles away. Even as we watched, the rain was moving toward Bien Hoa from the southeast with amazing quickness. "Call Bien Hoa tower. We're landing there!"

However, every other aircraft in the area had the same idea we did, which was to land at Bien Hoa as soon as possible, and the pattern there was filling up with aircraft. We were told to enter a right downwind for the north parallel runway, landing to the west. I pushed the throttles up as far as I dared. I didn't want to lose the race; I wanted to make it to Bien Hoa before the rain did.

I positioned the aircraft on an extended downwind, delaying the flaps and gear to keep our speed up. Directly ahead was the darkest, blackest curtain of rain I had ever seen. The ground between us and it was rapidly disappearing. We had just flown abeam the Bien Hoa tower when the rain struck us like a blow, the whoosh! of rain and wind like a blanket thrown over us.

"I'm flying on instruments," I told Major Hartwig. "You look out your side window and keep the field in sight." I was flying downwind on a compass heading, holding altitude and airspeed. "Tell me when we're past the end of the runway." Mike Jones came up to look out the copilot's side of the cockpit windows to help us maintain visual contact with the ground. Floyd Cupp kept an eye on the engine instruments.

Major Hartwig leaned over his right arm rest, straining to see out the copilot's side windows. Fortunately, the runway and taxiway lights were on. After what seemed like much too long a period of time, he said "We're just past the end of the runway."

"How's my heading?" I asked. "Am I heading in, or drifting out?"

"You're going a bit wide," he said. "Bring it back a bit."

I corrected back to the right. The tower called to say they couldn't see us, and what were our intentions?

"Tell them we're damn well going to land," I said. "Tell me when to turn base." The rain beat down upon the aircraft.

"You'd better turn now," Major Hartwig said. "I'm having trouble seeing the runway from this angle." The tower gave us landing clearance. We were the only aircraft still attempting to land at Bien Hoa. Everyone else had landed or gone elsewhere.

I turned to the right, letting the nose down slightly and reducing power. I called for the flaps and gear down. "Tell me when to turn final," I said. "I'm still on instruments."

"Turn now."

"How's my altitude look?"

"Looks okay. Hard to tell."

Thank god the runway at Bien Hoa was long. I glanced up to see if there was any sign of the runway. Then Major Hartwig and Mike called out, "There's the runway! Our position looks good."

I searched through the rain. Then I saw the runway lights and the runway centerline. "Full flaps," I called, and pulled the throttles back. As we touched down the rain began to let up. And as we reached the midpoint of the runway, we rolled out from underneath the rain. Ahead the air was clear, at least ten miles visibility. We turned off the runway to the right and then right again towards the parking area. As we taxied back to the ramp, the rain hit us again. The noise of the rain was loud over the engine noise, and the visibility forward was zero. We followed the "follow-me" truck all the way into our parking spot on the ramp and shut our engines down.

We apologized to the passengers for not being able to make it to Tan Son Nhut and told them to sit tight on the airplane until base ops sent out a bus. We cracked the doors and ramp as much as we could so we wouldn't melt in the humidity. The passengers were impressed with the rain as we waited.

"Wow," they said. "How could you guys see while you were flying through that?"

"We couldn't," we answered. They gave us a strange look, then laughed. They thought we were joking.

Finally the bus arrived and we all boarded it, running through the rain. Once inside, we said, as soon as the rain passes, we'll carry you to Tan Son Nhut. But we sat there for two hours, and finally, the duty officer told us to fly back to Cam Ranh.

"It's still a mess in Saigon," he said. "The radar's out and the rain isn't letting up. We'll have to bus them in or fly them over later."

We flew back to Cam Ranh, leaving the dark skies of Saigon behind. At the end of my second day on the shuttle, I still had to fly a complete mission as scheduled.

Chapter 12

Long Night over the South China Sea

The following day we were scheduled for a late afternoon departure, from Cam Ranh up the coast to Chu Lai. We landed at Chu Lai a little after seven in the evening, a little too early for excitement along the perimeter, but the flares were already falling with steady regularity. We offloaded our pallets, closed up the cargo compartment, and flew to Pleiku where we loaded some Army troops and carried them to Bien Hoa. At Bien Hoa there was a delay while someone tried to find our load. Eventually a few army troops boarded, and we carried them and some pallets on the short hop to Saigon.

We landed at Tan Son Nhut just after eleven o'clock. We parked in the loading area. It was a warm, humid night, and I opened the pilot's window, turned up the overhead light, and began to read my current paperback. After a while I realized there was no activity in the vicinity of our aircraft. I stepped down from the cockpit and walked through the empty cargo area to the rear of the aircraft. Brownie was sitting on the open ramp.

"Where's our load?" I asked.

"They're looking for it."

I walked to the ops shack. "Where's our load?" I asked. Someone shrugged. "We're looking for it. Someone must have been moving some pallets around."

"Great," I said. "Just what I want to do—sit on the ramp in the middle of the night at Tan Son Nhut. Where are we taking it?"

"Da Nang."

"Well, let's find those pallets and get on the road," I said. "We're wasting crew day sitting around here."

I looked at my watch. We had been on the ramp for nearly an hour and still weren't loaded. Oh, well. I was paid the same whether we flew or sat on the ramp. I bought a Coke from the machine and walked back out to the aircraft. I climbed into the co-pilot's seat and started to read some more, then, as my eyelids started to close, I tilted my seat back and went to sleep, the warm Saigon night breeze coming through the side window.

I awoke some time later and looked at my watch. One o'clock in the morning! I had been sleeping for almost an hour. What the hell? I sat up and looked around. The flight deck was deserted; so was the cargo compartment. I stormed into the ALCE shack. My crew members were sprawled over various chairs, most of them asleep. I strode over to the duty desk, and demanded, in my most impressive demeanor, "What is going on? Where is our load? Why all of this delay?"

Chapter 12. Long Night over the South China Sea

The duty officer gave me a tired look. "Da Nang is under mortar attack. The flight line and barracks areas have been hit hard. They got at least one C-130 and some F-4s. We're waiting to hear how bad it is."

I staggered back a step or two. I had completely forgotten I was in a war zone. I hadn't thought about mortar attacks in a long time. My first reaction was concern. I worried about how bad the damage would be, the casualties, the loss of aircraft. I could imagine the chaos on the airfield, which was busy day or night. I worried about the loss of the C-130. Was it one of our wing aircraft? What if it had been me?

Then I realized: it could have been me! If events had worked out differently: if we had gotten out of Bien Hoa more rapidly; if they had had our load ready for us at Tan Son Nhut; if we had flown on schedule, we could have been sitting on the ramp at Da Nang. Taking a mortar. Thank god for the slow system at Tan Son Nhut.

We waited two more hours. It was bad at Da Nang. They wouldn't know the extent of the damage there until morning. Go home. We flew back to Cam Ranh with a stack of empty pallets. Another incomplete mission.

The next day the single topic of discussion around Cam Ranh was the mortar attack at Da Nang. It had been one of the most serious attacks since I had been in Southeast Asia. The Viet Cong had breached a portion of the perimeter fence.

We were scheduled to fly again that night, Sunday night, the 16th of July. "We're sending you up to Da Nang," the duty officer said. "They'll decide what they want you to do when you get there."

Remnants of C-130 A-Model on Ramp at Da Nang. This aircraft was one of two C-130s destroyed by a mortar attack during the early hours of the morning of 15 July 1967. This mortar attack was one of the most destructive attacks launched against Da Nang Air Base; over 80 separate rockets slammed into the runways, ramps, and surrounding areas. Other aircraft destroyed included eight F-4 Phantom fighters and two F-8 Crusaders. Eight Americans were killed and 175 were wounded. Due to delays at Tan Son Nhut, I and my crew were not present during the attack.

We arrived at Da Nang just before eight o'clock in the evening. We taxied to the ramp carefully. Even in the dark, we could see debris off to the side, mortar shell fragments, aircraft parts. On one portion of the ramp rested the remains of a C-130, mangled, sagging, and burnt. An A-model from Naha. It was a sad and disturbing sight.

We walked into the operations building to find out what they wanted us to do. "Air evac," we were told. "We've got about sixty casualties that need to be airlifted to the hospital at Clark. We'll send some men out to help your loadmaster rig the aircraft for litters."

We returned to the aircraft for the slow, laborious process of reconfiguring the aircraft. The seats had to be stowed, stanchions installed down the center, and straps hooked up to hold the litters along the sides and in the center of the aircraft. The entire rigging had to be checked carefully, for we didn't want any straps to come loose and cause the injured men to spill out into the aircraft.

Mike Jones, Major Hartwig, and I walked to the flight planning section to prepare the paperwork for our flight across the South China Sea to Clark Air Base, in the Philippines. Mike came up to me, concern showing on his face. "Our radar's not working very well," he said. "It's practically inoperative. And the weatherman is telling us we've got a sky full of thunderstorms between here and Clark. All that bad weather we've been dodging here for the last two days is right on our route to Clark."

"And don't forget about our autopilot," added Major Hartwig. The autopilot had not wanted to hold a constant heading on the flight up from Cam Ranh.

I thought about what it meant that sixty wounded men needed to get to Clark. "We'll give it our best effort," I said. We filed our flight plan and walked back out to the aircraft. By this time two or three ambulances and buses with large red crosses on them were parked in the darkness around the rear of our aircraft, and in the illuminated areas of the ramp we could see men carrying stretchers carefully aboard and assisting with the slow process of securing the stretchers to the stanchions.

I tried to avoid thinking how uncomfortable the flight would be for them, having to lie strapped onto their hard canvas stretchers, suffering from burns and mortar wounds, bouncing around as our aircraft encountered bumpy taxiways and choppy air currents. Riding in the back of a C-130 was no fun, even for someone in the best of health. We walked through the cargo compartment, talking to some of the men. Many of them were wrapped in blood-stained dressings. The nurses were hooking up plasma bottles and ensuring that the dressings were holding. Finally a few more men, less severely wounded than the others, made their way onto the aircraft, finding seats along the side of the cargo compartment.

After three and a half hours of rigging and loading, we started engines. One of the base fire trucks followed us as we taxied out of the ramp area north on the east parallel taxiway to the departure end of runway 29 Left, to be ready if some kind of emergency should occur on the ground. As we taxied, I turned the nosewheel steering as gradually as I could, trying to lessen the discomfort of the men on board. I applied the brakes as smoothly as I knew how. When we were cleared to take off, I aligned us with the centerline and eased the throttles forward gradually. Fortunately, the runway at Da Nang was long and we had plenty of room for a slowly accelerating takeoff.

We turned left and proceeded to the east, climbing to our cruise altitude. Once we rolled out on our climb heading, our fears were confirmed. "The radar's not working worth a damn," said Mike. I could see what he meant on our radar repeater

Chapter 12. Long Night over the South China Sea

scope, which rested on top of the pilots' instrument panel. We couldn't see any clear returns; everything was blurred, hazy. Far ahead through our windows lightning flashed across the distant horizon from left to right.

The autopilot, too, was useless. Whenever I tried to engage it, the aircraft would slowly turn left or right, wandering aimlessly in the night, ignoring the intended compass heading. We agreed we'd better turn off the autopilot completely; we didn't want it to give a sudden surge left or right, or worse, up or down, once we engaged the altitude hold. There we were, flying across the South China Sea at midnight in a thunderstorm-infested sky with no airborne radar and no autopilot. And a full load of burned and badly injured troops.

Major Hartwig and I took turns hand-flying the aircraft. We had to continually maneuver our way around the tops and sides of the thunderstorms, according to Mike's best reading of the fuzzy radar and our own estimates of clear routes through the clouds. Whenever the lightning flashed, we attempted to locate a clear channel through the clouds ahead. But the clouds were so thick and evenly distributed that we could find no clear route through.

The lightning was both foe and friend. We didn't want to fly too closely to an area of active lightning flashes, for that meant heavy rain, turbulence, and the possibility of a lightning strike. But we needed the bright light of the sudden flash to illuminate our passage through the clouds. We found, to our dismay and discomfort, that an area of darkness did not necessarily mean a quiet sky and smooth flying; really dark areas more often than not were cloud buildups, surrounded by turbulent air. We relied on the lightning to guide us through, wincing when the lightning was so close that it blinded us, relieved when it flashed behind clouds in front or to the side, showing us a temporary route through.

We continually fought to keep the aircraft on its assigned course. We were in constant radio contact, first with Saigon radio and then with Manila radio, reporting our deviations from our scheduled flight path. Fortunately, there was little traffic that night, and we had the airways over the South China Sea to ourselves.

Major Hartwig and I found that our endurance initially was about fifteen minutes before we began to tire and the other pilot had to take over. After two hours of working our way through the storms, we began to tire after ten minutes. We were working so hard that I scarcely had time to think about how uncomfortable the ride must be for the people in the back. We had no opportunity to walk back to see how our passengers were doing. Mike Jones was working as hard as we were, for in addition to trying to read his radar, he had to keep track of our position in the night, no easy task because of our wandering, irregular path through the sky. At one point we figured we were moving one mile laterally for every mile of forward progress. Floyd Cupp was helping us too, looking for safe passageways among the boiling masses of dark cloud.

Finally, about a half hour west of the Philippine coast, the storm clouds began to thin, and we found ourselves in a steady light rain between cloud layers. At least the air was smooth. We could relax a little. As we crossed the coast west of Clark, I retarded the throttles to begin our descent. Suddenly, a yellow light illuminated on the forward instrument panel. "Prop low oil light, number three engine," Floyd Cupp announced. "It was written up before," he said. "Apparently it comes on after the throttle is retarded. Add power and see what happens," he suggested.

I moved the throttle on the number three engine forward. The light wavered, then went out. "It'll probably come on again in the landing pattern," Floyd observed.

Just what we needed. The prop low oil light signaled low oil in the propeller control mechanism. If the amount of oil were reduced to too low a level, there was a danger we could lose control of the blade angle of the propeller. The condition could result in a runaway prop, which would be catastrophic on a C-130 engine. There was probably nothing wrong, just a glitch in the warning system, but it was risky to ignore it.

We continued our descent to Clark, our airspeed higher than normal as a result of our increased throttle settings. But the air was smooth, and I didn't mind arriving as quickly as we could. As we descended, however, the rain increased, beating heavily on the cabin and cabin windows.

We were now talking to Clark approach control, who was vectoring us for a ground-controlled approach to land to the south. As we entered a downwind leg east of the field, the prop low oil light on number three engine flickered on again. It was unusually distracting in the darkness of the night. I focused on my assigned heading and altitude. We were directed to turn to a westerly heading and prepare for landing. I decided that it was better to be safe than sorry. "Let's shut down number three engine. Run the emergency engine shutdown checklist."

Major Hartwig read the checklist aloud and Floyd Cupp and I followed the instructions, punching the feather button for engine #3, pushing the #3 condition lever forward to the feather position, and retarding #3 throttle. It seemed unnatural to be sitting in the cockpit with glowing red and yellow lights, one condition lever far forward, and one throttle back. Fortunately, the affected engine was an inboard engine, and shutting it down resulted in minimal effect on directional control.

We notified approach control that we had shut down one engine as a precautionary measure, and then followed their instructions to turn on our final approach. The approach controller told us that the fire truck was already awaiting our arrival; the truck would have been there anyway, because fire trucks were called out on standby any time an air evac flight landed or departed.

The rain continued to fall; the closer to the ground we descended, the more heavily the rain fell. I concentrated on holding my heading and rate of descent as we approached the runway. I could vaguely see the lights of the ramp far off through the rain-blurred windows. "I've got the runway," Major Hartwig announced. Reassuring words. "There's the fire truck," someone else said. "Over the approach lights," Major Hartwig announced.

I looked up; we were safely over the runway. I reduced power first on #2 engine and then gradually reduced power on the outboard engines. We floated and floated and finally touched down smoothly. I avoided using reverse thrust to minimize the discomfort on the passengers. I prided myself on the fact that it was one of the two smoothest landings I had ever made, and certainly the smoothest landing I had made lately. We taxied slowly up to base operations, where a fleet of buses and ambulances waited in the rain on the lighted ramp.

After we shut down the engines I struggled to pry myself out of my seat and walked back into the cargo compartment. "How was the ride?" I asked one of the nurses.

She tried to be nice. "Except for some of the men getting a little airsick, not too bad. The last part was smooth." Before I could begin my detailed explanation about why the ride had been a little rough, she moved off to assist with the offloading of the injured men. "At least we got them here all right," I thought. But it must have been a hard, hard ride for them. A small army of ground personnel carried the wounded through the rain to the waiting vehicles.

Inside the base airlift center the duty officer waved some paperwork at us as we walked in. "Here you are," he said. "We'll have you loaded and ready for Cam Ranh in no time."

"No, you won't," I said.

"What do you mean?" he asked.

"We've got a sick bird: no airborne radar, no autopilot, and we had a low oil light on number three engine in the pattern and had to shut it down. We've hand-flown that beast all the way from Vietnam through two hundred miles of thunderstorms, carrying a load of injured troops, and we're worn out. We're calling it quits for the night."

"You can't do that. You've got four hours of crew duty day left," he said.

"Yes, I can," I said, "and I'm doing it. I hereby declare that this crew needs crew rest. Call us some transport so that we can get some sleep. And then you can call us when the aircraft is ready to fly." I had never felt so physically and emotionally beat as I did when I fell into bed in our crew trailer that night.

We flew directly back to Cam Ranh late the next afternoon and flew two night runs to Qui Nhon, landing finally at five-thirty in the morning, just as the sun was starting to come up over the South China Sea.

We launched again at eight that night for another series of shuttle runs, this time between Cam Ranh and Tan Son Nhut. Nothing exceptional occurred. Well, one aspect of the mission was exceptional; it was the first mission we had flown since I had taken over as aircraft commander that we flew the mission as scheduled without interruption or deviation.

The following night we flew once again, a direct flight back to CCK. I had survived my first in-country mission as an aircraft commander. My performance had not earned particularly high marks, had anyone been there to grade it, but if it was a test, I had passed. I guessed.

Chapter 13

Dancing
in the Alligator House

After flying a number of flights in the local area, we were scheduled to fly straight to Udorn for another ABCCC mission. It was a pleasure to spend a few days in the relative calm of Thailand. The late afternoon sky was filled with storm clouds as we climbed out to the east on our first mission, a night mission. We threaded our way through the buildups until we found a parcel of relatively open sky along a bend in the Mekong River. Through the clouds we could see the Mekong winding slowly past the low hills to the north and east. As the darkness increased, we could see lightning flashes to the north.

We leveled at 16,000 feet and began to fly a racetrack pattern from the northwest to the southeast. As the last of the sunlight faded, we lost sight of the river below, invisible in the bottomless blackness beneath. At first, our orbit pattern held us clear of clouds; but eventually, as the lightning flashes increased, we could see a massive wall of storm clouds moving slowly down from the northwest, and we began to drift south ahead of that intimidating mass. Our fuel burned off, and we climbed to higher altitudes, hoping to find clearer airspace above. And for a while we did, until the upper level winds brought more storm clouds toward us. We found ourselves being slowly forced south and east, toward Da Nang. The stormy weather was inhibiting activity on the ground as well, and the men in the communications capsule were having a quiet night on the radios.

The lightning continued to flash, to the north, to the east, above us. Finally, it began to flash to the south as well, and we had no place to maneuver. We turned in tighter and tighter circles. Then the rain fell on us. Even above the noise of the engines and the air conditioning system, we could hear the rain washing over the cockpit and the fuselage, inundating the aircraft. We soon began to pick up increasing turbulence.

"Mike, we've got to go someplace else," I said. "See if you can find any clear area on the radar. Floyd, go back in the back and tell the troops to strap in until we can get out of this."

Mike Jones searched for a clear area and finally suggested we head west. I turned out of our racetrack pattern and rolled out on a heading of 270 degrees. At first there was no change in the quality of the precipitation or the turbulence, but gradually the rain began to subside and the air grew smoother. Mike gave me adjustments to the aircraft heading as our path through the buildups became clearer on the radar.

Finally we reached a condition of smooth air and steady rain. In the darkness I

Chapter 13. Dancing in the Alligator House

couldn't tell if we were in thin cloud or between layers. The rain interfered with our visibility. I focused on the flight control and navigation instruments, trying to orient myself according to their readings. Suddenly, someone said, "Holy Christ. Look at that."

I looked up from the instrument panel. In the darkness surrounding the right wing a strange blue-green glow was emanating from the leading edge. As I watched, the blue-green glow progressed out the front of the engine nacelles to the tips of the propellers and then illuminated the arc of the props. The blue-green light moved in a regular pattern out away from the prop spinners until it described a perfect cone shape at a 45-degree angle forward from the plane of the props. The same phenomenon developed on the left wing and engines. It was as if we had a blue-green neon light system rigged along our wings and engines which we had turned on in some kind of dazzling night-time aerial display.

For a minute everyone on the flight deck was crowding up to the front to see the amazing sight. "What is it?" someone asked. "Saint Elmo's fire," I said. "The sailors on the old ships used to see it flashing from their masts during heavy weather." We were all engaged in watching the wonderful sights of Mother Nature when suddenly there was a blinding flash of light and we could see tracks of cloud-to-cloud lightning immediately in front of us.

"Whoops," I said. "About face." I grabbed the autopilot turn knob and turned the aircraft back to the left in a healthy bank, to get out of that area before more lightning occurred. We headed back to the east. Mike couldn't find any more promising direction than that from which we had come. We held on course for as long as we could until the rain began to increase again and the turbulence began to pick up. We could hold about seven to ten minutes in each direction before we had to reverse course. Time after time we turned and turned about. Finally I decided I had to get out of the seat.

As I stood behind the flight engineer's seat, watching the St. Elmo's fire fade, one of the troops from the back climbed the steps up to the flight deck.

"Quiet night on the radios?" I asked.

"Very quiet," he said, rubbing his ears. I could see the impression of earphones around his ears. Then came the inevitable question. "Where are we?" he asked.

I gave him the most truthful answer I could: "Halfway between the St. Elmo's fire and the moderate turbulence," I said.

About two hours later, the sky in the east began to grow light. The sun eventually shone through the dissipating layers of the night's storms. The air was calm. By the time we landed at Udorn at seven-twenty, the sky was clear.

We flew two day missions during the following four days, and then our ABCCC missions were done. We had flown three missions in six days, for a total of forty hours of flying time. We left for Bangkok at seven in the morning, stopping at Korat and Takhli on the way in. Flying across Thailand in the early morning was always a pleasure, especially when you knew you were going to spend the night in Bangkok.

* * *

The next afternoon we flew from Bangkok to Clark, with one stop at Takhli, arriving at Clark shortly before eleven in the evening. It was an unexpected pleasure to have a day at Clark as well as at Bangkok. The crew was in a party mood, and we agreed to go together into Angeles City.

About nine o'clock in the evening we caught a base taxi to the main gate, where we hopped into one of the Jeep-like jitneys lined up there. The five of us barely fit into one. Mike had been there before, so we put him in the front seat to make sure the driver's navigation was good. As we sped into town to Pauline's, a distance of about five miles, we passed the Philippine housing area. The streets were full of people walking and engaged in animated conversation. The men wore short-sleeved shirts, mostly unbuttoned, and casual pants, and the women wore light, thin dresses, their shapely brown legs extending below the hem.

The jitney swerved to a stop in front of a large white-washed building with a large bright neon sign that proclaimed "Pauline's Club." We could hear music playing inside. We paid the driver, and he sped off, presumably back to the base for another load of party-minded airmen. We entered the front door and found the place was already crowded, filled with men from the base. There were a few folks in Army and Navy uniforms.

We wedged our way up to the bar, standing room only, and ordered beers. The air was smoky, warm, and the noise was raucous. A band was playing loud over in the dancing area, and everyone was engaged in shouted conversations. Mike grabbed me by the arm and hollered something about finding a table. I said I'd be right with him just as soon as I went to the john.

As I came back into the bar area, I saw Mike and the others pulling up chairs to one of the few remaining vacant tables. He waved me over. I grabbed a beer from the bar and began to walk over. Along the dividing area between the bar area and the dance area was an open space with a railing around it. I passed along it as I made my way past several men standing with Philippine girls. I edged up against the railing to get around one group and looked over. I had thought there would be a miniature garden or some kind of tropical plants in there, but when I looked over, I saw nothing but darkness. And then, as my eyes adjusted to the weak light, I saw, way below, something that looked like a pool of water. And then, as I looked again, something moved in the water. And then another something. Several somethings.

Alligators! Jesus! I backed away. It wouldn't be too hard to fall into that pit. I wondered if anyone had. With the noise and shouting and beer-drinking that was going on around me, I thought it quite likely that someone, sometime, must have fallen in. Or even jumped in, if the money was high enough. I looked up. Somebody was standing by me looking in.

"Mean mothers, aren't they? See them thrashing around? They probably haven't been fed yet."

I looked again. The animals were moving constantly. "Are those alligators?" I asked.

"No, not alligators—crocodiles, you bet your ass, and they look hungry. They'll feed them a little later, when the crowd gets bigger. But don't throw anything down there. The owners get really pissed. They'll throw your ass in jail."

"Thanks," I said. "I'll remember that." I had no intention of interacting with alligators in any fashion.

When I finally made my way over to the table, I saw that we had been joined by a number of slender, good-looking Philippine girls. "Hey, AC," Mike said, "meet our chaperones for the evening. This is Yvonne, and this is Gloria, and this is Estelle, and this is.... I didn't get your name, honey. What is it again?" Mike waved his hand as he

Chapter 13. Dancing in the Alligator House

called out the names. He was going too fast for me to place the name with the face of each of our female companions, but I figured it would all sort itself out eventually.

We sat and started talking, the usual get-acquainted stuff. Yes, we were aircrew members, passing through Clark on our way back to Taiwan. No we didn't fly jets, we flew something much better, the C-130. Yes we flew in Vietnam, but right now we were coming back from Thailand. Yes, we were all single, and no, we didn't have any girlfriends anywhere else. Yes, we would be happy to buy them something to drink, and hey, we needed another beer too.

I was paired off with the tallest girl that had joined our table, an attractive girl with long dark hair—Estelle—who had a rather long, sad face. She seldom smiled, and when she did, she still looked sad. She was doing her part to support the club by dutifully drinking the tea we were buying for her and her friends. But she looked a little bored. I wasn't talking much, just looking around, studying the mass of people who were trying to talk or tell jokes over the noise of the band. I thought about Karla. The last time I had been in a bar, I had been with her. It had been a long time since I had seen her. I was impressed to think how accurately she had predicted the results of our night together.

I pulled out of my reverie to notice that Estelle and I were alone at the table. Everyone else was on the dance floor, dancing. Estelle looked at me. "You want to dance?"

I shrugged my shoulders. "I don't know how to dance. Not with this new kind of music. I'm not a very good dancer."

"That's okay. I show you. Come on."

I followed her out to the dance floor. Part of the dance floor was on an elevated area, which served as a stage for the floor show. As we made our way up onto the dancing area, I could see out over the large, noisy crowd. I looked around to see what the preferred mode of dance was. A few men were firmly holding on to their female counterparts, but most were gyrating vigorously in opposition to their partner. I didn't see how I could ever get the hang of that form of dancing. I planted my feet firmly so as not to lose my balance and began to wave my arms and hands in some kind of approximate rhythm.

"No, no, not like that," Estelle shouted. "Like this. Watch me." I continued to writhe mildly as I studied her movements. She made small, subtle movements with her arms, legs, and body. She made suggestive, flowing movements with her arms and hands while she moved her feet as little as possible. But her body was moving in syncopation with the beat of the music; her stomach especially was serving as the focus of her body movement, a pivot point between the movements of her hips and shoulders. I forgot about my dancing and bobbed up and down vaguely to the music as I watched her well-coordinated, rhythmic movements. She must have had lots of practice if she frequented Pauline's every night. "Now," she said, "follow my movements."

At first I was hopelessly uncoordinated in my efforts. I moved my feet in motions that were much too large, and I moved my head and body in jerky up-and-down movements, like a heavyweight fighter in training. I was waving my hands and arms in a dangerous fashion. I caught one unfortunate dancer in the side with one of my flailing hands. Just as I began to imagine I might be catching the hang of it, the band took a break. I was warm and thirsty.

We walked back to the table. The table was filled with new faces and people;

when I had walked off, I had left it unguarded. The rest of the crew spread around the room, shoehorning themselves in wherever they could find room. I found a chair for Estelle to sit in and waved at a passing waitress. "You want a beer?" I asked Estelle. She shook her head, no. I ordered two beers. "I don't want a beer," she insisted.

"I know. They're for me." When the waitress returned I drank one in a hurry, then started on the next. After a while the band began to play again. "Ready to dance?" I asked. Estelle smiled a weak smile. "Good," I said. "Let's go." I grabbed her hand and led her up to the stage.

I concentrated on the music, trying simultaneously to adjust to the rhythmic patterns of the music and then trying to develop movements of my body, arms and legs that caught the rhythm in as efficient and as coordinated a way as I could. I concentrated as intently as I could, closing my eyes and tuning out the wild assembly of bodies undulating around me. I began not to pay attention to Estelle, except when I lost my concentration.

Eventually I began to experiment with more varied body movements, always overdoing it at first and then figuring out how I could move more efficiently. The band was playing a variety of dances, a mixture of fast and slow, and I began to develop a series of rhythmic movements. Previously I had always preferred to dance to slow music, because I could disguise my awkwardness more easily. But tonight I wanted the music to be fast, and the rhythm to be complicated and vigorous. I began to grow impatient whenever the band played a slow dance, leading Estelle off the stage to our table, drinking beer after beer.

I never stopped dancing. When the band took a break, I fidgeted, drinking beer until it started again. When the band started, I wanted to be the first on the floor. When I began to dance I closed my eyes, moving with the music, disregarding everyone around me, eventually including Estelle.

As I danced, I began to listen to the music internally; it became more and more a part of me. I was not thinking about dancing at all. I was in synchronization with the music, I was moving with it. My mind, released from the effort of thinking about my physical movements, floated to other thoughts, never on anything concrete, specific, not on people, not on tasks, but drifting in a kind of free association.

An image began to take shape in my mind. I couldn't tell what kind of image it was at first. I wasn't aware that an image was trying to materialize. It was a kind of blank openness, a dark vista with approximate features. A geometric pattern, a long oblique line, was extending at an angle before me. A long line towards which I was slowly moving. A runway. A runway that shone vaguely in a blue darkness, in a kind of half-light as if under an overcast. A runway that seemed somehow familiar. And then I knew what runway it was. It was the runway at Phan Thiet, a long, wet strip with clouds overhead and hills behind and the sea in front. I was slowly moving closer to this shadowy dark runway, moving in time with the beat of the music. There were no aircraft, no people; I was not in an aircraft; I was the aircraft, and I was about to touch down on the runway at Phan Thiet.

The more the music continued, the clearer the vision became. There was no doubt, it was the runway at Phan Thiet, and I was there, I was touching down on that runway, in slow, suspended motion, as the vision slowly grew larger in my mind. But the sense of threat that had been associated with the vision when I had landed there was gone; not gone, exactly, but it was a vague sensation. It was being replaced gradually by a new sensation, a feeling of exhilaration, of pleasure, of physical release. I danced and danced and as I danced the runway slowly moved closer and the feeling of threat receded and the feeling of exhilaration increased, until I was dancing on the runway. The dance floor at Pauline's was gone, the people were gone. I was dancing on the runway at Phan Thiet, alone, moving to the beat of music, moving all of my body, my arms, my hands, my body, moving my shoulders, my torso, my stomach, all in an amazing exhibition of physical coordination, and my feet were light, lighter than they have ever been in my life, I might have been a ballet dancer, I was dancing on the runway of Phan Thiet, my toes were scarcely touching the dark shiny surface moving slowly, slowly past beneath me. This amazing sight, who could have thought that the vision of Phan Thiet would return to me here, at Pauline's, with the noise and the music and the beer, in a place I had never seen before and would never see again.

The vision stayed with me, remained with me, and I danced the remainder of the night not in Pauline's but on the runway at Phan Thiet, surprised by the agility with which I was dancing, excited by my new-found talent for physical coordination, delighted with my achievement. When I looked up, after I had been within myself for some time, Estelle was not there. I saw that another girl had materialized in front of me. She was smaller, younger, with a happier face. I smiled, nodded, and kept dancing. She too seemed to be concentrating on something inside her. When the band took another break, I asked her if she wanted a beer. She shook her head. When the music started, we went up to the dance floor together.

I was still on the runway at Phan Thiet when the loadmaster came to tell me that the crew was going back to the base and did I want to go with them?

I pulled myself out of my vision. It was late. The bar was closing. The place was deserted. The band had gone home. I was dancing by myself, along with one or two others, to music on the juke box.

"We thought maybe you wanted to spend the night with the girl you were dancing with and were going without you, because you didn't seem to want to leave. Do you want to go with her? It looks like she's waiting for you."

I looked down at the deserted tables. There sat Estelle, sitting next to the girl who had been dancing with me. "No," I said. "Wait for me. I'm going back to the base with you."

"Estelle," I said, "are you waiting for me?"

She nodded. "I didn't know if you wanted to go with me. You seemed to be having a good time with me. But then you didn't seem to pay attention to me. So I waited."

"Estelle, I am very happy you were here tonight. You taught me to dance. Dancing tonight was important to me." She gave me a puzzled look.

"I have to back to the base tonight with my crew. Maybe I'll see you here again some other time. Here; take this." I gave her some money, enough to have paid for a night together.

The crew members were sprawled over the jitney in various positions of exhaustion. The only remaining seat was in the back. I jumped up, sat down as best I could, and hung on to the overhead brace for support. As the jitney lurched off into the darkness toward Clark, Estelle and her friend came out of Pauline's. They looked in our direction, and I waved.

"Boy, that was some night," someone said. "Wasn't that a great place? Did you see those alligators move when they fed them? That was fresh meat they tossed in. Somebody said it was parts of some Philippine guy that owed them money."

I said no, I had missed that part. "Missed feeding the alligators? Jesus, AC, where were you?" But I couldn't tell them.

Chapter 14

Ground Pounder

Just when I felt myself emerging into some kind of confidence and competence as a pilot, someone pulled my name out of the squadron hat, and I found that I was scheduled to spend a month at Cam Ranh Bay, working as a kind of glorified administrative flunky. The squadron scheduling officer had said something about needing aircraft-commander qualified pilots to pull duty at various airlift command centers, or ALCEs for short. In addition, my flying time was high, and they needed to keep me on the ground for a while.

Although I let myself be convinced that my selection was fair and appropriate according to the criteria explained to me, my heart sank. Going to Cam Ranh for a month meant just one thing: I would lose the crew I had been flying with. And who knew what the crew situation would be in a month's time? I had the feeling that my tenure as an aircraft commander was going to be brief. It was already brief. I had been flying as an aircraft commander for only three months. And now I was going to spend a month on the ground at Cam Ranh.

When I arrived at the China Nights, few customers were there. It was a slow night, and only three or four girls were working. One of them looked at me and walked to the back; she must have called Karla. She came in after I had been there about a half hour, nursing my second drink.

She came in slowly, deliberately, as always. Tall, slender, in a one-piece silk dress. I looked at her as she came over. Her face was impassive. Her eyes studied mine as she walked over.

"Hi, GI," she said, as she seated herself carefully opposite me.

"Hi," I said. "You look nice." She barely acknowledged the compliment.

"I think you not come back." She said it evenly, without emotion, a statement, not an accusation.

"Me too," I agreed. "I didn't think I'd come back either."

"You go with other girls?"

"No. No other girls."

"Why you come back?"

"I'm not sure. I needed to see you again."

"How long before you fly again?"

"Two days. I have to go to Cam Ranh Bay for a month."

"A month? You fly Vietnam for a month?"

"No. I won't fly at all. I'll be working in an office. I'll be filling out paperwork. Answering phones. Making out schedules."

"You not happy to go?"

"No. It's boring work. I'll be wasting a whole month. I'd rather fly on the shuttle."

We sat for a while in silence. Finally, I asked "Hungry?" She nodded. "Want to eat at the MAAG Club?" She nodded again. She went to talk to the Mama-san. After a couple of minutes she returned. "Okay. We go."

The MAAG Club was almost deserted when we arrived. We sat in our favorite booth, on the right side. We both ordered steak. It seemed we were hungry. After we ate, Karla walked over to the juke box and punched a couple of buttons. Music began to play. On the dance floor we danced for a while, and then she stepped back and looked at me. "Where you go dancing?" she asked.

"What do you mean?" I said.

"You dance better now. Where you learn to dance?" She looked at me suspiciously.

"On the runways of Vietnam," I said simply.

She gave me a long look. "You different since last time."

* * *

I flew into Cam Ranh with Captain Kirk Waldron, one of the 345th instructor pilots. I deadheaded on the crew, an extra pilot, logging time but not flying. I sat on the crew bunk most of the time, watching Kirk check out a new pilot. It took us forever to get to Cam Ranh, ten hours from the time we took off at CCK. I didn't like it at all, riding on the bunk seat. I could feel my aircraft commander's status eroding like the sand that surrounded Cam Ranh.

My duties in the airlift control center were simple. I helped make up the crew folders for each day's missions, filled out the crew schedule on a large transparent plastic overlay, kept track of aircraft maintenance status, coordinated loading of the aircraft, helped to brief the outbound crews, debriefed the crews when they finished their duty day and poured the liquor ration for them, answered the phone, and filled out reports. It was enjoyable to be working at the heart of the Cam Ranh cargo airlift operation and talking with the crew members as they came and went, but my heart was not in it. I saw many of the crew members from the squadron and the other squadrons in the wing. They kidded me about the tough duty I was pulling.

My room was in a building in the RMK barracks area, on top of the hill that ran north and south between the main part of the base and the beach to the east. My room had no amenities, no air-conditioning. But the breeze blew through steadily, off the ocean, down the hallway, and I had the room to myself. Sand was everywhere, on every floor area, the room, the hall, the shower, but the feel of the sand on the concrete floor was pleasant. When I wasn't working, I spent hours on my bunk, the breeze blowing though, as I read one after another of my pile of paperback novels and listened to the noise of the F-4s and other aircraft to the west and the sound of the ocean to the east.

Early each morning I rode the van around the southern perimeter road from the main part of the base around to west side of the base, where the ALCE was located, a two-story building in a sea of sand, with the C-130s parked wingtip to wingtip on a concrete platform between the ops building and the north-south taxiway on the west side of the main runways. Walking up the steps to the second floor, where the day's schedule was posted, being briefed on lingering problems, looking over the mission folders for the crews to make sure they were complete.

Chapter 14. Ground Pounder

RMK Quarters, Da Nang, October 1967. This area was located on the east side of Cam Ranh Bay AB. Looking North; South China Sea to the right. An on-shore breeze provided air conditioning.

A C-130 A-model crew called in one night from Qui Nhon, where they had had a hard landing and had broken their right torque tube, the linking mechanism that held the front and rear wheels of the main gear together. With a broken torque tube, the front wheel would be pointing in one direction, the rear wheel pointing in another. They needed a repair team to help them fix their problem. I remembered my hard landing at Qui Nhon and was thankful for the sturdier gear design of the E-models.

A lieutenant colonel, fresh from the States, called in from a remote special forces camp with the news that one of his engines had failed to start and directed that we immediately send up a new engine and a maintenance team to change the old engine. The maintenance chief broke into hysterical laughter when I relayed the request; when he paused for breath, he said, "you tell that guy he better hunker down for the night and kiss his airplane good-bye; I wouldn't want to be within a half mile of it when the VC figure out it will be there all night. It'll be the biggest and best target they've had for a long time."

I told the colonel that if his maintenance problem was great enough to warrant sending a maintenance repair team, he should take everything of value from it including all classified material, because it would take several days before a maintenance team could be dispatched. In the meantime, perhaps he could take another look at the problem and see if some sort of interim repair might not suffice to bring the aircraft back to Cam Ranh, where a more complete investigation of the situation could be conducted.

I was tempted to tell him that he wasn't flying stateside anymore, but I realized that he was in the process of discovering that fact for himself. Later I learned that he had been able to get a buddy start from a passing C-130 who had heard his call for help on the radio.

I reviewed the folders in the crew flight planning area to learn the latest information on the fields into which I had flown, and especially those I hadn't yet flown into. Most of the pictures were old, and the data old. But there were two or three places that caught my attention.

The Khe Sanh folder informed me that the runway, which had been closed for improvements, was being rebuilt and soon would be open for landings again. Another folder described the field at Kham Duc, a special forces camp located about fifty miles west-southwest of Da Nang. Even the name of the field sounded abrupt, hard, final. As I studied the photograph, I could see a cut in a hill, a kind of groove through which the aircraft flew on final approach. The cut allowed the landing aircraft to use the full length of the runway (so the write-up said) rather than landing long because of the tightness of the approach. I had landed at LZ English, near Bong Son, where a cut in the hill had been made at the point of aircraft touchdown, but that was a relatively small rise that had been reshaped; at Kham Duc a very large notch had been cut in a relatively large hill a quarter mile or so from the end of the runway.

I studied the folder for Dak To. The field was located at a special forces camp at the base of a hill north of Pleiku and west of Kontum. From the photos, it was easy to imagine mortar fire descending on the base from the hill. The fact sheet in the folder indicated that could happen at any time. Dak To was the site of an on-going Army operation, and we were sending numerous into Dak To with supplies and ammunition. Operations were particularly hazardous at Dak To because of the limited space to offload aircraft and the almost continuous activity around the camp.

In September, while I had been dodging thunderstorms in Thailand, one of the wing C-130s had been involved in a bizarre and scary accident there. One crew had been carrying a load into Dak To. They took off empty, just as it was getting dark. They had just gotten airborne, were just lifting off the runway, when for some unknown reason an Army troop drove a bulldozer onto the runway. There was no question of stopping. The aircraft commander hauled back on the yoke, hoping to avoid hitting the bulldozer. There was a resounding THUNK! and the aircraft seemed to stagger through the air.

Fortunately, the aircraft was not loaded, and it maintained flying speed. The blow to the aircraft seemed to have come well back on the airframe structure. The aircraft was controllable, but the controls were strangely loose and wobbly. The aircraft commander gently turned the aircraft in the general direction of Cam Ranh Bay, gradually gaining altitude and airspeed. After they were away from the immediate vicinity of the airfield, he sent his loadmaster back to inspect the cargo compartment. The loadmaster could scarcely believe what he was seeing. As he stood at the front of the cargo compartment looking back, he could see the entire tail of the aircraft flexing in a gently rolling movement. As he watched, the entire interior of the aircraft aft of the rear jump doors was smoothly twisting and rolling, describing a corkscrewing motion as the ship flew through the air.

The crew decided to fly the aircraft back to Cam Ranh, hoping it would hold together until they got there. They didn't have much choice, really; there just wasn't any better field in the area. The aircraft commander figured that he shouldn't make any further adjustments to the aircraft configuration or speed; the gear and flaps

Chapter 14. Ground Pounder

were still down. So he aimed for Cam Ranh. He was approved for a straight-in landing to the south and decided to land on the dirt area between the main runways. As they approached Cam Ranh, they could hear the aircraft making more and more noises, the kind that suggested increasing structural failure. Finally they were on a long final. The aircraft commander very slowly reduced airspeed. They touched down a little hot, but under control. Once they were clearly on the ground, they feathered all four engines and cut the power. The aircraft slid to a stop in a small cloud of dust.

After the aircrew exited the aircraft, they could see where the Army bulldozer had struck the aircraft exactly at the front bottom of the right crew door, causing structural failure. Shortly after they landed, the large tail section slowly sagged and tilted back, leaning towards the right rear. The aircraft was damaged beyond repair. It was hauled to the C-130 ramp, its parts soon cannibalized for other aircraft.

Another folder described a place called Bao Loc, which was described as having a curved runway. A curved runway up and down, not left to right. According to the write-up, a C-130 at one of the field could not see a C-130 at the other end, the curvature was so great. I tried to imagine what that would look like, how it was possible, but couldn't.

I read the folders, visualized approaches to these new and strange fields, and wondered when I would be flying into them. Behind the ops counter, one day was much like another. I read in my room, drank beer in the O-club. Gradually, slowly, the days passed. Finally my month of desk duty ended and I returned to CCK.

Chapter 15

Gear and Flaps Man

In my mail box at CCK I found a set of orders assigning me to Major Edgar Smith's crew as copilot, dated over a week earlier. Ed Smith was one of the squadron's best pilots, an experienced instructor pilot. But I wasn't happy about being reduced to copilot status. My reward for a month on the desk at Cam Ranh.

The day following, Major Smith's crew was on alert. Early in the morning we were alerted to fly some supplies from CCK to Vung Tau, Vietnam. I sat in the right seat, a copilot once again, raising the gear and flaps. There was a high solid overcast all the way from CCK to Vung Tau, on the coast of South Vietnam, our first stop. It was unusual for the weather to remain the same throughout the full range of our travel from CCK to Vietnam and back. The weather matched my mood: overcast and gray. I had wakened feeling a little bit light-headed, and as the mission wore on I began to feel feverish. Ed asked how I was feeling. I told him I had a bit of a chill, but nothing I couldn't deal with.

I read the checklist, set the flaps and gear, and made the radio calls as we coasted in to Vung Tau. From Vung Tau we carried a load over to Bin Thuy, about a half hour's flight farther southwest, down in the delta. After we left Bin Thuy for the return flight to CCK, I began to shiver. The flight mechanic, bless him, said he had a can of cream of tomato soup he could heat up for me and did I want some?

I sat in the right seat, feet propped up on the foot rests, both hands wrapped around the cup of steaming soup, inhaling the aroma, savoring the taste, watching the slate gray skies, profoundly unhappy. Ed suggested if I was still feeling bad that I could take a nap on the top bunk. I slept for most of the five-hour flight back to CCK. After we landed I went back to my room, took a long hot shower and went to bed. I had celebrated my twenty-seventh birthday by flying as a copilot.

* * *

Karla's mood matched mine.
"What's the matter?" I asked.
"My boy sick."
"How sick was he?"
"He go hospital two days. He have pains in arm. Very hard to move arm."
"What's the problem?"
She paused before answering.
"My boy born with crooked arm. His arm bother him ever since he was born. Doctors say he will be all right, just have pains as his body grows." Her eyes were distant, tinged with pain.
"What's the matter?" I asked.

"When my boy born with crooked arm, my husband blame me. He say boy's crooked arm my fault."

"That's a stupid thing to say. Where is your husband now?"

"He live Taipei. He leave me, not see son."

"How long ago?"

"Three years. No can find work Taipei. Friend in Taichung say can work in bar for Mama-san. Mama-san good woman. Help me very much. Give me time to visit my son when he sick. Give me money, care about me."

I had never spoken much with the Mama-san at the China Nights, but I had often seen her sitting at a table at the rear, usually with two or three of the girls around her. She was older, reserved, and seemed like a pleasant person.

Karla was still, withdrawn. "Are you okay? Do you want me to leave?"

"No, no," she said quickly. She touched my hand. After a time we danced again.

* * *

When I checked the squadron scheduling board on the first of November, my mood worsened. I was scheduled to fly as copilot once again, this time for Lieutenant Colonel Charles Reece, our squadron operations officer, on a short night out-and-back to Naha. Then, a day later, another out-and-back to Naha, again as copilot.

Mortar attack on Dak To, 15 November 1967. Two C-130s were destroyed. Several C-130s were parked on the ramp at Dak To; they were carrying troops and supplies as part of Operation Junction City. Captain Joseph Glenn and Sergeant Joseph Mack received Silver Star awards for their actions in taxiing one C-130 away from two burning C-130s while the attack was in progress.

When I walked into the squadron building, I learned that some of the wing aircraft had been destroyed by a mortar attack at Dak To. Several aircraft had been parked on the small ramp at Dak To when mortar shells began falling. One of the 50th TAS aircraft commanders, Captain Joe Glenn, and a flight engineer, Sergeant Joe Mack, had started up the engines in one of the aircraft to taxi it away from another aircraft that was burning. I wasn't sure I would be able to function efficiently on a field if mortar shells began to fall around me.

News of the attack at Dak To darkened my mood even further. Here I was, motoring through the skies over Okinawa, Thailand, and Taiwan, raising and lowering the gear and flaps, making radio calls and reading checklists, while the war was intensifying in Vietnam. I consoled myself with a bottle of scotch, pouring generous portions as I sat in my room. But not even scotch and Verdi's *Trovatore* at full volume could cheer me, and when the room began to spin dangerously, I decided to step outside for fresh air. I sat on the concrete step outside the building, looking up at the stars, which were shining above in the unusually clear Taiwan night sky.

I tried to recall the constellations I had memorized in my youth when I used to lie on my back on summer nights in the middle of my grandparents' farm, observing the moons of Jupiter and the densely packed stars of the Milky Way through my primitive refractor telescope. I recalled the deer approaching cautiously as I lay engrossed in my studies, flashlight and star guide in hand, until they decided I was harmless, and they browsed in the grass in a circle around me while I lay fascinated by the brilliance of the night sky.

I was aware that Major Horace Pemberton, our jovial squadron scheduling officer, was standing beside me.

"What're you doing, Vaughan? Some astrological star-gazing?"

"Oh, hi, Horse," I said. "No, just thinking of better days." I didn't elaborate.

"Yeah, well, you're looking pretty philosophical, that's for sure. What's bothering you?"

"I'm not feeling especially productive. That's all." I was understating my feelings significantly, but I didn't want to bore Horse with my problems.

"Oh? Well, hang in there, sport. Things'll get better."

"Thanks, Horse. I'm sure they will." But I couldn't imagine how.

He patted my shoulder and moved on inside the building to his room, which was just across the hall from the room Les Fredericks and I shared. Horse was a cheery, friendly individual who automatically made you feel better just by being around him. After a while, I went inside.

Two days later I left on a trip to Naha and Qui Nhon, copilot once again. When I returned, I saw that I was on the board for an out-and-back to Naha with Captain Bob Smith, one of our squadron instructor pilots. I couldn't imagine why I would be flying as a copilot for an instructor pilot on a trip to Naha. Those Naha out-and-backs were usually reserved for squadron or wing staff types who needed a little flying time and a quick return to their office duties. I asked Horse why I was playing copilot for an IP on such a short trip.

"You're not playing copilot," he said.

What was I doing, then?

"You're being upgraded to instructor pilot. This is a practice ride to get you ready for your check ride."

Chapter 15. Gear and Flaps Man

I had difficulty understanding what Horse was saying. He seemed to be speaking a language I couldn't comprehend.

"You're being upgraded to instructor pilot," Horse said again. "I guess they decided that since you're spending so much time in the right seat, you might as well do more useful work than raise and lower the gear and flaps." He smiled broadly at me.

* * *

On the way over to Naha, Bob asked me some questions about the hydraulic and electrical systems. He asked me what I would do if such-and-such a failure occurred, testing me on my knowledge of the systems and especially of my knowledge of the locations of mechanisms that constituted the various aircraft systems. He mentioned some of the challenges I would probably be presented with on my check ride, like having three of the four engines experiencing (simulated) failures, so that I would be left with one useful engine to make my landing. I remembered my checkout pilot in C-130 school at Sewart Air Force Base east of Nashville demonstrating a one-engine landing, but I had never been in an aircraft when three of the four engines were retarded to flight idle and I was expected to make the approach and landing safely.

I had five days to prepare for the written test, which I had to pass before I would be able to take the flight check. I read the C-130 Flight Manual, the "Dash One," with greater interest than I ever had before. Having flown in-country enough to know what kinds of emergency situations could occur, I didn't have to imagine any problematic situations; our pilot read files were full of incidents and accidents that contained detailed accounts of system malfunctions. Attempting to clarify the physical layout of the various aircraft systems, I visited the maintenance hangars, asking the over-worked airmen and sergeants questions about maintenance problems and procedures.

As I reviewed the "Dash One," I noted the aircraft and engine operating limitations that I knew I would be asked about, either in written or oral form. Other calculations, such as takeoff distances and stopping distances at certain weights, altitudes, and temperatures, were to be derived from performance charts, as were maximum loads and center of gravity calculations.

On my next flight, Captain Kirk Waldron gave me and Captain Phil Rodke, another squadron pilot up for an IP checkout, one last run-through of the maneuvers and challenges that we would be expected to master on our check rides. Kirk put each of us in the right seat in turn, and then gave condition after condition that called for us to simulate shutting down an engine, reciting the associated loss of systems, simultaneously flying the aircraft in the traffic pattern safely to a landing at the airfield. Both of us seemed to perform at an acceptable level, and Kirk pronounced himself pleased with our progress.

The next day I walked into the Standboard office to take my written exam. I felt as if my head were bursting with the information I had stored, and I moved slowly so as not to have any tidbit of information fall out. The test lasted a little over an hour. As I worked on it, I felt increasingly confident that I would do well. And I did. The next step was the flight check.

A little over one month after my depressing birthday flight as copilot, I strapped myself into the right seat, as ready as I would ever be to take the IP check ride.

Captain Waldron was once again along as aircraft commander, but he sat in the back, on the crew bunk seat, as Captain Glen Wilson, one of the wing standboard pilots, sat in the left seat. We started up as usual, taxied out to the south end of the runway, and flew a departure routing to the local area, where Glen began to give me a variety of situations designed to test my knowledge of emergency procedures.

After demonstrating proficiency in some aerial maneuvers and instruction at altitude, I returned to the landing pattern at CCK. Soon I had one throttle retarded, simulating a failed engine, then another, and finally, a third. I was left with one throttle, for the left inboard engine, which I had shoved full forward as we staggered around the pattern for a final landing. I hoped to God I had done everything correctly. To my knowledge, I hadn't made any major mistakes.

As the engines wound down in the chocks, I realized that my shirt was drenched with sweat. When I walked in for the debriefing, Captain Wilson went through the phases of the check ride slowly, critiquing my actions. As he went through them, I could see he was finding only minor errors to criticize. He finally finished, stood up, held out his hand, and said "Congratulations. You flew a good ride." I smiled with relief as he shook my hand. Back at the squadron, Kirk said "I knew you'd do well."

I celebrated with Karla that night. But she couldn't understand why I was happy.
"You still sit in right seat?"
"Yes," I said.
"You fly airplane?"
"No," I said.
"Other pilot fly airplane?"
"Yes," I said.
"You still raise gear and talk on radio?"
"Yes," I said.
"Sound like you still copilot to me," she said.

Chapter 16

Taipei R&R

For the next two weeks Horse Pemberton kept me at CCK, flying proficiency flights in the local area for new pilots, practicing landings and low-level navigation. I flew two out-and-back cargo hauling trips, one to Iwakuni, Japan, and one to Naha. On the ground at Naha I persuaded the flight engineer to let me control every sequence of the engine start procedures, so that I could become more familiar with all of the systems operations during the engine start process. While the pilots initiated the engine start procedure by pushing in the engine start buttons and manipulating the engine condition levers, once the propellers started turning, the flight engineer normally completed the rest of the engine start activities.

There was another reason I was given the unheard-of luxury of nearly two weeks at CCK: I was being given a few days of rest and relaxation (R&R) time. Horse said I had better take advantage of my time off the in-country shuttle while I could; now that I had passed my Instructor Pilot checkout, I could anticipate many days on the road, checking out new pilots in-country. I decided to spend the weekend in Taipei. While I was enjoying myself in Taipei, Horse would be assembling the other members of my new crew, who would be flying with me for the next few months.

I left Taichung on the Friday afternoon train and enjoyed the leisurely ride to Taipei, the capital city of Taiwan, located about an hour's train ride to the north. I had brought a book to read on the train, but as the train made its way through the rice fields and terraced hills, I preferred to look out the window. My plan was simple: check into a good hotel, enjoy a complete Chinese dinner, and relax by walking around the city.

When I stepped off the train in Taipei, I asked the taxi driver to take me to the best hotel in town. He smiled, nodded, and drove straight to the Ambassador Hotel, a large, elegant structure in the heart of the city. I liked it at once. I walked into the spacious lobby, admiring the Oriental styling and art, the tall vases on pedestals, the large paintings on the walls. Yes, I thought, this is nice. Two hours out of CCK, into a totally different world, a world so unlike the world of a C-130 crewmember; I was a long way from anything remotely connected with the war.

My room was modest but stylish, one bed, tastefully if sparely furnished. I took a long hot shower, put on some casual clothes, and went down to the hotel dining room. The dining room was large and blue, the Ming Garden Dining Room. It was still early in the evening, and when I walked in, the room was practically deserted. It felt strange to be in an empty room. Everywhere I had been in the last eight months, there were lots of people around me, mostly in flight suits and other uniforms. To eat alone was not usual. But it did not bother me.

Ambassador Hotel, Taipei, Taiwan.

    I ordered a complete meal, rice wine, egg drop soup, an entrée with many side dishes, dessert, tea. I took my time. Because there were so few people eating, I had lots of attention from the waiters and waitresses. I indulged myself completely. I ate slowly, forcing myself to take my time. The food was excellent, nothing like the ubiquitous grilled ham cheese sandwiches which I normally consumed at every base's flight line snack bar. I drank my tea slowly, enjoying every minute. By the time I pushed my chair back from the table, the room was half-filled with diners. I had enjoyed my meal for an hour and a half.

I looked at my watch. Not quite nine o'clock. What could I do to round out this pleasant evening? As I waited for the elevator to take me up to my room, I noticed an advertisement for the Sky Lounge, a bar on the top floor of the hotel with a view of the city. I pushed the button for the Sky Lounge.

When the elevator door opened, I walked into a room with windows on three sides, offering views to the east, south, and west. Many tables, a bar along the north wall, some couples at tables, a few people gathered around a piano in the southeast corner. I made my way over to a table in the southwest corner, sat down, and admired the view. The sun had set in the west, but the city below was still visible in the fading light, the city lights just taking effect.

The streets of Taipei were laid out before me, fading into the smoke and haze of street life and cooking fires. From where I sat, I could see aircraft approaching the Taipei airport, which was located on the northeast side of the city. They circled around to the west, then headed to the east on final approach, briefly disappearing behind the north wall of the hotel, then reappearing on the east side, descending toward the runway, anti-collision lights flashing regularly in the growing darkness. As I drank my scotches, I followed the approach course of several aircraft, following one another to their landing.

I sat there, completely relaxed, watching the city lights grow stronger as the twilight faded. I let myself realize how unhappy I had been at the prospect of playing permanent copilot for the remainder of my tour at CCK, and how totally surprised and exhilarated I was to have been given the opportunity to upgrade to instructor pilot and pleased to have done so well in my brief ten-day checkout period. There was much in my mind I needed to process.

I had finished my third scotch (or was it my fourth?). By now the room was almost deserted. The nighttime view of the city was lovely, but apparently few local people cared to see it, and there were few Western tourists interested in coming up here for the evening. The only activity was over at the piano. Three or four people were sitting around the piano, requesting songs and approving the pianist's performance. I decided I would join these few, have one more scotch, and retire for the evening.

I sat down next to a slender, dark-haired woman, older than I was, but strikingly attractive. She was dressed in a simple black dress. She had been talking to a local man seated next to her. They had been together at the bar when I came in, and I had assumed they were there together. But she increasingly directed her remarks to me.

"Where are you from?" she asked.

"From the air base at Taichung," I said.

"Have you been there long?" Her English was excellent.

"Eight months."

"Why are you in Taipei?"

"Three days of R and R—rest and relaxation."

Her name was Tamiko. She did not have the Chinese look of most of the residents of the island. She looked almost European. When I asked her, she said that her father had been Japanese, and her mother had been one of the native Taiwan islanders. These people, I knew, were distinguished by their distinctly Polynesian features.

She seemed knowledgeable about the music the pianist was playing. She had taken piano lessons in Japan and had been fairly proficient in playing classical music. Chopin, Brahms. The few details suggested that she had a very unusual background. I was impressed. I said it was too bad the pianist didn't take a break. I would like to hear her play.

Oh no, she said. She hadn't practiced for a long time. Did I play a musical instrument? Yes, I said. The trombone. The what? The trombone. The slush pump. I gestured, holding my left hand near my mouth, as if were holding a trombone, moving my right hand in and out, as if I were moving the slide. Oh, she said, using the Chinese word for the instrument. No, I said, I wasn't very good. It had been a long time since I had played the trombone.

We had been talking together for a long time. The man seated on the other side of her seemed to be a little distressed that she was paying so much attention to me. I said I had to go to the bathroom and would be right back. When I finished my duties in the bathroom and stepped out in the hall, she was there waiting for me.

"Do you want me to spend the night with you?" she asked.

I was a little surprised by the abruptness of her question. But on very brief reflection, it seemed like an excellent idea.

"What about …?" I nodded in the direction of the bar, hidden from view by a wall.

She smiled and grabbed my arm.

"Don't worry about him. Let's go."

We made a quick exit, laughing together as we stepped onto the elevator.

Chapter 17

Christmas at Khe Sanh

After my return from Taipei, Horse Pemberton wasted no time placing me on the in-country shuttle schedule. We departed just after six in the evening on the fifteenth of December, bound for Tuy Hoa by way of Naha. Major Chick McWilliams was in the left seat, newly arrived at CCK and scheduled for his in-country checkout. The rest of the crew consisted of Captain Larry Fordham, navigator, Sergeant Irving "Ski" Torchinski, flight mechanic, and Sergeant Gerald P. Walker, loadmaster. I had inherited Captain Kirk Waldron's crew, the same crew that had flown with me on my check ride. Kirk was off with Lieutenant Colonel Tom Phillips, flying Bob Hope around Vietnam for his annual Christmas show. The rest of the crew complained loudly about the unfairness of a system that allowed Waldron to fly around with Bob Hope, Raquel Welch, Barbara McNair, and Elaine Dunn, getting the full VIP treatment, while they had to go on the shuttle with a brand-new IP.

After landing at Tan Son Nhut at six in the morning, we flew up the coast from Qui Nhon to Tuy Hoa in the bright light of a Southeast Asia sunrise. The sun illuminated the beach to the east and the hills beyond the valley west of Tuy Hoa. It had been over six months since I had landed at Tuy Hoa, and the place had changed significantly.

Gone was the narrow aluminum matting runway. In its place was a long, wide concrete runway that ran from the southwest to the northeast, ending just short of the sea. Several F-100s were parked on the ramp. We walked off the aircraft to the operations building, a small, white wooden structure at the edge of the ramp, and deposited our flight gear and survival vests. The crew van took us to our hooches, long low wooden and concrete structures with sides that lifted to allow the ocean breeze to filter through the screens.

The next morning we carried a load of Army troops from Phan Rang to Bao Loc, one of the most unusual fields in South Vietnam, located about 50 miles west of Phan Rang. Bao Loc featured a humped runway, significantly higher in the middle than it was on either end. The landing strip at Bao Loc had been created from the top of one of the smaller, more regular hills in the area. The men who made the field had tried to level out the landing areas at the ends of the field as best they could, but they had not been able to eliminate the large rise in the middle.

I had flown into runways that were higher at one end than the other, and a Dash One chart helped estimate landing or takeoff roll from a slanted runway. But no one had come up with a chart for a humped runway, one that was markedly lower at both ends than it was in the middle. Other pilots who had flown to Bao Loc said landing

Tuy Hoa Air Base from 15,000 feet, December 1967. Home to an F-100 unit as well as our C-130 operations.

C-130 A-model Landing at Bao Loc, December 1967. The far end of the runway is not visible due to the pronounced curved slope of the runway. Photograph taken from midfield.

and taking off there was almost normal—with a couple of exceptions. On landing, they said, you aimed for the end of the runway, as usual, and tried to disregard the fact that as touched down, you lost sight of approximately half of the remaining runway. And as you flared, you had to adjust your flare to anticipate the runway that was rising to meet you.

    Taking off, the reduction in speed suffered climbing uphill was (probably) compensated for by the speed gained going downhill. No one seemed to know whether the acceleration gained going downhill exactly compensated for the acceleration lost going uphill. Seemed to me it wasn't likely. Somebody suggested carrying ten percent less weight than you would normally carry.

These abnormal runways had abnormal numbers of accidents associated with them. Earlier that year, a C-130 with a load of ammunition on board had crashed at Bao Loc. The crew members had been unable to extricate the flight engineer from his seat and he had perished in the fire and explosions that had consumed the aircraft.

We saw a number of aircraft circling the field; the parking ramp was full of aircraft, and Army helicopters were busy moving in and out of the area. The off-loading ramp was relatively small; as a result of the unique nature of the runway there was a single access entry to the ramp, at the top center of the runway. As a result, the process of moving aircraft into and out of the airfield was slow.

A road and a small creek circled the field just outside the overrun areas. The runway touchdown stripes were painted in a big white block design, and those were my target. As we descended on final approach, I pulled the power to idle, pulled back on the yoke to flare, and realized that the runway immediately began to slope noticeably up. To avoid slamming into the rising runway, I had to apply even more back pressure, which helped to slow the aircraft as it helped to reduce the rate of descent. All I had to do was hold that attitude and let the ground come up to meet me. Which it did. Kablam! The aircraft and everyone on it gave a collective oomph! Ski Torchinski cleared me to reverse.

We rose to the top of the hill, the top of the runway, and saw the taxiway and the ramp pass by us on our right side. As we looked ahead to the end of the runway, a disturbing vision presented itself: the downward slope of the runway made it seem like we were accelerating, not decelerating. There was a limited amount of overrun beyond the end of the runway. And beyond that, the perimeter fence, a drop-off, another stream bed, shrubs, trees, rocks—an unfriendly environment for aircraft. But we stopped with room to spare and used reverse thrust to turn around and taxi back to the middle of the runway, where we turned left onto the loading ramp.

We took off empty, but even though weight was not a problem, the takeoff was as visually unsettling as the landing. When we positioned ourselves at the west end, we could see only to the center point of the runway and had to remember that the rest of the runway was really there. The curvature of the runway was so marked that you could not see the tip of the vertical stabilizer of one C-130 parked at one end of the runway from the seats of the cockpit of another C-130 parked at the other end. Occasionally one 130 would taxi down to takeoff position just after another 130 landed so that the arriving aircraft would have room to unload on the ramp. It was an impressive sight, as you sat at the end of the runway, to see a C-130 gradually appear from behind the rise in the runway before it turned off into the ramp area.

Once we released the brakes, the aircraft seemed to leap ahead. As we rose over the top of the runway, we saw that we would have plenty of runway left to take off. But it was a disturbing perception to be taking off from a runway that now tilted downhill noticeably. You again had to remind yourself that the C-130 was fully capable of clearing the fence, shrubs, trees, and hills which surrounded the departure end. From Bao Loc we returned to Phan Rang, where we picked up a load for Phan Thiet.

Phan Thiet, the field that had caused me to sweat six months earlier, offered no challenge today. Not after the peculiarities of Bao Loc. We landed towards the sea, towards the crowded ramp at the end. We were empty and stopped with little problem. We waited our turn to load. As we waited in line to return to Bao Loc, we watched one E-model give another E-model a buddy start, in which one C-130 ran up its engines to provide adequate wind force to start turning the blades on the balky engine of a C-130 parked immediately behind it. The wind force generated by the engines of the aircraft parked in front gradually caused the balky propeller to start turning, but the aircraft with the balky engine paid the price by being bombarded with rocks and pebbles loosened by the force of the wind blast of the engines in the lead aircraft.

"What's the problem?" asked Chick. "Why won't the prop turn over?"

"Probably a stuck bleed air valve," said "Ski" Torchinsky, our flight engineer. "Sometimes, in these small field operations, if you shut down an engine, the heat and dust will cause the valve to stick shut. The bleed air valve allows pressurized air from the other engines to start the turbine turning. But if the bleed air valve won't open, you're screwed. A buddy start is the only way to get it started without having to take the side panels off the engine. And you don't want to delay your departure in remote fields."

"If you can't get an engine started," I said, "you might be able to do a three-engine takeoff, if the aircraft is empty and the field is long enough. But you are supposed to get approval from the Air Division at Tan Son Nhut before doing so."

I told Chick about our procedure for making a three-engine takeoff, in which we ran up our two symmetrical engines to full power, released brakes and brought in the good engine as airspeed and controllability allowed. But we used that procedure only in an emergency, and then for a one-time flight to the nearest base capable of fixing the problem.

Buddy Start, Phan Thiet, December 1967. The loadmaster sitting on the open ramp of the aircraft on the right is reporting on the progress of the engine start on the aircraft on the left. The wind blast from the lead aircraft can result in small rocks, pebbles, and loose sand blasting the surfaces of the aircraft behind it. This effort was a success.

Chapter 17. Christmas at Khe Sanh

I asked Ski what was the most common reason for an engine failing to start besides a stuck bleed air valve. "Blown O-ring seal on the oil line," he said, without hesitation. The O-ring seals were installed at crucial junctions in the oil feed line, the large, one-inch diameter line that fed oil to each engine. "You lose an O-ring seal on an oil line, your engine will overheat and seize instantaneously."

Ski reached down and pulled out his dog tag chain from underneath his flight suit. He held them out for us to see. "I always wear one on my dog tag chain. See?"

In addition to his small metal identification tag, we could see a small round flexible rubber ring, about an inch in diameter.

"What's that other item?" Chick asked.

"That's my P-38," Ski said. The P-38 was a small folding metal tool with a sharp pointed edge that we used to open our C-ration cans when we wanted something to eat at remote fields. Our favorites were scrambled eggs and bacon, peaches in syrup, and pound cake. Like Ski, I had a P-38 on my dog tag chain. But I didn't have an O-ring seal.

"Got a spare?" I asked.

"Always," he said. He reached into his small tool bag, pulled out two seals and gave one to each of us.

We returned to Tuy Hoa by six o'clock in the evening. I had almost forgotten how challenging flying in-country was.

* * *

The next morning our first stop was Da Nang. Da Nang was the airfield that supported all operations in the northern third of South Vietnam, and it was always busy. Lately, Da Nang's traffic pattern had proven harder to break into than the pattern at Tan Son Nhut. The pattern was full of many different kinds of airplanes, C-47s, O-1s, C-123s, other C-130s, and of course the Air Force and Marine jets that were based there, F-4s, A-7s. Plus Army and Marine helicopters.

We shoehorned our way into the pattern and landed without incident. We parked with our nose to the south on the parking ramp on the east side of the field and shut our engines down. I walked with Chick into the Da Nang ALCE, a two-story wooden building on the north side of the ramp, where we learned we would be making runs to Hue and Khe Sanh. "What's going on?" I asked.

"Seems like there's a lot of enemy activity in the north—the NVA is getting ready to celebrate Tet," the duty officer said.

Our first shuttle took us to Hue Phu Bai, located just south of the city of Hue. It was a short trip north with a simple route: a south takeoff, turn left and head east to the sea, turn left up the coast, head in to the northwest when the coastal mountains ended, and you were on a straight-in for Hue. The approach to the runway at Hue was clear and the runway itself was of a good length, so landing there was not a problem. Chick made the landing easily. The hills began to rise again just beyond the city of Hue. We landed to the northwest and turned off to the left to enter the loading ramp. There were many aircraft on the ramp, mostly Army Hueys and other helicopters. We returned to Da Nang and two hours later we were off again, this time with a load for Khe Sanh. I had been to Khe Sanh before, five months earlier, when I was flying co-pilot with Passarello. But that was at night, and landing there had seemed to me to be a suicide mission. I had been certain the unseen controller was trying to fly us into a hillside. I had never really seen Khe Sanh; but I had seen the photos in the crew file when I had been the duty officer at Cam Ranh.

Khe Sanh was located in the extreme northwest corner of South Vietnam, with Laos to the west and North Vietnam to the north. The field sat on an elevated plateau surrounded on three sides by rolling hills. Immediately east of the field, the land dropped off abruptly. At the base of the drop-off a river flowed down from the hills to the north. The west side of the runway was about one hundred feet higher than the east side. The preferred method was to land to the west (upslope) and take off to the east (downslope); gravity helped us slow on landing and assisted our takeoff. The loading ramp was located near the southwest corner of the runway; two taxiways led into the ramp, one just west of midfield, and the other at the west end of the runway. The main part of the Marine base at Khe Sanh was situated south of the runway.

The weather at Khe Sanh was typically cloudy or hazy. Today the visibility was good, and the Marine camp stood out clearly. The red dirt of the base camp area contrasted markedly with the surrounding green vegetation. To the southwest, we could see the village of Khe Sanh, which sat, our maps told us, practically on the Vietnam-Laos border. A few miles to the north was the imaginary line that separated North and South Vietnam. Hills to the south, west, and north surrounded the base. The Ho Chi Minh Trail was just on the other side of the hills to the west.

As we descended to the east end of the runway, a great chasm opened up below us, created by the steep west bank of the river wall. At the bottom of the chasm was a fast-flowing stream, with green trees and bushes along the white water where it fell

Approach to Khe Sanh, December 1967. Runway extends at an angle from the edge of the valley. Hills dimly visible in background.

Chapter 17. Christmas at Khe Sanh

to lower elevations. The overrun on the east side was practically nonexistent; the runway ended where the drop-off began.

After we landed, we walked around the ramp. The air was cool and refreshing after the Da Nang heat. The hills looked green and pleasant through the mild haze of the late afternoon. We walked over to the airlift center on the edge of the ramp. No load out. As we walked back to the aircraft, we observed the neatness and efficiency of the installation, at least as much as we could see from the ramp: airfield tower to the east, even a fire truck for emergency, rows of low, long wooden buildings to the southeast, a line of helicopters in revetments along the north side of the runway.

We returned to Tuy Hoa just before nine. As we walked into the ops shack, we noted a Coke machine outside the building. "All the comforts of home," someone said. "A chaser for our liquor ration," someone else said. I remembered the first time I had sampled my combat ration. The longer I flew in-country, the better it tasted.

* * *

The next day we were off early, a seven-thirty departure to Phu Cat, where we picked up a load for Da Nang. We arrived in the Da Nang area just after ten. An hour and a half later we were heading north again, up the coast to Dong Ha. Dong Ha was our northernmost airstrip, just south of the line separating North and South Vietnam. It was actually farther north than Khe Sanh, but most of the fighting in the area occurred in hills to the west.

The runway at Dong Ha was good by in-country standards, over 3000 feet long, straight, narrow, and flat. We let down under a cloud layer, turned west from the

Loading Cargo at Dong Ha, December 1967. These loaded aluminum pallets often sat in unprotected conditions on the open ramp; the sacks of mail on this pallet are protected by plastic sheeting and held in place by tie-down straps.

coast, and Chick landed easily to the east. Next to the ops building, a makeshift wooden structure on the north side of the runway served as base operations. A forklift maneuvered behind the aircraft, removing a pallet of mail. The mail sacks were covered with plastic sheeting and then strapped down with webbed straps to keep them dry and intact. In the hazy distance I could see a few trees, some towers, and flat fields stretching away for miles. Less than ten miles to the north was North Vietnam.

From Dong Ha we went back to Da Nang, where we picked up another load for Khe Sanh. The visibility at Khe Sanh was good, even better than it had been earlier, and we could see the plateau and hills surrounding the field clearly. To the west and north tall hills dominated the view, looming over the river valley and the base at Khe Sanh. Farther to the west, the hills rose higher. While the ground crew offloaded the aircraft, we walked around the ramp, admiring its orderly appearance. The landing C-123s, the helicopters arriving and departing, were part of a perfect picture. From Khe Sanh we flew straight home to Tuy Hoa, our crew day at an end.

The following morning we flew north once again, direct to Da Nang, where we picked up a load of food, meats and vegetables, for Khe Sanh. The weather this time was hazy, and we had to use the stair-step TACAN approach, in which we descended to Khe Sanh in 500-foot increments as we approached from the east. The visibility increased as we reached final approach altitude, and the ravine appeared below us as we descended through the clouds on short final.

We returned to Da Nang with a few passengers and then carried some Army equipment to Quang Tri, another small field up the coast, just south of Dong Ha. It was seven miles in from the coast; the runway ran roughly southeast to northwest. The terrain around Quang Tri was like that of Dong Ha, flat in the middle of what normally would have been farm lands. The runway there was shorter and narrower than the one at Dong Ha.

Returning to Da Nang, we were once again scheduled to take another load of supplies to Khe Sanh. We arrived about five thirty, just as the light was beginning to fade. We shut down the engines while we offloaded, our usual practice, and as the forklift removed the pallets, the light grew darker. The hills seemed to grow larger and more threatening as the darkness increased. We took off in the half light of late evening. The lights of the camp came on, and as we banked right, we could see the field growing fainter in the darkness. We stopped at Da Nang to let a few passengers off and flew home in the dark to Tuy Hoa.

* * *

The schedule that was posted in the crew barracks the next day was just like every other crew schedule with the exception of a seasonal sentiment:

C-130 Operations Schedule
for 25 "Christmas" December 1967

Block Time	Aircraft Commander for Crew Scheduled
0500	Capt Riggins
est. 1300	Capt Smith
0630	Maj Shanahan
0700	Lt Col Munsey
0730	Lt Col Rizer
0800	Maj Lewis

Chapter 17. Christmas at Khe Sanh

Block Time	Aircraft Commander for Crew Scheduled
0830	Maj Martin
0900	Maj Wharton with Capt Wilson
0930	Capt Vaughan
1000	Lt Col Pavlica
1200	Maj Anderton
2100	Capt Anz
Alert	Capt Turner

Happy Christmas to one and all. Marry [sic] Christmas.

Our first stop was Cam Ranh Bay. From Cam Ranh we flew to Da Nang, arriving just before one o'clock. The traffic seemed to be a little less hectic, perhaps because it was Christmas. It was no surprise to learn that we were taking some supplies to Khe Sanh. We made our way up the coast and across to Khe Sanh without incident. The sun was shining brightly through scattered clouds and the visibility was excellent. But the field seemed to be deserted. There were a few helicopters coming in to land or refuel, but something seemed different, strange.

We shut the engines down while we offloaded our cargo of mail and supplies. "Come on," I said to Larry, Chick, and Ski; "let's have our Christmas dinner."

Larry gave me a funny look. "Where?" he asked.

"With the troops," I said. "Did you see all that fresh food we've been carrying around for the last few days?" They all nodded. "Christmas dinner," I said. "The Army and the Marines feed their troops well on holidays. You can bet they've got good food here too. I don't know about you, but today I'd rather have something else besides that grilled ham cheese we get at the Da Nang flightline snack bar. I'll bet these Marines are going to eat turkey and mashed potatoes. Cranberry dressing. Giblet gravy. Chocolate ice cream." We walked over to the ops shack to ask where the chow hall was.

"Right down that way," a sergeant said, pointing due east. "But what about your schedule? Aren't you supposed to head back to Da Nang?"

"What about our schedule?" I said. "It's Christmas."

We walked eagerly down the dirt road toward the chow hall, anticipating a good meal. Inside, the food was set out in metal trays on a long counter, steam curling up from beneath the tin covers. But except for a few men standing behind the food racks, the place was deserted. One of the Marines behind the counter noticed our flight suits. "Yessirs, what can we do for you?" he said.

"Would it be okay if we had some of your Christmas dinner? We're not likely to get any today."

"Sure, go right ahead."

I had to make sure. "You're sure it's okay? We don't want to take somebody else's food."

"No, it's okay," the Marine insisted. "Nobody's here to eat it anyway. The food's just getting cold." We walked up to the steaming trays. Sure enough, there it was, just as I'd advertised: turkey, mashed potatoes, cranberry sauce, giblet gravy, fresh bread, fresh coffee. Even chocolate ice cream.

I was puzzled by the fact that the chow hall was empty. "Where is everybody? Have they eaten already?"

The Marine shook his head. "No, they haven't eaten at all. They're out there." And he waved vaguely at the hills to the north and west.

On the ramp at Tuy Hoa. Major Chick McWilliams in the background.

"What's going on?" Larry asked.

"Lots of movement out there. They think there's a whole NVA battalion out there. They're expecting a big attack for Tet. So our boys are out on patrol."

"When will they eat their dinner?"

He shrugged his shoulders. "Nobody tells us nothing. We just do the cooking."

We ate quietly, absorbing this information, and our Christmas dinner didn't taste quite as good as we thought it would. We sat alone, our crew in the chow hall at Khe Sanh, eating Christmas dinner in silence, the only noise the regular "whop-whop-whop" of helicopter blades as the Marine helicopters hovered near the runway.

When we walked back out to the flight line, the sun was starting to set behind the hills to the west. The air smelled fresh and clean, but I felt a bit of chill. A C-123 landed and turned into the ramp. As it taxied by, one of the crew members opened a top hatch and stuck out a flag that said "Fuck Communism." We gave them a thumbs-up high sign. We took off to the east, heading back to Da Nang, as the helicopters continued to maneuver in and out of the refueling pit. The roads of Khe Sanh were deserted. There was still no line into the chow hall.

Two days later Chick Mac Williams was scheduled for his in-country check ride. "Don't worry," I told him. "You'll do fine." And he did.

Chapter 18

Bao Loc in the Fog

We returned to CCK late in the afternoon on New Year's Eve. I knew that the girls at the China Nights wouldn't be celebrating their new year's yet; the Chinese New Year celebration—Tet—was coming up in another month. But I thought maybe there would be a new year's celebration for the Americans, who would be coming into town to celebrate. I waved at one of the red cabs at the gate and headed into Taichung.

The China Nights was full of activity. The music was loud, men and women were dancing, talking, laughing, having a good time. I asked one of the girls if Karla was around. She told me she'd check. I walked over to the bar and ordered a drink. The girl came back after a while and said Karla was on her way over. When she walked through the door, she was upset. She walked directly towards me. "Why you no tell me when you come to town? You think I sit around all the time, wait for you?" She was really angry. I must have interrupted something.

She studied me for a moment. "Okay. You wait here. I make phone call." She walked quickly, determinedly toward the back of the bar, where Mama-san was sitting. After a few minutes, she walked back, frowning.

"Let's go." She grabbed my arm.

"Where are we going?"

"We leave. Change clothes. I hungry. You buy dinner."

We walked out the door and turned left down the sidewalk. We made our way the two blocks to her room. I sat on the bed and watched while she changed from her evening dress into something more traditional. I moved toward her, but she pushed me away. "No. Eat first." While she was dressing, there was a knock on the door.

Without hesitating, she said "Come in."

In walked Sue, another girl who worked at the China Nights. Sue was older than Karla, in her thirties. She was an attractive woman, always with a smile and a friendly disposition. Sue was eating with us. Her boyfriend, one of the majors in the squadron, was in-country, working in a C-130 ALCE for a month. He and Sue had a permanent arrangement; while he was gone, she paid only social visits to the China Nights. We walked downstairs and into the street. Karla grabbed my right arm, Sue the left, and we headed toward the train station to find a taxi. The streets were filled with people in a festive mood.

"What's the occasion?" I asked.

"New Year's Eve."

"Chinese?"

"No," they laughed at me. "American. We have two New Year's, one for Americans, one for Chinese."

"Where are we going?" I asked.

"You like Mongolian Barbecue?" We stopped a taxi and piled in. We drove to the edge of town and stopped at an outdoor restaurant, a large building in front, tables spread out under trees in the back.

We sat at one of the tables set out under an awning, decorated with Chinese lanterns. We ate and drank for over an hour, enjoying the uncommonly warm night air. Suddenly there was a burst of light overhead and a loud Bang! My survival instinct, by now well-developed, kicked in, and I ducked instinctively, sober in an instant. But Karla was laughing at me, pointing through the branches of the trees. Fireworks.

Another burst went off overhead, the sparkling fragments blossoming over us like fragile flowers. Red and green and orange. Rockets shot off into the air, hissing and swirling. There was noise and shouting. Men and women were embracing. I reached for Karla. "Happy New Year!" We kissed. Sue waited patiently. "Me too!"

Later we said good night to Sue, who walked down the hall to her room, as we walked into Karla's room. Karla sat down on the bed and patted the bed beside her. "Okay, GI. Now tell me why you gone so long."

* * *

My new, permanent crew consisted of Captain Al Williams, navigator, Technical Sergeant Edwin Scholes, flight mechanic, and Airman Michael Morris, loadmaster. Al Williams was a long-legged string bean with an easy lope, whom nothing seemed to fluster. One of the few black officers in the squadron, he was quiet and soft-spoken, and his smile seemed wider than his face. He and I had come into the squadron about the same time, and he was now an instructor navigator. Ed Scholes had been in the unit a while, and had a quiet, even disposition. Mike Morris was quiet and efficient, so we constituted one of the most laid-back crews in the squadron. The other pilot for this in-country shuttle was Captain Jerry Figgins, who had been in the squadron for a while, and who was building time for his upgrade to first pilot. We were flying out of Cam Ranh this time.

Our first mission took us around the corner of the coast to Nha Trang and then down to Tan Son Nhut, where we arrived just as it was growing dark. Then to Qui Nhon, back to Nha Trang, and then over to Cam Ranh. From Cam Ranh we flew another run down to Tan Son Nhut and back, arriving at Cam Ramh about one o'clock in the morning. After a day off, we flew again in the evening, from Cam Ranh to Nha Trang to Pleiku, back to Nha Trang, then down to Binh Thuy and back to Cam Ranh. The next night we flew again, flying three shuttles between Qui Nhon and Chu Lai, south of Da Nang. As usual, at Chu Lai, the flares fell on the perimeter all night long. We got back to Cam Ranh in time for breakfast. I was beginning to wonder if our entire tour was going to be taken up with uneventful night missions.

The following night we had a takeoff time of three-thirty in the morning. After a stop at Phu Cat in the pre-dawn darkness, we flew up to Da Nang as the sun came up. From Da Nang we carried a load to Dong Ha, just south of the DMZ. I thought we were going to fly back empty to Da Nang, but the loadmaster said we had a special load. A truck pulled up to the rear of the aircraft and some Army troops carefully placed three long black bags on the rear ramp, where Mike Morris secured them as best he could.

Chapter 18. Bao Loc in the Fog

Even before the bags were secured, I knew what they were: body bags. Three dead soldiers. Although the bodies had been kept in a refrigeration unit, the decomposition process had begun. The smell worked its way up into the flight deck. The smell was over-powering, like exceedingly ripe cheese. We opened our side windows, but the breeze seemed to be blowing forward from the tail of the aircraft. Even after we started engines and the prop blast pulled fresh air in through the cockpit windows, the smell was there. It seemed inappropriate to complain. Once we were airborne, I unhooked my belt and got out of the seat.

"You've got it," I told Jerry. He nodded. I walked back to the rear of the aircraft, to the ramp where the three body bags were lying side by side. In spite of the smell, I had to examine them. I squatted down, studying the bags. I tried to imagine the bodies inside the black, rubberized, zippered bags. But I couldn't. For some reason I had an urge to unzip one.

My mind was blank. I felt a numb, heavy sadness, but somehow the fact of what I was looking at couldn't sink in. I had carried live soldiers, wounded soldiers, and now dead soldiers. A C-130 had probably brought them into their unit, and now a C-130 was taking them out, but not in the way that any of them would have liked. It didn't seem right that they should be lying flat on the ramp without a mattress or a pad of some sort underneath. They really weren't the equivalent of a pallet of mail or a load of ammunition. I squatted there for several minutes, trying to sort out my thoughts.

At Da Nang we exchanged our KIAs for four pallets of ammunition for Khe Sanh—105-millimeter shells, which the Marine artillery would fire into the surrounding hills. The ammunition was crated inside wooden boxes, strapped to the pallets. It was a heavy load. I didn't like the looks of that load. The situation must be getting serious at Khe Sanh. We left Da Nang, flew up the coast, and into Khe Sanh. The sky was overcast, but the visibility was good under the clouds. We landed to the west, turning off at the first taxiway. We shut down the engines while a forklift removed the pallets of ammunition. Helicopters were flying continuously in the area. We left as quickly as we could and flew directly back to Cam Ranh, our crew day over.

* * *

The next morning we left Cam Ranh just after sunrise on a clear, bright morning. We flew directly to Bao Loc, the field with the humped runway. We were one of several C-130s involved in moving some Army units from there to Song Be, an Army camp close to the Cambodian border. The weather was perfect: clear air, excellent visibility. I knew there was a problem when we arrived in the area and saw two other C-130s circling the field. We were the first aircraft to arrive, so I couldn't imagine what was causing the delay. When I looked down at the field, I immediately saw what the problem was.

The cool air that had moved in overnight had had a unique effect; in the low-lying areas around the field, patches of thick fog were gathered in the valleys and depressions. At the field itself, the ramp areas and center section of the runway were absolutely clear, bathed in sunlight, but fog lay thickly over the ends of the runway, those portions of the runway that dipped down towards the small river valley that bordered the field on the west, north, and east sides. While thick fog sat on the ends of the runway, the center of the runway basked in the early morning sunshine. I had never seen anything like it. The middle of the runway was VFR, and the ends were IFR. And it was a relatively short runway, about 3500 feet long. What a strange phenomenon. What a predicament.

I and the two aircraft commanders in the other aircraft, Captain Dennis Ward and Captain David Risher, discussed our options over the radio. It was clear the fog wasn't going to burn off soon, and we didn't want to orbit the field indefinitely. Finally Dave Risher made a decision. "What the hell," he said. "I'm going to land."

Dave set up on a left downwind on the north side of the field. I could see him drop his gear, then flaps. He turned base to the south, losing altitude. Then he turned on final approach, heading east, descending into that white patch of fog at the end of the runway. He disappeared into the white cloud, except for the tip of his tail, the top of the vertical stabilizer, which stuck out of the fog. We followed the progress of his plane by the movement of the tip of his tail. We could see it level off, move forward, then begin to rise out of the fog.

The entire aircraft emerged from the pool of fog, engines clearly in reverse, shrouds of fog spinning forward through the props from the force of the reverse thrust. Up the slope it came, then over the top, now fully in the clear. Past the turn-off point, traveling too rapidly to turn off.

Dave's aircraft continued to decelerate on the downslope side and entered the fog at the far end. Once again the plane disappeared into the fog. Only the tip of the vertical stabilizer was visible. About the time we imagined the aircraft would be running out of runway, the plane came to a stop. Then we saw the tip of the vertical stabilizer move back and forth, slowly turning to the left, as the aircraft executed a series of backwards and forwards movements, so that it could taxi back up the runway.

The aircraft reappeared from the thick fog, wisps of fog streaming off the props, as it taxied, slowly, proudly, up the runway to the top of the rise, where it turned left, taxied to the offloading area, and stopped in the bright sunshine. "No problem," Dave announced over the radio. I wasn't so sure.

Dennis Ward was next. I was happy to let him have the next go at landing. I was hoping that the efforts of the two aircraft would help to dissipate the fog. Dennis followed Dave's example, set himself up on downwind, dropped his gear and flaps, turned base, then final. Into the fog. Then out, props in reverse. Over the top. Then back into the fog. Slow stop at the end. Back and forth in the fog. Out of the fog, slowly and proudly. Turn off at the top and park. My turn.

Well, I thought, if they can do it, I can too. I flew down the center of the runway, hoping that I could see evidence of the fog thinning out. Through the fog I could see the white markings at the end of the runway. As long as there was some visual reference once we got in the fog. Oh well. Onto a crosswind. Downwind. Gear down. Flaps down. Slow the aircraft. Try to judge where to turn. How do you decide where to turn when the end of the field is covered by fog? Turn base. Pull the power back. Hold a little extra altitude until lined up on final. Turn to final. Flaps full.

The white stripes and line at the end of the runway are just visible through the whiteness of the fog. Thank god. Line up on those marks. Lock onto them with my vision. Pull the power back. Slow the airspeed. Closer and closer to the fog. Into the fog.

Suddenly surrounded by dark, greyish-white environment. Shit! The white runway markings have disappeared! Where the hell is the runway? Then suddenly, the markings are there in front of us! Flare! Pull the yoke back, hard. Here comes the runway. Power off. Yoke back some more. Wham! Definitely a firm landing. But no worse than many others I've made in perfect weather. Power to idle. Pause. Into reverse pitch range. Clear to reverse. Full reverse. How's my directional control? Hard to tell in the fog. Looks okay. On the brakes. Slow this sucker down. Wish I could see where we're going.

Then, suddenly, out of the fog. Blinding, bright sunlight. Hard to see. At least we're under control, slowing, more or less in the center of the runway. Here comes the top of the rise. A quick look to the right, at the two planes parked there. On the wings, on the ground, the crew members of Risher's and Ward's crews, waving at us as we tear past, handkerchiefs in their hands. Bastards. But no time to dwell on their cute antics. A quick obscene gesture from one of us, then we turn our attention to completing the landing roll.

Over the top of the rise, now downhill. Still on the brakes. Into the fog again. Whiteness, no visibility. Oh man. Where is the end of the runway? Are we still in the center? Then through the fog appear the white hash marks at the east end of the runway. We can see them coming up at us, but slowly. Yes, we can stop in time. We will stop. We stop. Son of a bitch. Don't want to do this again any time soon.

Like the others, I slowly move the aircraft back and forth. Forward thrust. Turn to the left. Edge of the runway. Reverse thrust. Back up, turning to the left. Forward thrust. Reverse thrust. Back up the runway. Finally, out into the sun. After the grey denseness of the fog, the sunlight is too bright. Slowly, steadily, up the slope, to the top, then off to the access ramp. Park it. Shut it down. Out of the aircraft, to swear at Dave and Denny. You bastards. They are laughing, tears in their eyes. They swear they could see the whites of our eyes as we thundered past.

"Risher, you crazy bastard." What can you say? Probably the most bizarre landing I'll ever make at the most unusual field I'll ever see. Only in Vietnam. Only at a place like Bao Loc, with its strangely, excessively humped runway. But Dave and Denny and I and our crews, we did it. I think about it now, and I shake my head.

By the time we were loaded with Army troops, the fog was gone. We carried a load over to Song Be, near the Cambodian border. Song Be was easy to spot from a distance, for it was located east of one of the few large hills in the area. When we arrived, the air over the field was filled with dust, raised by a variety of landing and departing aircraft, and numerous Army troops were moving around the perimeter of the loading ramp. We off-loaded our troops and equipment without incident.

Later we heard about the problems that Louis McAdory and Horse Pemberton had when they tried to deliver an unusually long load of timbers there at night. They had just landed and were preparing to offload when the field came under attack. They had to secure their load in a hurry and beat it out of there. Fortunately, they did so without damaging themselves, the aircraft, or the load. They returned a little later and completed their offload successfully.

But our excitement at Bao Loc wasn't over. We returned to Bao Loc a few hours later. The sun had dissipated the fog, and it was now uncomfortably hot. The loadmaster, Mike Morris, expressed some concern about the weight of the load the Army was putting on the aircraft. The load looked normal to me—a six-by Army truck, a trailer loaded with a water tank, and about fifteen troops.

"What's the matter?" I asked.

"They're supposed to empty the fuel and water out of their trucks and trailers when we carry them. But I'm not sure they've emptied all of their tanks. Sometimes they don't want to because they have trouble filling them when they get to their next location."

"Can't you check their tanks?" I asked.

"Yeah, but you can't really see anything. And it's hard to tell by hitting the sides."

"Well," I said, "don't load as much on board. Reduce our load."

"I have. But for some reason, I don't think they're telling the truth about emptying their tanks."

"Well, let's take this load," I said. "Let's close it up and get going."

"Yes sir." Mike walked back to the rear of the aircraft.

Jerry and I strapped in and started engines. As we taxied out to the runway, I tried to detect any signs of an unusually heavy aircraft. But our taxi distance was too short for a decent check. We moved out to the center of the runway, then turned left and proceeded down to the west end of the runway for a takeoff to the east. The aircraft rumbled along as it normally did with a load on board, rocking slightly from side to side. I could tell we had a load, but the rough runway made it impossible to tell for certain if the load was especially heavy.

We positioned ourselves at the end of the runway, looking up to the top of the rise. It was particularly disconcerting to be able to see only half of the runway. I backed the aircraft as far as it could go and ran the engines up to full power, standing on the brakes. When Ed Scholes said the power looked good, I released the brakes.

Normally, when we released the brakes at full power, the aircraft gave a lurch forward, even when it carried a load. But this time there was no lurch, not even a hint of one. A bad sign. The aircraft started to move slowly forward. It picked up speed at a decent rate until we hit the upslope of the runway. Then I could tell for sure that our rate of acceleration was not what we wanted. Once again the old dilemma: would the increased acceleration on the downslope compensate for the reduced acceleration on the upslope? I hoped to hell it would.

We went over the top of the rise at about fifty knots. Definitely slow. But the additional weight on a downhill roll ought to work to our advantage. The aircraft accelerated as we went downhill. Here came our calculated rotate speed, about eighty knots. "Rotate now!" Jerry said from the right seat. I pulled back on the yoke, hoping for the usual reaction: that the nose would lift into the air and that as we gained speed, the aircraft would fly off the runway.

But the nose did not lift. The aircraft did not show the least inclination to leave the ground. If we had had adequate runway left I would have called for an abort. But there was little runway remaining and essentially no overrun. Trying to stop now was not a good idea. So I decided to do the only thing we could do: keep the aircraft on the ground, building up airspeed until we ran out of runway, and then take off. I eased the nose back down—no sense adding unnecessary drag with my elevators up.

We sat and watched the end of the runway approach. No one said anything. There was nothing to say. There was no clever advice to give. We had to hope the aircraft would fly when we reached the end.

The aircraft bounced and rolled from side to side. The airspeed was fluctuating somewhere around 105 knots. The end of the runway was directly in front of us. A few yards beyond the end, the perimeter fence stuck into the air, a few strands of barbed wire strung on iron posts. Trees and shrubs grew sparsely in the rocky ground beyond. I kept the nose wheel on the ground right to the end, then as the aircraft

Chapter 18. Bao Loc in the Fog

bottomed out on the front end of the turnaround area, I pulled back on the yoke as firmly as I could.

The aircraft bounced heavily and staggered into the air. The yoke felt heavy, so heavy in my hands. I had never felt such weight on the aircraft. The aircraft wallowed through the air. I felt as if I were holding the aircraft in the air single-handedly. We were airborne, but barely. "Gear up!" I said, tensely.

Fortunately, the ground at the east end of the runway sloped down, following the course of the stream bed. I followed the course of the stream bed, turning as little as possible. Thank god the stream bed was more or less in line with the runway heading. "Don't touch the flaps!" I told Jerry. Slowly, slowly, slowly, we gained airspeed. We climbed 50 feet, 75 feet, 100 feet. Two hundred feet. Finally, after following the stream bed for about a mile, we were able to begin a slow turn to the left. After we had gained five hundred feet of altitude, I told Jerry to raise the flaps ten degrees at a time.

I don't think I exhaled for five minutes. I began to relax only after we were cruising at 4500 feet on course for Song Be. Then we all looked around at one another, smiled weakly, shook our heads. It was the most helpless feeling I have ever had, committed to a takeoff that could well have ended in disaster. Unlike landing, where you have some control over the movement and configuration of the aircraft, on takeoff, there's not a damn thing you can do except sit there and sweat.

I was reminded of the story Captain Ross Kramer told me about flying out of the Golf Course at An Khe. Ross was one of the most experienced squadron pilots and had returned to the States before Christmas. On one of his missions out of the Golf Course, he had been similarly overloaded, and found himself running out of runway, bouncing down toward the low north end of the field. As I had, he kept the aircraft on the runway until the last second, then lifted it off at a much lower than normal airspeed. The propwash of the aircraft blew down tents and shacks located off the end of the runway as it roared through, getting maximum benefit of ground effect. Barely airborne, blowing dust and debris out behind him for the better part of a mile, Ross gradually gained adequate altitude to maneuver out of the valley. He, too, was going to Song Be, and when he landed, he found pieces of shrubbery embedded in the gear doors. Both he and I had survived the unique experience of living on ground effect.

At Song Be we glared at the Army troops when they moved their equipment off the aircraft. We didn't say anything to them about our close call. "Okay, Mike," I said. "Next trip we give ourselves a 25% safety factor." We figured out that the air temperature had increased much more than we had estimated, and that factor, added to the higher elevation of the field at Bao Loc, contributed to our decreased takeoff performance. But we were through with Bao Loc that day. For the next three missions we flew Army troops and equipment on nineteen hops to five fields, Cam Ranh, Ban Me Thuot, Bao Loc, Song Be, Bien Hoa.

On our final landing at Bien Hoa I had an experience that greatly upset me. About fifteen miles out of Bien Hoa, I contacted Bien Hoa approach control and asked for artillery firing advisories, as was my custom. I had not forgotten the advice Duke Williams had given me many months earlier, about avoiding active firing areas around Bien Hoa. We did not want to fly through an outgoing artillery barrage. Now I was especially concerned about the danger because I had just seen a story in the far east edition of *Stars and Stripes* (the American newspaper that was reported news to

Friendly fire accident. An Air Force C-7 Caribou is falling out of the sky after an outgoing army artillery shell severed its fuselage near Duc Pho, 3 August 1967.

the military personnel in Southeast Asia) about an American C-7 Caribou that had just been shot out of the sky by friendly fire near Duc Pho. The Caribous were small and slow but could land on some really short fields. It had taken a direct hit from artillery fire in its thin empennage section just in front of the tail. The disturbing part of the story, besides the deaths of all aboard, was the fact that the artillery fire had been American; the Caribou had been shot down by friendly fire. A real waste, to be killed by friendly fire. As if the occasional enemy bullet or your own carelessness weren't hazards enough.

We were starting our descent to 2500 feet, and the outbound shells could arc as high as 5000 feet. The army artillery unit at Bien Hoa was often called upon to provide artillery support for army units operating north of Bien Hoa.

"Roger," answered approach control. "Active firing from 270 to 300 degrees." Outbound firing was taking place west to northwest of Bien Hoa. As long as we continued our approach on our southerly heading, we should be safe.

But when I called Bien Hoa tower frequency, the controller advised "Avoid the northeast quadrant on your approach. Army artillery is active."

Shit! We were right in the middle of the northeast quadrant at 2500 feet. I was instantaneously furious. How could Bien Hoa approach control and Bien Hoa tower provide us with dangerously different advisories? I grabbed the controls—Jerry Figgins had been flying the approach—and banked hard right then hard left, looking for tell-tale signs of artillery fire. But I could see no sign of smoke or dust rising from any location near the airfield. I told Jerry to continue the approach. We landed without incident.

At the Bien Hoa base operations counter, I asked the duty officer about the dangerously conflicting information. He shrugged. "Sorry," he said. "We pass the information along as soon as we get it. The artillery unit fires first and tells us afterwards. There has been a lot of enemy activity lately. Something big is going on."

I resolved that I would not allow myself and my crew to be put in such a hazardous situation in the future.

Our mission the following day was different. An A-model had taken some hits going into An Hoa, a special forces field a few miles southwest of Da Nang. We were tasked to carry a replacement engine, propeller, miscellaneous parts, tools, and a repair crew from Cam Ranh to An Hoa. "Be careful," the duty officer said; "the guys who shot that A-model full of holes are still there. Keep your pattern high and tight."

I had never been to An Hoa, so wasn't sure what to expect. I wanted to stay well above the terrain. I planned to fly into the field high and land out of a circling overhead approach. But a low, thin cloud deck extended inland from the coast at Chu Lai as far as we could see, and I had to abandon my plan. We let down over the shoreline near Chu Lai, then flew in under the cloud layer, heading on a north-northwest heading to An Hoa under a thousand feet, too close to the ground for my comfort. Any enemy troop with a rifle could hit us. The clouds remained thick with no sign of breaking up. The flat terrain below was thick with trees and bushes. I kept looking for tell-tale signs of muzzle flashes.

Al Williams was following our progress on his map. "Should be about ten miles ahead," he said. "There's a hill just to the south. The runway is on the north side, running east-west." Soon we saw a dark shape sticking up above the surrounding terrain. The hill south of An Hoa. And then I saw sunshine. The clouds were breaking up. Clear sky over An Hoa. We could have flown at a higher, safer altitude after all.

I was furious in an instant. I swore, "Goddammit! Goddammit! Goddammit!" pounding the top of the instrument panel. "Shit! Goddamn clouds!" Jerry Figgins gave me a funny look. Why was I so upset about a little thing like a cloud layer with a hole in it?

We approached the hill from the southeast. The tower cleared us to land to the east. We were set up on a right downwind. I called for the gear and flaps down and slowed the aircraft. Looking across Jerry and out the copilot's window, I could see the field to our right: decent length, about 3000 feet, flat. The only problems were trees; there were trees at both ends, the sides. And mud. Mud everywhere. They'd had a lot of rain in the last few days. It looked like the aluminum matting runway was afloat in a sea of mud.

The end of the field slipped past on the right, and I reduced power and descended in a right turn. On final. Full flaps. Power back. Trim the aircraft. The nose rising slightly. Over the threshold. Power to idle. Flare. Touchdown. Throttles to idle. Cleared to reverse. Hand on the nosewheel steering. Full reverse. Brakes. We're there.

"Nice landing," someone said, and I belatedly realized it had been a smooth touchdown. At the time I hadn't thought about it one way or the other. As we taxied from the runway onto the ramp, I could see why it was a smooth landing. The runway rippled on the mud base beneath. I felt like we had to keep the aircraft moving or we would sink into the mud beneath, runway and aircraft and all, swallowed up by a massive mudhole.

The A-model sat, abandoned and still, an unnatural sight on a forward operating strip. A large target for enemy mortars. After we shut down, we walked over to look at the disabled aircraft. Al, Jerry, Ed, Mike, and I stood under the open cargo ramp, looking in awe at the shot-up aircraft.

The A-model had several bullet holes in the fuselage and wings. Someone had whittled a wooden peg and shoved it into a hole on the bottom surface of the right wingtip. Fuel was steadily dripping down the peg onto the ramp below. The covering had been removed from the inboard section of the number three engine. We could see how perfectly a single bullet had pierced the main oil feed line. We unloaded our cargo and left the repair crew staring at the wounded aircraft, trying to figure out where to begin.

We flew directly to Khe Sanh, where we were directed to carry some passengers to Da Nang. We arrived at Khe Sanh just before three o'clock. It was strangely quiet when we arrived; you could feel tenseness in the air. A cloud layer over the hills gave the camp a thin, filtered light. The place looked much more war-weary than it had a week previously; there were smudged spots on the runway and taxiway where mortar rounds had hit and holes filled in. The buildings south of the runway showed signs of having been hit by mortars. We kept our engines running, and Jerry and I scanned the perimeter nervously, looking for signs of mortar fire. The ALCE troops said the Marines were waiting for the big VC probe of the perimeter they felt sure would come soon. We picked up our passengers and departed promptly for Da Nang.

On the ramp at An Hoa. Discussing procedures for repairing a shot-up A-Model, January 1968. Al Williams, second from left in baseball cap; Jerry Figgins, third from left in flight cap.

Chapter 18. Bao Loc in the Fog

An Hoa, January 1968. Bullet hole exactly in middle of engine oil feed line, number three engine of the disabled A-Model.

The next day was our final shuttle for this tour. We flew to the English LZ to pick up a bunch of Army troops, whom we carried to Hue Phu Bai. Then back to Da Nang. Then back to English for another load to Hue Phu Bai. Lots of troop relocation during the last week or so: west to Song Be, north to Hue. From Hue to Dong Ha to drop off some other troops, then back to Cam Ranh.

When we reported to the operations building late the following evening to fly back to CCK, we heard the news: Khe Sanh had been heavily mortared. Numerous casualties. The Marines' ammo dump had been blown up. All those 105-millimeter shells we had carried in there had exploded in a gigantic fireworks display. Debris from the exploding ammunition had rained down on the camp for an hour. "When did it happen?" I asked the duty officer.

"Yesterday afternoon." January 19. One day after we landed there when we flew up from An Hoa.

"No more C-130 landings at Khe Sanh until further notice," he said.

Chapter 19

Tet

We returned from Vietnam on a Sunday. My sudden, unexpected arrival for once did not interfere with Karla's schedule. When I left the next morning, I told her confidently I would be back to see her soon. Just a short out-and-back trip to a Marine base at Iwakuni, Japan. Good, she said. Finally, one time I know when to expect you.

We departed for Iwakuni early in the afternoon of January 23. The day was bright and clear. We flew for four hours and forty-five minutes, a straight shot up the Kurile Islands. Iwakuni was located just south of the Japanese city of Hiroshima. As we descended in clear weather, I tried to imagine what it might have looked like when the atomic bomb "Little Boy," dropped by the B-29 *Enola Gay*, detonated. After a delay of three and a half hours, we flew back to CCK, landing just after one o'clock in the morning. A simple flight, nothing exceptional. But when we landed, the mood of the base, and the world, had changed, the result of one bizarre, unusual incident: the capture of the U.S.S. *Pueblo*.

While we were en route to Japan, the U.S. Navy vessel U.S.S. *Pueblo* had been captured by the North Koreans, and by the time we returned to CCK, the world had learned about it. The capture of the *Pueblo* and the imminent arrival of Tet, the Chinese New Year, created a nervous, uncertain feeling in all of us. The duty officer told us that we were scheduled to return to Vietnam for an in-country shuttle immediately. We were to be flying down on an aircraft flown by another crew. So much for my return visit to Taichung.

The pilot assigned to our crew on this trip was none other than Captain David Risher, the brash young captain who led the way into the fog at Bao Loc. Dave was scheduled for upgrade to instructor pilot, and my task was to give him a workout in the right seat. I had a new loadmaster on this trip as well: Sergeant Virgis "Virg" Hill, an eager, enthusiastic troop, had replaced Mike Morris. When we landed at Tuy Hoa later that day, we received another relevant news item: C-130s had just resumed landing at Khe Sanh. "It looks like we came in-country just in time," I said to Dave.

"Just in time for what?" he said.

For our first mission we shuttled Army troops between Cu Chi and Hue. Cu Chi was located west of Bien Hoa, less than fifteen miles from the Cambodian border. The field at Cu Chi was short, less than 3000 feet. Landing in that distance was not a problem as long as we carried a small load. The approaches were free of obstructions, but the runway was an oil-coated dirt strip. The tower cautioned us to watch out for vehicle traffic on the approach end; the perimeter road bordered the end of the runway. As we whistled in on short final, I could see an Army military policeman standing off to the left of the approach end of the runway with his hand up in the air and two or three trucks waiting in the curve of the road, GIs leaning out of the windows watching our arrival.

We stopped quickly, kicking up dust on the runway. We taxied to the loading area and shut down, waiting for the Army troops to board. Several aircraft were involved in the airlift; the field and ramp area were small, and we were told to stay onboard during the loading process so we could depart promptly once loaded. Suited me. Dave and I sat in our seats, side windows open, joking, enjoying the early morning breeze as it blew through. We were drinking coffee from the coffee jugs stored in the galley.

"What was that song you were singing on short final?" he asked, leaning towards me from the co-pilot's seat.

"What do you mean, singing?" I demanded. "Are you putting me on?"

"No, really, you were singing something. What was it, Sergeant Scholes?"

Ed Scholes scratched his head. "Can't place it. Something familiar, though. I know I've heard it before."

"You guys are putting me on." Me singing on final approach? Not likely.

I started to say something, but just then Ka-rump! An explosion shook the ground, and a column of dust rose from the ground less than a quarter mile directly in front of us, outside the camp perimeter but near enough to be of serious concern.

"What the hell was that?" Dave and I yelled simultaneously. We looked anxiously out our cockpit windows for signs of activity. The Army troops continued their loading tasks as before, showing no obvious signs of concern. But Dave and I were distressed. That had been a mortar explosion, no doubt about it. There had been too many incidents of mortar attacks occurring any time a 130 landed for us to treat the matter as casually as the other Army troops seemed to be doing. But nobody else around appeared to be concerned; none of the troops was running for cover.

"I tell you what, we see another of those and we start engines and get the hell out of here," I said. Dave nodded vigorously, in total agreement. But no more explosions occurred.

Shortly the troops boarded and we were ready to depart. We departed to the north. As we roared down the runway, engines kicking up dust, we could see the guard to our right, once again holding up his hand, dutifully stopping traffic. I could see why the guard was necessary. Even though we had a reduced load, we needed all of the runway. If there had been a vehicle on the road in front of us, we would have left tire marks on it.

It was an hour and a half flight up the coast to Hue Phu Bai. Al Williams sat back at the navigator's position, giving us the necessary headings to the coast. When we cruised past Da Nang about ten o'clock, we could see smoke rising west of the field. Some sort of excitement was going on there. We turned in to Hue, shooting the usual straight-in approach from the coast. At Hue the troops we had carried up from Cu Chi filed off, looks of concern showing clearly on their faces.

Back to Cu Chi. After we taxied off the runway, Dave turned to Ed Scholes. "What was the song Vaughan was singing on short final?"

Oh, for Christ's sake, I thought.

"Rock of Ages," he said.

"Yeah. That's it! That's what it is. Rock of Ages."

This had to be a joke. And both of them were in on it.

"Listen, you guys...." I said.

"Al, you heard it, didn't you?" Dave asked.

"Yup. Sure did." So Al was in on it too.

"What do you mean, you heard it?" I said. "You sit back there at the nav desk. What do you mean you heard me?"

"Don't forget, AC," Al said, "you've got a hot mike."

"You guys are serious," I said finally.

"We're serious," Dave said. "Let me give you a sample of what you've been serenading us with: Rock of Ages, cleft for me, let me hide myself in thee." He sang it approximately in tune.

And then I realized I had in fact been singing it low, under my breath, as we had come across the threshold, just as I flared before landing.

"How long have I been doing that?" I asked.

"I don't know," Al said. "But I heard you doing it our last trip into Khe Sanh."

As the troops came on board, we asked about the explosion earlier in the morning. One shrugged his shoulders.

"Oh, they're always blowing up stuff around here. Probably tunnels. The whole place is nothing but fucking VC tunnels."

The MP stopped traffic once again and we roared off for Hue, where we offloaded with our engines running, and then we headed back to Tuy Hoa, our duty day done.

When we flew next, a sense of nervousness was evident even in the relatively secure confines of the ops building at Tuy Hoa. We flew all day in the northern area—from Da Nang to Dak To and Khe Sanh. Our first hop was a short one to Qui Nhon, where we picked up a load of supplies for Dak To. Dak To had a history of vulnerability to attack—less than two months previously mortar attacks had destroyed two C-130s and damaged two others. The airfield was laid out against one high hill and flanked by another. The hills were covered with heavy foliage.

The Army used the field as a staging and supply area for operations to the west, where Army troops scouted the Laotian border and the Ho Chi Minh trail. The runway at Dak To was of decent length—well over 3000 feet. The only problem was the large hill on the west side. There was a lot of activity around the field when we arrived—Huey helicopters in for refueling were raising dust to the south. But our landing was uneventful, and we departed for Pleiku in twenty minutes. We offloaded a few troops at Pleiku with our engines running and then flew northeast to Da Nang.

At Da Nang we became part of a stream of C-130s carrying supplies to Khe Sanh. The ALCE duty officer told us that Khe Sanh had come increasingly under fire in the last week. It had been ten days since my last visit there. For four of those ten days C-130s had not landed due to runway damage and intense mortar attacks. Now C-130 landings had resumed, and we were bringing supplies and ammunition to the Marines. Ammunition was in short supply since a VC mortar shell had blown up their ammo dump. In addition to the continuous threat of mortar attack, winter weather had begun to move in, reducing visibility and lowering ceilings.

We were one of the first 130s to land at Khe Sanh that day; the morning haze and fog which had restricted visibility had cleared. We flew directly up to Khe Sanh, where we could see the field through broken clouds. Marine helicopters were maneuvering north of the runway. As we descended on final, I spotted the darkened, blasted area which had been the Marines' ammo dump. Debris from that explosion littered the area.

We turned off to the left at the east entrance to the ramp and positioned ourselves parallel to the runway. The new procedure was to leave engines running during offload. This meant a little more dust in the faces of the forklift drivers and other ground crew. But it also meant we could depart quickly if necessary. Everywhere we flew these days, but especially in the north, an engines-running offload seemed to be the standard procedure.

We positioned ourselves at the west end of the runway and took off to the east, climbing as rapidly as we could. In an empty aircraft, we could establish a pretty good climb rate. We had just pulled our gear up and were about to turn on course for Da Nang when the loadmaster, Virg Hill, came on the interphone, his voice excited and animated.

"We've taken a hit! We've taken some hits!"

Dave and I looked at each other quickly. "What's been hit? Where?"

"In the left rear section of the aircraft!" Virg responded.

"Is there any damage? Do we have any leaking fluids? What about our hydraulic system?" I asked. The hydraulic pump sat above the upper cargo door. If we had received fire in the aft section, the hydraulic pump was vulnerable. And without hydraulics we could have problems operating the flight controls, flaps, gear.

After a pause, Virg said "No, the hydraulic system looks okay."

"Do we have any visible holes?"

"No, no holes. At least I can't see anything."

I looked at Dave. "Then how do you know we've been hit?" I asked, wondering what evidence there might be if there weren't any visible signs.

A slight pause, then: "I heard the bullets hit! And it sounds different," Virg said.

"It sounds different?? What do you mean it sounds different? What sounds different?" My tone of voice reflected my strong sense of disbelief. Dave and I checked the engine instruments for any sign of irregularity. But we didn't see any abnormal fluctuations.

"It's mostly back here by the left paratroop door. It sounds different."

That was it. That was his evidence. The aircraft sounded different. I looked at Dave and shook my head.

The back end of a C-130 is the noisiest environment imaginable. There are innumerable squeaks and rumbles, hisses and roars, thuds and bumps, noises of all kinds. How in god's name could one detect any difference in that cacophony of loud sounds?

"Okay," I said. "Take another look around and let us know if you see anything leaking." Virg had certainly spent much more time in the back end of a C-130 than I had, and if he said it sounded different, then I had to believe it sounded different. Besides, why would he say it if he didn't really believe it? Well, we'd find out one way or the other after we landed.

Virg came into the cockpit a few minutes later and said that he had rechecked the cargo compartment and everything looked okay.

"But it still sounds different?"

"Yessir." He nodded emphatically, a big smile on his face.

Dave and I continued to monitor the instruments as we descended into Da Nang, but all systems worked normally. When we lowered the gear and the flaps, we kept our eye on the hydraulic pressure gauge. But it remained in the green.

At Da Nang, we taxied into the parking area and shut the engines down. Scarcely had the engines stopped turning when Virg bounded up the steps of the crew entrance door and into the cockpit, vibrating with excitement.

"I told you we took some hits! Look at this. Hold out your hand."

I put down the Form 781 I had begun to fill out and held out my right hand, in which Virg deposited a small hunk of metal.

"What is it?" I asked.

"What's left of a 30-caliber bullet," he said. Proof that Virg has been correct in his assumption. It had sounded different. The small piece of metal was twisted and lopsided, like a small mis-shaped ball bearing.

"Where did you get it?"

"I dug it out of the aircraft skin just behind the left rear paratroop door. There's a bunch more holes. They really peppered us."

I studied the spent bullet carefully. I tried to imagine its progress. If we had been hit on the left side after takeoff, that meant it had come from one of the hills that sat immediately to the north of the runway. Some VC gunner had watched us start our takeoff roll to the east, elevated his gun to the appropriate height, led us with pretty good accuracy, and fired before we had come abeam his position. Fortunately, our climb had been steep enough to cause him to miss any vital parts. He could easily have hit the engines on the left side. He hadn't missed them by much. And a little forward of the engines was the pilot's position. Where I sat.

A message from the opposing forces. We see you. You are fair game. Bang. You're dead. Almost. I could interpret the sign logically. But the meaning wouldn't register completely. It was like seeing those black body bags on the cargo ramp when we flew out of Dong Ha. There was an emotional disconnect.

"Do you want it?" Virg asked.

I looked at the piece of metal in my hand. "No, I don't think so," I said. "You can have it."

Several groundcrew members had gathered around the left paratroop door, examining the bullet holes. There were several holes to the rear and a few more in the lower cargo door, maybe twenty in all. "Well, you don't need any repairs until you get back to Tuy Hoa, anyway," one of them observed. "Then you can put the aircraft in for a Purple Heart."

On our second trip to Khe Sanh the weather had improved, but the field now had a sinister aspect that increased with every trip. The field had received mortar fire while we were gone. Black smoke was rising on the west side of the field, and F-4s circled overhead, the sun glinting off their wings. Once again we offloaded with engines running. No mortars fell while we were there. When we returned to Tuy Hoa, my outlook on life had changed. Flying in Vietnam was no longer business as usual. I drank my combat liquor ration in a gulp.

The next day we flew down to Cam Ranh where we were loaded with supplies for Da Nang. As we were flying up the coast to Da Nang under grey, overcast skies, we heard voices on Guard Channel: calls for help, comments from aircrews flying top cover. The calls piled on top of one another, and no clear pattern of communication was evident.

"Two six, two six, say position, over ... the lead aircraft took a hit ... fire light on engine ... roger, thirty clicks south of ... negative chute, negative chute ... say again, over."

Chapter 19. Tet

And when there was a pause in the radio calls, the faint sound of emergency beepers, weep, weep, weep, weep, weep. It was too sad, too depressing. I turned the emergency channel off. Nothing we could do to help anyway.

We arrived at Da Nang late in the afternoon. Just time for one run to Khe Sanh. A caution from the controller to avoid using the TACAN step-down approach from the east, as those who tried it had received ground fire from the hills on the north side. I could believe it.

We landed uneventfully and backed up to the south edge of the ramp so that our load of ammunition could be removed with minimum ramp travel on the part of the ground crew. All four engines were running, kicking up dust and dirt. I was in the left seat, Dave in the right. The aircraft was pointing north, and as we sat in our seats we could look at the hill which had been the source of ground fire that hit us the preceding day. Light from the setting sun was coming across the ramp through my left side window, but I was not inclined to think how beautiful! any longer. I just wanted the offloading to proceed as quickly as possible.

Suddenly, without warning, the number two propeller began to unwind and the engine RPM fell off. We could hear the engine winding down. The number two engine was shutting itself down! What the hell? What weirdness was this? One of our engines had decided not to run? While we're sitting on the ramp at Khe Sanh?

Without thinking, without hesitation, sensing that the bleed air valve had closed, I immediately punched in the number two starter button, located above me on the overhead panel. That should cause the bleed air valve to open. Not the normal procedure at all. I probably should have let the engine unwind and then re-start it after it had completely shut down. But I was in no mood for delays or complications. Fortunately, after an instant's hesitation, the engine RPM began to increase and the prop came back on speed. The number two engine appeared to be running normally.

"As long as it keeps running until we get back to Da Nang," I said to Dave and Ed, who had been observing my rapid movements with interest. "Then it can fall off the wing for all I care." They both nodded, I assumed in agreement.

We kept looking at the instruments every ten seconds or so, but the engine kept running as if nothing unusual had happened. After a few more minutes, we were ready to depart. We flew directly back to Tuy Hoa, our crew duty day done.

The next day Dave flew back to CCK for further training in preparation for his upgrade to instructor pilot. "You'll do well," I told him. I was sorry to see him go. I enjoyed his irreverent sense of humor, his positive approach to life.

* * *

Using the phone in the ops building, I called my brother, Lantry, who had just been assigned to an Army unit located just to the south of our base at Tuy Hoa, to see if he could make it up that evening. I would buy him dinner. Yes; he would be there.

Lantry arrived early. He had been able to find transportation and his supervisors had let him off early. We ate at the chow hall and then went to the small, air-conditioned club, where we started drinking. We had pitcher after pitcher of beer. We drank to our mother, Peg, widowed early, suffering through a northern Michigan winter, wondering if her two boys would make it safely home from Vietnam. We told jokes and stories about our experiences. He told me about his adventures with the

Army as he moved from Saigon to Nha Trang and then from Nha Trang to Tuy Hoa. I told him about the perspective of the war as seen from the cockpit of a C-130. I began to relax and laugh. I was enjoying myself immensely; I felt good. Some time during the evening I began burning scrip, the funny money we used in Vietnam instead of real American money. It was much smaller than American bills, on the scale of play money. It was flimsy and disintegrated easily.

I started first with my small change, several crumpled and soiled one dollar bills. I folded each one lengthwise and held it in the flame of the candle that sat on the table between us. I held it as long as I could, before the flame reached my fingers, then dropped it into the ashtray. It was a great game.

When I finished all my ones, I started on my five-dollar bills. "This is great!" I announced to Lantry, who seemed to agree. "I always wanted to have money to burn." I encouraged him to join in, and he did burn a few ones, but he didn't seem to fully engage in the spirit of the game. I drank some more beer and burned a ten, then a twenty. The whole exercise was hilarious. I laughed and laughed. I felt like I was lightening my spirit as I burned each bill. I hardly noticed the few other men in the room looking over at us as we kept sending money up in smoke.

Lantry reminded me that he needed to return to his unit before curfew. We walked outside and I waved him off into the night. After he left, I walked back to the hooch where the crews slept; I noticed the sky was full of bright lights. I looked up, wondering who turned the lights on. Flare after flare dropped nearly overhead. I should have realized something unusual was occurring, but I walked on, assuming we were dispelling the darkness of the night. The wavering fall of the flares cast moving shadows on the ground around me as I walked back to the hooch, where I peeled off my clothes and collapsed into bed, dead to the world.

I was wakened early in the morning by the commotion in the crew hooch. We had the early go that morning, a three o'clock get-up for a five o'clock departure. But all the crewmembers were talking excitedly as they dressed. What was the excitement? I asked.

They all looked at me. "Where were you last night?" In the club, drinking. Hadn't I seen the flares? Oh, yeah, it was awfully bright when I walked back to the hooch. Hadn't I heard the noise? Noise? They looked at me again.

Didn't I know what night it was last night? Tet. Chinese New Year. The VC had welcomed the new year in grand style. There had been an attack on the perimeter of the base: in fact, the attack was still in progress. A number of VC had made it through the wire on the west side of the base. Some VC intruders had made it almost as far as the F-100s parked on the ramp. The security forces had called out reinforcements from the maintenance and supply troops. The fighting was serious. At one point there were fears a portion of the base might be overrun, but the situation seemed to be under control now.

I was suddenly wide awake. I vaguely remembered hearing some noise as I walked back in the light of the flares. In my condition the previous night, I would have been little help in defending against an attack. If the VC had made it to the hooch and cut my throat, I wouldn't have felt a thing. I hoped my brother had made it safely back to his area.

When we arrived at the squadron ops building on the flight line, increased activity was evident on the flight line and on the far side of the runway. The fences were being repaired. There were a number of dead VC. Fortunately, none of our troops had been killed, though there were a few injuries.

The duty officer gave us the surprising news that every American airfield had been attacked during the night. Only Cam Ranh had been spared any serious fighting. The American embassy in Saigon had been attacked and fighting was still going on.

"We've got a load for you to take to Nha Trang," he said, "but we're not sure if the field is open there. Be prepared to return here." My new pilot was a captain fresh from the States with little C-130 experience. And he was going to get his first in-country ride on the first day of the 1968 Tet offensive.

I put the new pilot in the left seat, figuring that he should be able to make a landing at Nha Trang without difficulty. But when we arrived, the Nha Trang tower informed us that the runway had been mortared and the field was not open. We returned to Tuy Hoa. At Tuy Hoa we were told to fly to Da Nang. Khe Sanh was under heavy attack and needed supplies badly.

When we arrived in the Da Nang area, we saw black smoke rising west of the field. There were numerous vehicles with beacons flashing, near the runway, around the perimeter of the base. The duty officers in the command post told us that the western perimeter had been breached and clean-up actions were in progress.

Khe Sanh had been heavily mortared and the tower had been destroyed. Radio contact was with ALCE personnel in one of the bunkers. Only one cargo aircraft at a time was allowed on the ramp. We were to do a really rapid offload: drop the pallets on the ramp ourselves. It was too hazardous for the ground troops to operate the forklifts due to exposure to enemy fire. "I'd better fly it in," I told the new pilot.

We were off with our first load, ammunition in wooden crates secured to pallets, just after eight o'clock. When we arrived in the area, haze and clouds partially obscured the field. Smoke was rising from fires burning southwest of the field. We landed to the west, as usual. I angled in from the south, turning to land at the last possible moment. I was lower than normal as well, hoping to throw off the aim of any enemy gunners who might be on the hill to the north. Small pieces of shrapnel lined the edges of the runway, and two or three blackened spots indicated where mortar shells had hit recently. The tower was gone, a pile of rubble where it had stood. Only a few buildings remained standing. The area had become one large target for VC mortars.

We slowed and turned left into the ramp. A few helmeted heads watched us from a bunker that had materialized on the southwest corner of the ramp. We taxied as close to the edge of the ramp as seemed safe, then turned to the west. I stepped on the brakes. Virg Hill opened the rear cargo doors. He raised the top door to the fully open position and lowered the lower door until it was about three inches off the ground.

"Ramp is open."

"Roger," I said. "Get ready to unlock the pallet locks."

I shoved the throttles forward, and the aircraft surged ahead. It moved a few feet, and then I retarded the throttles and stepped on the brakes. The aircraft rocked forward slightly. "Okay, unlock them."

"Pallets unlocked."

"Roger." I added power once again, moving the throttles rapidly forward to the takeoff power setting. The aircraft accelerated swiftly, and as it did so, the pallets rolled off the rear of the aircraft, one by one. Virg called out their progress.

"First pallet out. Second pallet out. Third pallet out. Last pallet out. All clear and in good order. Hold your position."

We had effectively taxied out from underneath our load. There might be a little damage to the trailing edges of the pallets as they exited the aircraft, and the trailing edge of the lower cargo door might receive a few nicks from the departing pallets, but if we had executed the procedure smoothly, the damage should be minimal.

We paused for a short count to see if anyone needed a ride out. Anyone who wanted to leave would come on a run and climb aboard through the lowered cargo door. In the meantime, we sat in the cockpit, nervously looking around for signs of mortars or hostile fire. Though smoke was rising along the western perimeter, it was a steady rise of smoke, something burning steadily, not the sudden black smoke associated with a mortar hit.

"No one's coming. Let's get out of here," Virg called out.

I taxied onto the end of the runway and added full power. We were airborne quickly and I climbed out with maximum climb airspeed, aiming for the safety of the broken cloud deck overhead. Only after we leveled off on our way to Da Nang did we begin to relax.

"How does it sound back there, Virg?"

"It sounds fine, sir. No problem."

The aerial port personnel at Da Nang worked rapidly, and we were soon loaded with ammunition for another run into Khe Sanh. The weather was good: clear with high cloud. But just as we arrived in the vicinity of Khe Sanh, the controller told us to return to Da Nang; Khe Sanh had just come under attack again and was receiving more mortar hits. We could see a number of Air Force F-4s and Navy A-7s maneuvering in the area. We returned to Da Nang, half relieved not to have had to land at Khe Sanh and half worried about what would await us when we did land there again.

We were sitting under the wing on the ramp at Da Nang, waiting for the word to take off again, joking around. F-4s and other aircraft were landing and taking off to the south. Then I saw an F-4 on the west runway heading south, on the go with his tail hook down. F-4s were supposed to take off with tail hooks up, not down. I was puzzling this vision in my head when the noise of the F-4's engine abruptly changed into an eerie whine. That was definitely not normal.

We scrambled out from under the wing to get a better view of the runway. When I moved out from under the wing, I saw that the F-4 was pointing straight up, flying in what appeared to be slow motion, stalled out five hundred feet in the air. It was turned slightly, angling to the west. As I watched, the nose of the aircraft slowly fell over, as if the aircraft were executing some sort of slow motion loop. Then one pilot ejected from the aircraft, then another, Bang! Bang! The parachutes deployed immediately, but the direction of travel of the seats was down, not up. One seat, pilot still in it, slammed into the concrete ramp in front of the Marine aircraft hangars. The parachute of the other seat was almost fully opened, but not in time to slow the speed of the other seat, as it slammed into the concrete as well, and the parachute settled over the pilot, still in his seat, like a shroud.

The aircraft continued its strange slow motion combination of loop and roll and fell near the Marine hangar on the west side of the field, smoke and fire erupting instantaneously. Fire trucks and emergency vehicles raced to the west side of the field. After a while, aircraft once again began to land and depart. When we departed for Khe Sanh half an hour later, smoke was still rising from the burning wreck of the F-4 and a helicopter was hovering over the wreckage.

We had our usual load, four pallets of ammunition. It was hazy in the Khe Sanh area, but some of the clouds had thinned out, and the sun was shining. The voice from the bunkers at Khe Sanh cleared us to land but warned us that mortar attacks had been occurring all morning and that we should be prepared to do an immediate go-around if an attack occurred prior to the time we touched down. The voice was tight and so was my gut. Smoke was rising to the west and north of the runway. I positioned the aircraft on a low, turning final approach. We were apparently the first cargo aircraft to arrive after the last mortar attack, as there were no other cargo aircraft on the ramp.

Smoke was rising from the camp area immediately to the south of the runway, and large pieces of shrapnel littered the runway. Most of the large pieces had been cleared away. While I was concentrating on our final approach, an F-4 flashed past the cockpit on the left, making a run to the west. Two large objects dropped away from the aircraft, and then black smoke rose suddenly from the impact of his bombs hitting the ground, just to the southwest of the field.

I landed on the end of the runway, hoping the small pieces of shrapnel we were rolling over would not puncture our tires. As we turned left to the ramp, a Navy A-7 zoomed past on the west side, flying from south to north. An astounding amount of smoke rose around us: black smoke, brown smoke, dust. The noise of our engines prevented us from hearing any of the explosions that appeared to be occurring at various locations around the field.

Khe Sanh, January 1968. C-130 taking off while American aircraft suppress ground fire from enemy forces in immediate area. Official Air Force photograph, taken by Sergeant M.L. Ray, appeared in many American publications.

We pulled into the offloading ramp; Virg Hill called "ready to unlock the pallets," and I depressed the brake pedals slightly. "Pallets unlocked."

I added power, suddenly and rapidly, and the pallets left the aircraft one by one. "Load clear. Checking for passengers." Pause. "Hold it. A couple of guys are coming on the run." Pause. "Okay, they're on board. Closing the ramp. Let's go."

I added power and we moved to the west end of the ramp, turned north onto the taxiway and then out onto the runway. "Cargo compartment secure," Virg called. Flaps set. Full power. Smoke drifted across the runway. We charged through it. Nose up. Airborne. Climbing right turn. Aiming for Da Nang, out of the inferno of Khe Sanh.

When we returned to Da Nang we expected to carry another load to Khe Sanh. But after we landed we discovered that once again landings at Khe Sanh were on a temporary hold. Nobody had to tell me why; the combat activity at Khe Sanh had been the most intense I had ever seen. We dropped off our passengers and after a short wait returned to Tuy Hoa.

We were landing from southwest to northeast, towards the coast at Tuy Hoa. Tuy Hoa tower told us to space ourselves between the landing F-100s. One F-100 was turning final from a right downwind in front of us while another was on initial above us. We managed to land between them. After we landed we taxied to the ramp and shut down. When we stepped off the aircraft, we could see the F-100s taking off in a regular string, one after the other.

"What's going on?" we asked.

"They're pounding Tuy Hoa village," the duty officer explained. "A number of the men who attacked last night live in the village. Viet Cong sympathizers, apparently."

After we turned our paperwork in, I waited impatiently for our combat ration to be poured. I downed it in an instant. God, it tasted good. Then we walked back outside to watch the show. We plugged quarters into the Coke machine that sat outside the building and sat down in some gray padded office chairs which had been placed along the west wall of the ops shack. A few maintenance and ops men were sitting there, talking, joking. We joined them, drinking our Cokes, tipping back in the chairs, watching the procession of aircraft flying in the late afternoon sunlight.

After each F-100 was loaded with bombs, it taxied out to the main runway and took off to the northeast, over the shoreline. After takeoff, each F-100 raised its flaps and gear, made a 180-degree climbing turn to the left, back towards the south of the base, then entered a steep dive on a northwest heading toward Tuy Hoa village, some five miles west of the field. We watched as the bombs fell from the aircraft and struck the ground. When the F-100 engine noise subsided, we could vaguely hear the dull roar of the explosions; black smoke rose slowly and steadily from the west. As each aircraft completed its bomb run, it circled back to the base, lined up over the runway, pitched out to the right, and landed. Then it loaded up and took off again, following the same profile.

"Seems a little like shooting fish in a barrel, doesn't it?" said one of the maintenance men.

"Not very neighborly, if you ask me," said another.

"Wonder how long we'll keep it up?" asked the first.

"Until we run out of bombs," suggested someone else. "Or crew duty day."

"Think they'll still do our laundry in the village?" asked another.

"Prices will probably go up," observed another.

We sat there, rocked back in our chairs, drinking Cokes, watching the F-100s pound Tuy Hoa village. There were high clouds in the sky to the west, and as the sun dropped, the sky took on a soft orange-red hue, while the F-100s continued their routine. After a while we finished our Cokes, went back into the ops building and caught a ride up to the hooch.

Chapter 20

Rising Dust at Dak To

The word was that the C-130s going into Khe Sanh were taking terrific beatings: receiving hits inbound, some with flat tires, engines out of commission. I couldn't imagine what it would be like to have to change a tire or repair an engine on the ramp at Khe Sanh.

On the 4th of February, we were on the schedule again. Since our last flight, the aircrew members had been issued steel pots (metal helmets) and flak jackets as well as the usual survival vests containing .38 pistols, emergency radios, and first aid kits. We were loaded down unbelievably. As we trudged on board the aircraft we looked like a bunch of refugees. The steel pots and flak jackets couldn't really be worn in the aircraft. I assumed they were intended to be worn if we got stranded on the ramp at Khe Sanh. Or, these days, just about anywhere. I threw my stuff down in the narrow aisle just behind the copilot's seat where I intended to sit. I wanted the new pilot to sit in the left seat so he could gain a little experience.

When he climbed up into the cockpit, he was wearing his flak jacket and his steel pot. I watched as he worked his way around the lead-shielded pilot's seat and struggled valiantly to fit himself into the seat. After watching him struggle for a few moments, I told him that he probably wouldn't be able to fit in the seat wearing all that equipment, and that he should follow my example and throw his gear in the aisle. It really was a comic sight. Then I remembered my clumsiness when I first arrived in the unit, when I wasn't required to deal with flak jackets and steel helmets. I wondered what my reaction would have been if, when I first arrived in-country, I had flown into places like Cu Chi or Bao Loc, much less Khe Sanh under fire. I recalled that the sight of the Tuy Hoa runway in the sand had caused me to swallow hard.

Our first hop was down to Nha Trang to pick up a load of ammunition. Our destination out of Nha Trang was Dak To. The field at Dak To was much more challenging for a newcomer, but it was long enough that I decided to let him make the landing there. We departed Nha Trang on a direct route to Dak To, heading north-northwest. The sky was cloudy and grey, a high overcast above us as we cruised up at 4500 feet.

About ten miles southeast of Dak To, I called the tower and requested landing information. There was no answer. I called again. Still no answer. I rechecked the radio frequency. Dave Risher and I had just flown in there six days earlier, so I was confident we had dialed in the right frequency.

Suddenly a breathless voice on the radio said "Aircraft calling Dak To tower, be advised we are under mortar attack. Do not land. Hold your position and wait for further instructions."

I looked towards Dak To. I could see the hills that provided the backdrop to the

Chapter 20. Rising Dust at Dak To

field. Over the field there was a dark cloud of smoke. As I looked another burst of black smoke appeared against the base of the south hill.

We were now within five miles of the field and could more clearly see the details of the scene. The smoke was beginning to thin, and two helicopters were in the process of lifting off. Men and vehicles were moving about on the runway. The voice came on the radio: "Aircraft calling Dak To, say type and position."

I responded that we were a C-130 five miles southeast of the field.

"What cargo do you have on board?"

"Four pallets of ammunition."

A pause. I imagined they were debating the value of running the risks of having us land. The decision probably depended on how badly they needed ammunition.

Then: "We are still in a state of alert, although mortar fire has ceased for the time being. There is a large enemy force in the hills north of the field, and another attack could occur at any time. Be advised we received a mortar hit just past the midpoint of the runway. There is a large hole in the runway with numerous mortar shell fragments around it. You'll have to land within the first 2000 feet of the runway. Advise intentions."

"What about mortar fragments on the good part of the runway and the ramp?"

"We've got men out right now sweeping the affected areas. If you avoid the area of the direct hit, you should be okay."

"We'll give it a try."

"Roger. Cleared to land at pilot's discretion."

"Looks like we'd better change seats," I told the other pilot. He eased out of his seat, squeezed past me, and I moved in. We tried to avoid tripping over the pile of gear each of us had thrown in the aisles next to our seats. Once I was squared away in the seat, I disengaged the autopilot and leaned forward for a better look.

The approach to the field was clear. But there was no question of setting up any kind of downwind, for that maneuver would have placed us in the vicinity of the hills where the attack had come from. So we would have to shoot a straight-in approach. Fortunately, I remembered the layout of the field from our visit to Dak To the previous week.

As we descended on final approach I could see the large black spot ahead where the mortar round had hit, dead center on the runway. Numerous large shell fragments lay on the dirt strip around it. I aimed directly for the end of the runway. Gear and flaps down. Touch down at the edge of the runway. Idle power. Over the stops. Brakes. Into reverse. Full reverse. On the nose-wheel steering. More brakes. We slowed with runway to spare.

After we landed, men with brooms and shovels returned to their clean-up tasks around the mortar hole. They had wisely moved to the sides of the runway during our approach. Smoke was rising from two other locations in the camp.

I taxied slowly into the offloading area to the south, scanning the ground in front for large pieces of metal. There were too many pieces of debris to avoid; I hoped that none of them were large, sharp fragments. We pulled into the ramp and Virg opened the cargo doors. We left our engines running. They kicked up dust in the faces of the ground troops, but that couldn't be helped. The tower cleared us to taxi and take off any time we thought it necessary if the mortar attack should resume.

While we were stopped during the offloading, I asked Ed Scholes to inspect the tires to see if any fragments had become embedded in the tires. After a quick check, he reported that as far as he could see, our tires were clean.

While we sat on the ground, I scanned the hilly terrain in front of us for signs of smoke or fire that might indicate that a mortar had been fired. It occurred to me that had the mortar attack taken place ten minutes later, or had we arrived ten minutes earlier, that still-smoking hole in the runway could have been us. Or what was left of us.

"Cleared to taxi," said the tower, after we had been offloaded.

We taxied slowly to our right and moved out on the runway. I positioned the aircraft at the end of the runway, almost on the overrun. We were taking off toward the mortar hit and needed all the room we could get. While we were offloading, the men with brooms and shovels had cleared away most of the large fragments, so we could use the runway up to the edge of the hole the mortar shell made. I hoped we would be fully airborne before we neared the mortar strike. I also hoped that the mortar crew that had launched that shell so accurately wouldn't decide to launch another one while we were taking off.

I ran the engines up to full power, depressing the tops of the rudder pedals with my feet to hold the brakes. Then, about the time I knew Ed would be worrying about the engine temperatures, I released the brakes. We leapt forward with that comforting lurch that indicated we had good power and no load. We accelerated rapidly, moving rapidly toward that crater in the runway. Then I lifted the nose and we were up and over the mortar hole, climbing rapidly.

The tower alerted us to helicopter activity on our right side, so I held the take-off heading to the northwest, even though we would be flying directly across the hills that bordered the field. As we climbed out of the valley, two Army gunships maneuvered on our level to the right. While we watched, one of them fired two rockets directly into the ridge line; the rockets slammed into the trees just below the peak of the hill. The white smoke that trailed in the wake of the rockets looked like a rope tied to harpoons that were being fired into the humped back of a passive, immobile, tree-covered leviathan. Another Huey was firing its machine guns into the ridge line farther to the east.

We continued our climb and then began a gradual turn to the right, rolling out on a northeast heading. As we looked back to our right, we could see the Hueys hovering around the top of the hill like bees attacking an intruder of their hive. Beyond the ridge line, smoke continued to rise over the field at Dak To. Al gave us the heading for our next stop, Da Nang.

It was no surprise where we were going from Da Nang. We had our usual load—four pallets of 105 mm rockets—for Khe Sanh. But just as we leveled off on our climb out of Da Nang en route to Khe Sanh, the fire light on number two engine flickered briefly, then blinked on.

Just what I needed—a fire on number two with a full load of ammunition. But when I looked out the window at the engine, the prop was spinning as usual. The engine appeared to be operating normally, and we could see no sign of fire.

Ed Scholes picked up the Form 781 and said, "The engine has been written up before. Apparently the sensor wire works itself loose and rubs against the side of the engine."

"So the problem is with the sensor and not the engine?" I asked. Ed nodded.

Chapter 20. Rising Dust at Dak To

So what should we do? Ignore it and go to Khe Sanh? Or return to Da Nang and get it fixed? If the problem was only a loose wire, it really was a small problem. But what if it was something else, not just a loose wire? And did I really want to land at Khe Sanh with a malfunctioning fire warning system on one of my engines? Damn.

"Let's go back to Da Nang and have it looked at," I said.

That was probably a good decision. What was not as good a decision was my telling Da Nang approach control that we had "sort of an emergency."

Approach control said either it was an emergency or it wasn't. I said okay, then, it was. That meant ten minutes of questions: how many people on board? what was our cargo? how much fuel? what exactly was the nature of the emergency? and so on. We orbited for about a half hour while some other aircraft landed in front of us. But the fire light remained illuminated the whole time, though it did flicker once in a while. I decided we'd better shut the engine down or they wouldn't believe we had an emergency. When we lined up on final, I could see the fire trucks waiting for us at the side of the runway, about halfway down. The fire trucks followed us all the way into the ramp area.

"Well," Ed Scholes said, "at least maintenance will pay attention to this write-up."

A half hour later we were on our way to Khe Sanh again. "How'd they fix it so quickly?" I asked. Ed gave me a wink, and answered, "Duct tape."

The weather at Khe Sanh had deteriorated. There was a thin low cloud deck over the field, about 500 feet above the runway. Above it was more layers. We had flown into the area at 6500 feet, between broken layers. We couldn't fly the established instrument approach into Khe Sanh, because any aircraft that had tried it had received intense ground fire on short final. At a place like Tan Son Nhut, landing under a 500-foot ceiling was almost VFR conditions. But a 500-foot ceiling at Khe Sanh provided no sure clearance from the hills that surrounded the field on the south, west, and north.

How could we get into a field that was blanketed by clouds and with no usable instrument approaches? The advice from the air controller, operating from one of the bunkers, was "look for a hole in the deck and come in underneath." Were there any holes in the deck in the vicinity? "Other pilots have reported small breaks in the clouds to the west." The west: over the Laotian border. Above the hills that extended into Laos. Right on top of the Ho Chi Minh Trail.

We flew over Khe Sanh, which we could vaguely see through the cloud deck below us. Smoke was rising from one or two locations, but otherwise the field seemed quiet.

"Al, can you get a fix on Khe Sanh on your radar in case we start wandering around over here?"

"Roger. It stands out real good."

We continued on a westerly heading, scanning the deck below us for breaks in the clouds, doubtful we would find a decent hole to let down through. The controller had been talking to two other C-130s since we checked in on frequency, one on the ground about to depart, the other inbound to the field. Suddenly we saw a C-130 far below us about to drop through a small hole in the clouds. It dipped through an opening little larger than the aircraft itself and then vanished from sight, heading toward Khe Sanh. It seemed totally unlikely that such an approach was feasible.

We continued to orbit in the area for the next fifteen minutes. I kept my eye on that small hole; from our altitude it appeared tiny, too small, and if I had not seen another C-130 drop through it I would have bet it couldn't be done. Then came the go-ahead call from the controller—the other 130 had departed. We were cleared in. I called for the gear down and half flaps and began a descent at 145 knots. Once again I found myself led onward by my unofficial in-country guideline: if the aircraft in front of us had made it, we could, too. As we approached the opening in the clouds—which still seemed preposterously small—we could see that the cloud layer was relatively thin, though solid, and that we could probably maneuver safely beneath it. We dropped down through the hole heading for Khe Sanh, committed now whether we liked it or not.

The visibility beneath the cloud deck was good. We had come down above a plateau which stretched northeast towards Khe Sanh. We could see hills above us on our left. I doubted we were two hundred feet above the scrub and bush that covered the ground. We were approaching the field over relatively flat and open terrain, countryside not likely to harbor any large gathering of hostile forces. At least I hoped not; we were so low that it seemed anyone on the ground could have hit one of our props with a well-thrown rock.

"How are we doing, Al?" I asked. "What's our position?"

"Six miles to the field. Come right five degrees." His steady, even voice gave me confidence.

"How are the engine instruments, Ed?" Other than quick glances at airspeed and heading, I wasn't looking inside the cockpit.

"Everything looks good."

"Stand by to set full flaps," I said to the new pilot in the right seat. I was a little worried about him; he was moving his hands nervously next to the yoke. I was afraid he might grab the controls and give a vigorous pull up to get away from the ground. Ed ran the rest of the before-landing checklist while I scanned an approaching ridge line.

"The field should be on the other side of that rise," Al said.

I pulled the throttles back slightly to reduce the airspeed. It dropped to 135, then 130. I hesitated to reduce the speed any further, because I wasn't sure what we'd see when we cleared the rise. In my mind I envisioned what it would look like from the other side, a picture I had had ample opportunity to imprint in my mind on my previous trips into Khe Sanh.

Here came the low hill that marked the western boundary of the field. The cloud layer appeared to be resting on it. We were so low that we would have to climb slightly to clear the rise. Just as we came up to it, I could see the east end of the runway extending in the distance.

"Flaps full!" I called. We cleared the rise by feet. There was the runway, stretching away at a 20-degree angle to the right. We were in the process of over-shooting it. Throttles to idle. Right bank—too much for this low altitude, but I was not about to circle around if I could help it. Back pressure. Airspeed falling off. Adjust the trim. Hold the nose up. A little right rudder. We were lining up with the runway and descending down the east side of the rise towards the west end of the runway. Left bank. Add a little power.

Ed called out the airspeed for me: "One twenty. One fifteen. One ten."

We were over the end of the runway. A little more back pressure to slow the

Chapter 20. Rising Dust at Dak To

descent. Landing assured. Power to idle. Riding the thin edge of controllability, we touched down within 100 feet of the west end of the runway. A firm touchdown. Power to ground idle, stop, lift into ground idle, then reverse thrust range, pause. Feet on the brakes. Release the yoke. Left hand on the nose wheel steering.

"Clear to reverse," Ed called.

I pulled all four throttles back as far as they would go. The props growled into reverse pitch, and as I stepped on the brakes, the aircraft slowed noticeably. We were thrown forward slightly against the shoulder straps attached to our seats.

We slowed to taxi speed and turned off at the far taxiway. Our ground roll was somewhere between 1000 and 1500 feet. Probably my best landing at Khe Sanh, and certainly my shortest. Not bad considering I had never landed to the east there before. Downhill at that.

"Clear to open the cargo door," I called, and Virg Hill had the cargo door coming open even before we turned into the ramp. We taxied to the southeast corner of the ramp, pausing for a few seconds for the upper cargo door to raise fully and the lower cargo ramp to lower to within three inches of the ground.

I taxied forward slowly, throttles in ground idle, riding the brakes. "Ready to offload," Virg called. I depressed the brakes slightly, and the forward-rocking motion of the aircraft temporarily released pressure on the cargo compartment pallet locks, which Virg quickly unlocked.

"Pallets unlocked," he called out. I released the brakes and advanced all four throttles. The aircraft accelerated quickly, and the four pallets dropped out, one behind the other, plop! plop! plop! plop! on the ramp.

"Pallets clear," called Virg. "Hold your position while we see if anyone wants a ride out."

As we waited nervously, I surveyed the area around us, looking from the south on my left around to the north on my right. The skies were gray and dark; wisps of fog and cloud were attached to the hills to the north. There were a couple of mortar shell holes off to the left. It was a scene of complete destruction and desolation.

A few weeks ago I had parked the aircraft and walked over to the chow hall for Christmas dinner. Now the chow hall was gone—pulverized by repeated mortar attacks. Then there had been maintenance and supply shacks, a tower, rows of helicopters in neat revetments. Now all except a few revetments had been leveled by the mortar and rocket attacks, and the entire population lived in bunkers, trenches and tunnels, below the surface of the ground like burrowing animals. Enough heavy equipment had survived to keep the runway and ramp in operation and to repair a few revetments. But the place now looked literally like a dump, a collection of refuse and garbage.

It was strangely quiet. The low-lying clouds cast a muted, gray-blue light over the field. The cloudy weather prevented any close air support from Air Force and Navy fighter-bombers, and the only flying activity that I saw was some helicopters nosing around the ridges to the north. The clouds seemed to have an inhibiting effect on the North Vietnamese forces as well, for we had not seen any explosions or other signs of hostile action while we had been on the ground. But then, we had not been on the ground all that long—probably no more than three or four minutes.

"How long do you think C-130s will continue to land here in these conditions?" Ed asked.

Khe Sanh, January 1968. Offloading ramp at left end of runway. Helicopter revetments across from ramp. Southern perimeter trench visible at bottom of photograph.

"As long as they need supplies," I said. "Or until they get one of us."

"No one's coming," said Virg. "Let's get out of here." He closed the cargo section, and we moved out onto the runway. With no cargo and a reduced fuel load, we accelerated quickly and were soon airborne. We left the flaps down until we entered the protective environment of the cloud deck, where the lights of our anti-collision beacon illuminated the darkness that seemed to be enveloping Khe Sanh. There were no more aircraft into Khe Sanh that day—ours was the last mission of the afternoon. We flew back to Tuy Hoa in relative silence.

That night my brother came over from his camp. He said getting back to his unit had not been a problem. Apparently all the fighting had been on our western perimeter, and the route to the Army camp was on the south side.

The next day we flew back to CCK, arriving shortly before eight in the evening. When we went through the squadron ops building, we saw that we were scheduled to go back to Vietnam in two days. My fourth in-country shuttle in a row. We had a day and a half to rest, relax, and recuperate.

"Oh, by the way, did you guys hear about Dallman?" someone asked us. No, we hadn't heard.

Howard Dallman, my old KC-97 squadron commander at Selfridge AFB, and a member of the 345th for several months, had flown into Khe Sanh on 5 February, the day after our last flight there. He had apparently flown a straight-in approach to the west, descending out of an overcast, and had taken heavy ground fire that had started a fire in the cargo compartment. The wooden crates that contained the 105 shells they were carrying started to burn. While he was maneuvering the aircraft on the ground, his copilot, Captain Roland Behnke, the navigator, Gerald Johnson, and the flight engineer, Sergeant Charles Brault, had gone back into the cargo compartment to help the loadmaster, Sergeant Wade Green, put out the fires, spraying the smoldering crates with their on-board fire extinguishers.

While they were putting out the fires and unloading the pallets of ammunition, an enemy bullet put a hole in one of the tires. With some help, they were able to change the tire, all the while under mortar attack. Eventually they flew the aircraft out of Khe Sanh. They had experienced my worst nightmare. Later Dallman was awarded the Air Force Cross, and the other crew members received Silver Stars.

Chapter 21

Blind Descent to Kham Duc

By the time I walked into my room it was nine o'clock at night. I didn't bother to shower, but changed quickly into civilian clothes, stuffed some clean underwear and my toilet kit into a gym bag, and headed for the gate. The taxi driver delivered me to the Taichung Hotel, where I requested a room, and tossed my bag on the bed. Then I walked over to the China Nights. I hoped Karla wouldn't be busy. I should have known better.

Sue, Karla's friend, came over when I walked in. No, she said, Karla was not there. She and some other girls had gone to a big party for some Air Force VIPs who were visiting the base. Could you get a message to her? Tell her I have a room at the hotel. Tell her I leave again in two days. Sue said she would try.

I stopped at the hotel desk. Could I buy a bottle of scotch? Yes, I could. They would send out for it. I went up to the room, disappointed. But I had realized Karla would probably be busy. In the bathroom was a large porcelain bathtub. It had been a long time since I had sat in a bathtub. I turned the water on. There was a knock on the door. It was an attendant with a bottle of scotch and a bucket of ice.

I lay in the steaming water, a glass of ice-cold scotch in my hand, a few soap bubbles around the edge of the tub. I finished one drink, taking my time, sipping it slowly, letting the hot water warm me on the outside and the scotch warm me on the inside. After a while I stepped out of the tub, refilled my glass of scotch and ice, and stepped back in. I ran some more hot water into the tub. Wow. This is the life. I could feel the tension drain out of me.

I was awakened by a knock on the door. I was in the tub, water barely warm, my full glass of scotch on the edge of the tub. I had no idea how long I had been sleeping. Come in, I called. The door is open. Hello? It was Sue. I'm in here. In the tub.

Sue came in, smiling when she saw me. Then she frowned. I'm sorry, she said. Karla is at big party and cannot leave. Visitors. Important persons from C-130 wing in Japan. I'll be damned, I thought. Out-of-towners down to fight the Battle of Taichung. Well, it couldn't be helped. I'm sorry, she said. She shrugged her shoulders, as if to say, What can I do?

I gestured towards the tub. "Care to join me?" She smiled but shook her head. No. She had to get back to the China Nights. Had to help Mama-san.

I blew her a kiss. Thanks, Sue. Thanks for your help. She went out, closed the door after her. So. One more drink. Then I dried and fell into bed.

Sometime during the night I felt Karla climb into bed. She snuggled up to me and gave me a hug. I could smell the liquor on her breath, cigarette smoke.

I take bath, she said. When she came back into bed, she smelled fresh and clean.

Chapter 21. Blind Descent to Kham Duc

How long you here, she asked. I leave in two days, I said. After a while we fell asleep. In the morning we ordered a big breakfast. She told me about her life and I told her about mine.

The following morning I was awakened in my room by a strange dream. I was dreaming that one of the squadron drivers was standing over me, shaking me, saying Captain Vaughan wake up, wake up. You have to go fly. Time to get up. He continued shaking me. I opened my eyes. No one was there. The room was empty, and the gray early morning light came through the solitary window.

The bed was moving across the floor, ever so slightly. The floor was shaking. The earth was shaking. It was a mild tremor, one of Taiwan's frequent earthquakes. After a while the shaking stopped, the bed stopped vibrating. I looked at my watch. It was time to go fly.

* * *

Our guest pilot on this shuttle was Major Harry Crozier, a new arrival to the unit and one of those individuals who had been in a staff job when he received the call to report to Southeast Asia. We departed CCK at nine-thirty with stops at Naha and Nha Trang before terminating at Cam Ranh, our home for the next sixteen days. When we landed at Cam Ranh after seven in the evening, we heard more bad news from Khe Sanh; a Marine C-130 had received enemy fire and had exploded and burned. Most of the crew had been killed or injured. I envisioned the awful scene, a burning wreck on a bleak, trashed airstrip. On the following day, an Air Force C-130 received damage from a mortar shell which hit it while it was parked on the ramp. The mortar killed two passengers and wounded the loadmaster.

I tried not to think about flying into Khe Sanh. When we reported to the ops building the following morning for a late morning block time, we learned that all C-130 landings at Khe Sanh had been halted. "Too dangerous." Uh-huh. But not too dangerous for the C-123s, however, for they continued to land there until one of them crashed into the ravine wall with a load of replacement Marines. Then all cargo landings ceased and airdrops became the sole means of supply.

Our first shuttle mission took us over to Ban Me Thuot, where we picked up a load of troops for Dong Xoai, near the Cambodian border. Dong Xoai was an improved dirt strip a few miles south of Song Be. We offloaded there with our engines running. We flew next to Bien Hoa, where we should have had a quick offload. We were landing to the east, towards the shoreline, at Nha Trang. As we flew past the big white Buddha on a right downwind, we saw a C-47 on final approach to the runway low to our left. We spaced ourselves well behind him as we turned left on our base leg before turning left again on our final approach. The Nha Trang tower cleared us to land behind the C-47. We watched the C-47 descend towards the runway. And then we witnessed the most unusual landing maneuver I had ever seen.

No sooner had the C-47 touched down on its main gear than it suddenly veered sharply to the right, crossed over the flat ground to the parallel taxiway and continued down the taxiway at a high rate of speed. Fortunately, no other aircraft were on the taxiway or even in the general area. No other reason for this bizarre maneuver being evident, I thought for a moment that the pilot was in a hurry to get to the parking area and did not want to waste time completing his landing roll on the runway.

Then the C-47 suddenly veered back across the ground and returned to the runway, where it continued its landing roll as if nothing had happened.

By this time we had realized that we had better not land the aircraft while this performance was in progress. We leveled off about 500 feet above the runway. Sitting in the right seat, I had the perfect location to view the entire incident. As we flew past overhead, the C-47 came to a stop on the runway. I was amazed that the C-47 had not scraped a wingtip or worse, collapsed a gear in its abrupt, high-speed turns to the right and left.

In the meantime, after an extended silence from the tower operator, whom I assumed had been as fascinated by the events unfolding in front of him as we had, announced "The field is closed!" and directed us to hold well to the east while order was restored. After we landed we learned that the Air Force was training South Vietnamese pilots to fly the C-47 at Nha Trang.

From Nha Trang we flew back to Dong Xoai with another load of troops. The remainder of the day's hops were routine: back to Nha Trang; up the coast to Qui Nhon; down the coast to Cam Ranh; over to Tan Son Nhut; back to Cam Ranh and done for the day.

Flying into Qui Nhon on his first stint in the left seat, Harry worried me briefly when he waited for what seemed to me to be an unusually long time before beginning his descent to the runway. The runway had just about disappeared under the nose of the aircraft before he started his descent. I thought to myself, he won't make it; he'll be too high and we'll have to go around.

My philosophy as an instructor pilot was to let the other guy fly the aircraft the way he wanted to as long as the situation didn't become dangerous. If he made a mistake, he'd learn from it much more quickly than if I were to tell him his maneuver was a bad idea. So I let Harry proceed with his high and steep approach. But he surprised me and Ed Scholes, who had seen a lot of landings from his engineer's seat, when he made a good approach and landing at Qui Nhon. Well, I'll be damned, I thought. I would have bet money he wouldn't have made it.

* * *

Our cargo two days later was two pallets of diesel fuel in barrels to be delivered to Kham Duc. The load was termed "mission essential." "They need this fuel up there," the duty officer said; "It powers their radio beacon, which they use to navigate at night and in bad weather. We've been trying to get this fuel in to them for the past several days, but the weather has been bad—cloudy, foggy, rain. Hope you guys have better luck."

I studied the pictures in the Cam Ranh crew file. The field at Kham Duc sat next to the Laotian border, in the middle of a ring of mountains, like a corn flake in the middle of a cereal bowl. The runway was decently long, over 3500 feet. But the approaches were difficult. High mountains to the west and north, a large hill to the south. A successful landing would require a steep descent to the end of the runway.

When we departed Cam Ranh the sun was shining brightly over the South China Sea. We headed up the coast until we reached Chu Lai, south of Da Nang, and then turned west. Even before we turned, we could see a layer of clouds extending to the west and north. We maintained our altitude, 6500 feet, as we flew over the top of the clouds. The layer was thick and extended many miles inland. "Kham Duc is somewhere under that layer," Al said.

Chapter 21. Blind Descent to Kham Duc

We orbited for a while to see if the late morning sun would burn off the clouds. But I knew that the likelihood of that happening was small. Those clouds were solid and thick.

"Well, what now?" I asked myself. I told Harry, who was sitting in the left seat, to fly a gentle orbit pattern to the left. I got out of the copilot's seat where I had been sitting and moved back to look at Al's map. It showed Kham Duc sitting squarely among some of the highest mountains in the north central section of South Vietnam. The field sat in the westernmost portion of the bowl-shaped valley. The elevations of some of the mountains on the northeast side were a little lower than those of the mountains to the west.

"What if we set up a right-hand race track pattern and descend to about 4500 feet over the lower hills to the north?" I asked Al, tracing the route on his map with my finger. "Is the radar altimeter working okay?" That altitude would keep us just above the mountains in the area.

"We can do that," he said. "We can establish a heading in the general direction of Kham Duc by tracking out on a radial of the Da Nang TACAN and use the mileage readout for a cross-check. At least, as long as the signal holds."

"Okay, Al," I said. "You track us on the map and we'll see what happens. Harry, you'd better play copilot for a while." Harry climbed out of the pilot's seat and I climbed in. He settled into the copilot's seat.

I turned the aircraft to the right, picking up an inbound heading to the Da Nang TACAN, which showed us about 50 miles out. "Okay, that's good," Al said, after a few minutes. "Track outbound now."

I turned the aircraft to the right again, rolling out on the outbound radial of the TACAN. I pulled the throttles back and trimmed the aircraft for a slower airspeed. When the airspeed dropped, I called for gear down, then half flaps. I trimmed the aircraft again, holding the airspeed at 150 knots. We descended gradually through 5000 feet. "Time to turn inbound, towards Da Nang," Al called.

I turned to the right again. We were just above the layer of clouds with the sun on our right. The light reflecting off the cloud deck just beneath us was bright, almost blinding. Harry and I both had lowered the sun screens over our windows. Then we slipped into the cloud deck, the light lessened noticeably, and we flipped our sun screens up. We were floating through a world of white nothingness. We could see drops of moisture form on the windows and roll past. Fortunately, there was no turbulence. The air was as smooth as vanilla pudding. It was like flying instruments in the simulator. The drone of the engines was steady and constant and the flight controls responded easily.

"Coming up on 4500 feet," Harry called.

"Roger." I added power slightly as we leveled off. It was unreal, sitting there, surrounded by gray whiteness, all sensation of speed and progress through the skies gone.

"Time to turn," Al said. His calm, deliberate tone of voice once again was reassuring.

I turned the aircraft to the right, using a gentle bank. We intercepted the TACAN radial again and I tracked out on it. We sat there saying little. We might not have been moving, for all we could tell. All we could see was continuous, uninterrupted grayish whiteness. But now my attention was focused on the radar altimeter, a strange little instrument that I had never paid much attention to.

It was a round gauge which sat in the lower left of the pilot's instrument panel. Its indicator was a squiggly bright circular line on a red background that showed the differential distance between the aircraft and the terrain beneath. As I watched, it was wiggling rapidly, showing between 800 and a thousand feet in altitude difference between us and the terrain beneath. I knew we were flying over the mountain ridge on the north side of the valley. Then the radar altimeter showed a sudden drop off. We were over the narrow opening in the valley to the northeast of the field. I tried to keep my eyes on the flight instruments and the radar altimeter simultaneously.

Suddenly, out of the corner of my eye, I noticed a brief opening in the clouds to my left. I looked out quickly and saw a valley below, a stream running down from the north, thick vegetation growing on the sides of steep hills, a greenish-brown world clear of clouds. I had a sudden urge to retard the throttles and make a diving left turn into the valley below. But before I could do much more than think about turning, the opening in the clouds was gone and we were back in the white world of solid cloud.

"Al, I saw it! I saw the valley! It looks clear! I think we can make it in! Could we try it again and drop down another 500 feet?" I was practically yelling into the headset.

"Yup," Al replied laconically. "But first we've got to climb 500 feet or we're going to have an unpleasant encounter with a hill."

Oh yeah. The mountains that bordered the west side of the valley were coming up, and their altitude was higher than ours. I added power and pulled back on the yoke. But somehow I wasn't worried about those mountains. We needed only another 500 feet to reach a safe altitude, and we gained 500 feet in short order. I leveled off, maintaining 150 knots. "Time to turn," Al said.

I turned to the right, and we flew a northeast heading towards Da Nang. Once again all was whiteness and silence. "Cleared to descend 500 feet," Al said. I reduced power slightly and started a descent. I looked back at Al; he had his head stuck in his radar screen, cross-checking our position on radar and on the map on his desk. "Okay, time to turn again," Al said, "and wait for me to tell you when to drop that final 500 feet."

"Roger." I had a great feeling of warmth for Al. Without his skill and knowledge we would not be able to make this approach. I trusted his directions absolutely.

We rolled out on the outbound radial. My eyes moved from the airspeed indicator to the attitude indicator to the TACAN needle, to the radar altimeter, to the engine instruments. The radar indicator began to show an increasing distance between us and the terrain beneath. "Okay, cleared to descend another 500 feet. But when I give the word, begin to climb in a hurry. We've got a thousand feet to gain if we don't make it in this time."

"Roger." I pulled the throttles back slightly and the nose dropped. As we descended, it grew darker outside the cockpit. The additional depth of clouds, I hoped, and not some mountain looming over us. I dropped the additional 500 feet and leveled off. The TACAN signal began to waver. We were now too low to receive it clearly. For a few moments, nothing happened. I began to worry that my plan was not going to work.

"Any time now," said Al. I looked at the radar altimeter. It showed a sudden increase in distance. Suddenly, we were out of the clouds. Not just a little hole; this time, the whole aircraft was briefly out of the clouds and in the clear. We were in

Chapter 21. Blind Descent to Kham Duc

a bubble of clear air over the small valley through which the stream below was flowing.

"Here we go," I said, pulling the throttles back almost to idle, banking sharply to the left. We descended into clear air underneath an umbrella of clouds that covered the larger valley like a lid. We had little room to maneuver; the area inside the larger valley appeared to be only two or three miles across. I descended until we were a few hundred feet above the tops of the smaller hills that came up from the center of the valley. I had to keep turning the aircraft so we wouldn't run into a hill. I was worried that I had put us into a trap.

Soon we saw the Kham Duc runway off to the west, to our right, located between the wall of mountains to the west and north and one of the hills to the south of the runway. We flew over the camp, trying to spot a windsock, so we could tell which way the wind was blowing, which way to land. But the windsock on the ramp hung limp, showing little if any breeze.

As we passed over the field, I noticed a notch cut in the hill which sat close to the south end of the runway, to allow something like a normal descent and approach. "We'll land to the west, through that cut in the hill," I said.

I banked the aircraft to the left on a kind of downwind. The gear and flaps were already set, had been set for about the last twenty minutes while we motored through the clouds. "Full flaps," I called, as we turned more to the left. I aimed for that cut in the hill. Over on the ramp ahead and to the right I could see green smoke; the Army guys had set out a flare to let us know which way the wind was blowing. The smoke drifted slowly to the southeast; a light right quartering head wind. We rolled wings level and settled through the cut in the hill; the peaks of the hill passed above us to the left and right. I aimed for the end of the runway in front of us.

We passed through and down the large dark hill. Power to idle. A steep, rapid descent. The end of the runway. I heard myself humming "Rock of Ages" under my breath. Time to flare! Back on the yoke with more than normal pressure, because of the extreme change in attitude caused by the steep descent. More back pressure. Throttles all the way back. Bam! Touchdown. Firm but safe. Throttles up over the detent, into the ground idle position. Feet on the brakes. "You've got the yoke!" I yelled to Harry, who grabbed it immediately to keep it from flopping around.

I waited impatiently for Ed to yell "Clear to reverse," as usual, but instead he said, "Hold it! Number three is hung up!"

Shit! Of all the times to have a prop fail to go into reverse pitch. I pulled throttles one and four into the full reverse range and left them there while I moved throttles two and three forward, into the flight idle position, paused briefly, then brought them back over the detent position once again. I couldn't be bothered looking at the engine torquemeters; I had other things to look at, the runway, for instance.

"Okay! They're in this time. Clear to reverse two and three," Ed called out.

Thank god. Two and three into full reverse. The aircraft began to decelerate noticeably. With all four props in reverse and my feet heavy on the brakes, the aircraft slowed rapidly. We had lots of runway left and managed to turn off into the first taxiway with room to spare. We pulled up into the center of the ramp, which sat on the north side of the runway. The green smoke from the flare the Army troops had set out drifted across our position.

Virg lowered the ramp and we waited for some assistance from the ground troops. Apparently we had caught them by surprise. Finally several green-suited troops gathered around, and someone drove a forklift up. A staff sergeant wearing jungle fatigues came into the cockpit.

"Hey," he said, "are we glad to see you! We need that diesel fuel bad! But we didn't think anyone would land today. Where'd you guys come from?"

I could see Al pointing his finger at the sky, a grin on his face. But the only thing I could think of saying was, "Cam Ranh Bay." Not a particularly clever response.

After the forklift offloaded the pallets, we closed up the aircraft and taxied to the west end of the runway, ran up our engines, and departed to the east. We aimed for that strange cut in the hill. I couldn't get over it. Out here, in the middle of hill country, Vietnam, all that dirt cut out of a hill so that we could deliver diesel fuel to the Army troops so they could run a radio beacon so aircraft could land at Kham Duc. The logic of it dazzled me.

We continued our climb, through the cut in the hill, up into the air over the bowl-shaped valley, into the solid layer of clouds, out of Kham Duc, climbing to worlds unknown. Finally, we broke through the clouds, into the bright, blinding sunshine. I told Harry to raise the flaps, and I pointed the aircraft in the general direction of Da Nang.

From Da Nang we flew to Dong Ha, and I moved out of the left seat so that Harry could fly the aircraft. From Dong Ha we hopped down to Hue, then to Da Nang as it grew dark, then back to Cam Ranh Bay. We had the next two days off. Why such an easy schedule? I asked the duty officer. Too many aircraft and too little cargo to haul, he said. All the spare C-130s in the States had been sent over as a result of the *Pueblo* incident and the Tet offensive, and now there were many aircraft but not enough cargo to fill them.

Chapter 22

Low Visibility at Quang Tri

The next mission involved hauling Army troops north. We flew first to Bien Hoa, where we were to pick up a load of troops. I recalled the vow I had made on a previous visit to Bien Hoa, where I had found myself flying through an active army artillery fire zone. Then I decided I would not let myself be placed in such a hazardous situation again.

"I'll fly the approach," I told Harry when we were about 25 miles out. I descended to 5000 feet and aligned myself with the active runway, towards the southwest. When I contacted Bien Hoa tower, I said that we were on initial for the southwest runway.

"Request overhead approach," I called.

"Roger," replied the tower operator. "Continue approach. Not in sight." I knew why we were not visible to the tower operator: he was looking to the northeast, above the horizon. He should have been looking up.

I called for gear down and half flaps. We were still at 5000 feet and now we were directly over the east end of the runway. One advantage of this approach: I could see any aircraft in the vicinity. I reduced the power and started a banking descent to the left.

"What's the plan?" asked Harry.

"This is my new approach, specifically designed for landing at Bien Hoa to avoid artillery fire: a circling descent from 5000 feet." I explained why I was flying such an unusual approach.

When I called on downwind, I could tell the tower operator was concerned; he still could not see me. I was well above the normal downwind altitude for any aircraft.

"We are at 2500 feet on downwind," I replied. I imagined him scanning the skies overhead.

Finally, after a momentary pause, he called "In sight. Continue approach. Call final."

While I had been descending, a flight of two F-100s had entered on initial, pitched out, and landed. I had widened my pattern slightly to allow adequate spacing on final. I rolled out on final, a little high, but I wasn't worried. I knew Harry was good at landing out of a high approach.

"On final," I called.

"Cleared to land."

"Your aircraft," I told Harry.

At Bien Hoa we loaded our army troops and headed for Hue. The winter weather was beginning to bring clouds and rain, reducing visibility. We had to pick up a radar approach to Hue. Then down to Landing Zone English, near Bong Son, where Harry landed through another cut in a hill, but a smaller one. We left English with a load of troops for Quang Tri. Once again, we were in poor visibility after we passed Da Nang. The haze was thick; we couldn't see more than a half mile in front of us.

"Bogey at twelve o'clock," Al called out. We were about five miles out over the sea, on a northerly heading. Harry and I strained to see through the haze.

"Can't see a thing," I said.

"He's out there about two miles," Al said. "Going in the same direction we are, only a little slower."

Two miles. Normally we would have been able to see him. But all was haze.

"One mile."

We were gaining on this aircraft in a hurry. My fears of running into another aircraft began to make me nervous. But I didn't know whether we should turn left or right, climb, or dive. The wrong maneuver could make the situation worse. We had to hold course and wait.

"A half mile."

I placed my left hand on the autopilot control, my right hand on the yoke, ready to disengage the autopilot and make whatever emergency move might be necessary.

"He's starting to turn to the right. Looks like a Caribou."

How could Al be so sure? I wondered. Our airborne radar wasn't that good.

Suddenly, Harry said, "There he is, turning right, like you said." Then I saw it, a Caribou, a two-engine, high-wing awkward-looking, slow-moving aircraft, lazily turning to the right as if he were out sightseeing.

"Damn," I said, "that's too close. Thanks, Al."

We checked in with Quang Tri tower and were directed to contact their radar approach unit. We were going to have to fly a radar-controlled approach into Quang Tri. Normally a radar-controlled approach was a no-sweat, high-confidence type of maneuver. But not when it was an approach to a place like Quang Tri. If we had to fly a radar approach into Quang Tri, that meant the visibility was really poor. And the radar control unit was probably sitting in the back of a trailer that had been trucked or airlifted into the field. Quang Tri was much too small a field to merit permanent radar approach equipment. Oh well. We just had to trust to their skill to lead and our ability to follow.

We were one of the last C-130s in the string of 130s waiting to arrive, and we were directed to hold at altitude in a circular orbit on a radial off the Quang Tri TACAN well out to sea while other aircraft in front of us were brought in to land. Apparently the Army wanted its troops moved into Quang Tri pretty badly. To complicate the situation, only two or three aircraft could be on the ground at a time because of limited ramp space. For every aircraft that landed, another had to depart. Any delays on the ground would cause delays in arrival. We had lots of fuel, but it was after five o'clock in the afternoon when we began to orbit, and in another hour or so it would be dark. I did not relish the idea of shooting a radar approach to Quang Tri in the dark in bad weather, under the control of two or three guys sitting in the back of a trailer hunched over a portable radar screen.

This would be good experience for Harry, I told myself, and sat back in the copilot's seat while he flew the plane. We orbited for a half hour inside the darkening environment of the clouds, then heard the controller tell us it was our turn for an approach to Quang Tri. The controller brought us in well south of the field, then turned us in to the final approach on a northeast heading. Having flown over the area often in the past, I knew that the terrain we were flying over was flat and free of obstructions. I told Harry not to worry and to concentrate on flying a good approach. Harry, calm and unflappable, nodded.

The controller informed us we were on final approach. Harry called for the gear to be lowered and half flaps to be set. A different voice came on the radio for the final segment of the approach. The new voice told us we were about to start our final approach. Normally, if I had been flying, I would have set full flaps just prior to beginning the descent to the runway. Then I wouldn't have to worry about changes in aircraft attitude during the last crucial phase of flight, the transition to flaring for landing on the runway. "Want full flaps?" I asked.

"Not yet." Okay, Harry was flying the airplane. He had been doing a good job of it so far. Half flaps it was.

The controller guided us in with calm, unhurried, clear instructions. These guys had been bringing aircraft into Quang Tri all day, but you'd never have known it from their tone of voice. Just another day in the Air Force. Harry kept the aircraft on course, using a minimum of corrections. All we could see outside our windows was slowly darkening whiteness.

We started our descent, passing through 500 feet above ground level, then 400 feet. No sign of the ground below. All we could see was grayness outside our windows. We were about 200 feet above the runway. We should have been able to see something! I strained for some sight of the ground but could see nothing. Finally, just as the controller announced "Over the runway, take over visually and land," I saw the end of the runway through the ragged and broken clouds. "There it is!" I yelled at Harry.

"Full flaps," said Harry. I lowered full flaps.

Wups. Back up into the clouds we went, and the end of the runway passed beneath us. The added lift from the full flaps pushed us back up into the cloud deck. The runway, which we had glimpsed briefly, disappeared. Harry began to push over on the yoke.

"Don't do it!" I yelled. "Go around! Add full power."

Fortunately, Harry did not argue. He added full power and we sailed even higher into the soup; we were up to 500 feet. "Hold your altitude and heading while I bring the flaps up."

Harry nodded and focused on the instruments. As I milked the flaps up to the half-flap setting, I called the controller, who had probably been wondering where we had gone and why he hadn't heard from us.

"We're on the go," I told him. "We couldn't get it on the runway."

"Roger. Climb to a thousand feet and turn right to a heading of 090."

"Roger."

"Was there a problem with the approach?" the controller asked.

"Negative, negative. It was our fault. You guys did a great job. We would appreciate it if you would bring us around so we can try it again. I think we can get it right this time."

"Roger. We've got one in front of you, but we should be able to get you in soon."

"Well, Harry," I said, "now you can see why I like to set full flaps before starting final approach. You avoid the kind of thing that just happened." But I didn't tell him that I had never seen such a dramatic illustration of the lesson.

The light coming through the clouds was turning steadily darker, and I didn't want to think about landing in the darkness at Quang Tri under these conditions. But at least I knew what to expect.

"I think I'll fly the approach," I told Harry.

"Want to change seats?" he asked.

"No. I'll fly it from the right seat," I said.

The controller gave us a wide pattern while the aircraft in front of us landed. Then it was our turn again. We were now the last aircraft to land. I had left the gear and half flaps set as they had been since we executed our missed approach. The controller turned us onto a base leg. The sky was growing darker. It was now almost six o'clock. Then we were on final. "Stand by for final approach."

The second voice came on the frequency again, with the same steady, measured tone. "Stand by to begin descent."

"Roger," Harry said. "Full flaps," I said. Harry lowered the flaps. The rear end of the ship seemed to lift slightly, and with my thumb I added nose up trim with the trim switch. The aircraft leveled and slowed.

"Begin descent." I reduced power slightly, working the throttles with my left hand and controlling the yoke with my right. I was much more used to the opposite situation, throttles in the right hand, yoke in the left. But things seemed to be going okay. I concentrated on the airspeed, the heading, the rate of descent. Once again, there was no turbulence; the air was smooth. Thank God.

We descended steadily. The altitude at Quang Tri was just above sea level, so when we reached zero altitude, we had to be close to the ground. Five hundred feet. On course. On the glide path. Three hundred feet. Two hundred feet.

"I'm on instruments all the way," I told Harry. "You tell me when you see the ground."

One hundred feet. The light outside the windows grew darker and darker. Then, simultaneously: "Take over and land," from the final controller, and "There's the runway," from Harry and Ed Scholes.

I looked up. There it was. The end of the runway. The narrow, aluminum matting runway of Quang Tri. Little to no overrun. Power to idle. Back pressure. Thump! on the runway. Throttles over the detent. Pause. "Clear to reverse." Full reverse. On the brakes.

Harry had his hand on the nose wheel steering. "Want me to take it?" he asked.

"Nope, I've got it," I said. For some reason I wanted to take the aircraft all the way onto the ramp from the right seat. I maintained directional control with relative ease using differential braking. When we reached the end of the runway, my biggest challenge was to make a 180-degree right turn onto the off-loading ramp. I braked hard on the right brake, adding power on engines one and two. I was probably blowing mud and dirt into the poor ground crew guys behind us, but I was determined to manhandle the aircraft right to the end. When we completed our turn, I saw a ground crewman off to our left, signaling us to park in front of him. It would be a real task for me to make the small turns necessary to do so. Harry looked at me.

"Okay, you've got it," I said. I decided I'd proved whatever it was I was proving. Harry easily maneuvered the aircraft using the nosewheel steering.

We offloaded with our engines running. "Well, anyway, now you see what I mean about full flaps," I said. Harry nodded.

Before we left Quang Tri we congratulated the controllers on their excellent work bringing us in in difficult conditions. "You guys do really good work," I said as we left.

"Thanks," they said.

From Quang Tri we flew back to Da Nang in the darkness, then flew on to Cam Ranh, done for the day. I was happy to let Harry fly the plane the rest of the way home. It didn't occur to me until later that we had landed with a full load of troops on a very small runway in visibility that was less than an eighth of a mile and a ceiling that was less than a hundred feet.

If someone would have told me before I arrived in Southeast Asia that I would be making the kind of landings I was making, flying into the kinds of fields I was flying into, I would have shaken my head in disbelief.

* * *

A day or so later Al and I were walking together through the Cam Ranh O-Club. It was late in the afternoon, and we had come in to get an early start on happy hour. I was wearing my short-sleeved Air Force fatigues, and Al was wearing his Army jungle fatigues. We walked in the door and saw that the club was well filled. As we walked past one of the tables, a man rose out of his chair and stood in front of us, and conversation at his table paused as he stood. He had the longer hair indicative of one of the few civilians who worked at the base. At first I thought there was some kind of a problem.

He made a gesture of welcome, a can of unopened beer in one hand, and spoke directly to Al. "Buddy, I think you guys are okay. I don't care what anyone says." I wasn't aware that we C-130 crewmembers had any kind of stigma attached to us. But it turned out that wasn't what he meant.

"You colored people are okay. You're over here doing as good a job as any of us white guys, and I take my hat off to you. Buddy, have a beer." He handed the can of beer to Al.

Al was uncomfortable. He tried to refuse the beer the happy white guy was trying to offer him. "Hey, it's okay, I don't need it, really," he said.

"No, this one's on me. After all the time that you people have been repressed. I insist." We could see this was quite an emotional moment for the happy white guy. By now the eyes of many club inhabitants were on us, wondering how this little drama would turn out.

Al took the beer, smiled awkwardly, said thanks, and the happy white guy slapped him cordially on the shoulder. "There's more where that came from." We made our way as quickly as we could to a table in the corner.

"This kind of thing happen often?" I asked. I was smiling at Al's discomfort.

"Shee-it. Was that guy crazy, or what?" Al was wiping his face with his handkerchief.

"Well, at least you got a free beer out of it."

"You drink it. Who knows what's in it?" He pushed it towards me.

"Hey, you don't know how great this stuff is," I said, holding the can of warm beer up in the air. "The brew of social equality, the spiritus fermenti of brotherly love. You can't find this stuff just anywhere, you know. Only here. Only at Cam Ranh Bay, Vietnam, in the month of February in the year of our lord one hundred nineteen sixty eight."

"Shee-it," Al said. "Shee-it," he said again, relaxing. "This has been a weird fucking day."

"It's been a weird fucking month," I said.

* * *

At nine the next morning we were airborne. Harry Crozier sat in the left seat and headed the aircraft over to Ban Me Thuot, where we loaded the largest bulldozer I had ever seen. It was huge. I don't know how we loaded it on board. There was no room for the loadmaster to get by it on either side. We flew it to Nhon Co. The C-130 swayed heavily from side to side as we taxied out to the runway. I couldn't recall carrying a load that was so obviously heavy. Fortunately, the runway at Ban Me Thuot was long enough for us to get airborne without any trouble.

Nhon Co was a special forces camp near the Cambodian border. The runway led up to the camp, surrounded by concertina wire. The dirt strip was about 3500 feet long but was enclosed with high trees on the side and approach end. A bunker surrounded with wire sat at one end. The bulldozer was going to widen the area around the landing strip.

"This is the kind of place where you don't want to have any problems," I told Harry. "Conditions are pretty primitive. If you get stranded in a place like this at night, you have to go inside the bunker, and the VC will try to drop a mortar or two on the airplane. Then you've got a long walk home and a lot of explaining to do."

We offloaded the bulldozer at Nhon Co without tearing up the airplane, a miracle in itself. From Nhon Co we flew empty to Nha Trang, where we picked up a load of supplies for Song Be. From Song Be we went directly up to Hue. At Hue, the weather was still bad, and we had to fly a radar-controlled approach into the field again. This time, however, Harry dropped full flaps before beginning the final descent, and we landed without incident.

Many wounded Vietnamese soldiers were resting outside the airport building at Hue. They had been involved in some of the heavy fighting that had been taking place in and around the old city of Hue, about ten miles north of the field. They looked weary and drained, as if they had been engaged in heavy fighting for an extended period of time. Most were assisted by Vietnamese and American medical personnel; they carried a few litters on board, but most of the wounded sat in the troop seats. Blood showed through the temporary bandages, the white gauze and linen wrappings that had been placed around their arms and legs. We watched them load; I couldn't help looking at each one as he made his way slowly and painfully on to the airplane. It would be an uncomfortable ride, but at least it would be a short ride to Da Nang, not a four-hour ride across the South China Sea in the middle of a thunderstorm-infested sky.

"Be gentle," I told Harry, as we prepared to start engines. The flight back to Da Nang was less than thirty minutes long, but it seemed to take longer. We made a special effort not to be abrupt on the controls in our turns. At Da Nang the fire trucks escorted us into the offloading area. We watched helplessly as the wounded men stepped painfully off or were carried off the aircraft into waiting Army buses with big red crosses painted on their sides.

The next day we were flying again, this time with a bread-and-butter itinerary, landing at fields with good approaches and long runways. This was the last mission before Harry was scheduled to fly his in-country check ride. "Okay," I said to Harry, "this is your mission. You fly it and make all the decisions as if you were the aircraft commander. I'll sit in the left seat and play copilot for you. It's your show." He nodded, all smiles. I knew he would do well.

Our first stop was Qui Nhon, where Harry made his usual high straight-in approach. We approached from the north, and Harry kept us at en route altitude until the field began to disappear under the nose of the aircraft. Then he called for gear and flaps and descended straight for the end of the runway. I never saw anyone make a steeper approach than Harry did. I always said to myself that we would overshoot the field, but we never did. Nor did we this time. Harry brought us in right on the mark.

Our next stop was Nha Trang, and then down to Tan Son Nhut, where the biggest challenge lay in breaking into the traffic pattern. After only two hours of waiting for our load, we were off again, back to Qui Nhon. Harry had been flying the aircraft very well.

We were carrying one of the flight examiners from the wing, a captain a little older than I. He had come down from CCK to fly check rides with some of the pilots. He had been on the aircraft all day, evaluating my work as an instructor pilot. With Harry as a student, it was a piece of cake. Harry made me look great. Finally, though, the examiner got bored sitting on the bunk seat making notes. After we arrived at Qui Nhon, he asked, "How about if I fly it for a while? I don't get to fly much doing these evaluations all the time."

"Sure," I said. And I told Harry he could take a break and sit on the crew bunk for a while. I sat in the right seat to play copilot for the evaluator for the flight up to Da Nang. I figured it would be a relaxing way to wind down our crew day.

We took off to the south, heading out over the Qui Nhon harbor. But instead of making a climbing turn to the left after takeoff, the check pilot pulled the power back slightly and leveled off about 100 feet above the surface of the water. Oh, I thought, he wants to do a little sightseeing on our run up the coast. Well, the scenery is pretty interesting.

He headed to the northeast, taking us on a route that was parallel to the coastline. But as we left Qui Nhon behind, he eased the nose of the aircraft lower and lower. Uh-oh, I thought, I don't like the looks of this. Soon we were skimming along just above the surface of the sea. A few gulls and sea birds dove out of our way as we buzzed along. Lower and lower he took us, until we were practically on the water. Our props were kicking spray up on the windows.

I couldn't believe what I was seeing. This guy had the nerve to endanger an entire crew, a crew that was assigned to someone else. As if we didn't have enough ways to kill ourselves. I was tense. The crew was tense. If the check pilot thought he would impress the crew or generate words of praise or approval, he was greatly mistaken. I glanced back quickly. Everyone, including Harry, who was now standing behind Ed Scholes, had his eyes locked forward, scanning for any object that might be an obstruction. As casually as I could, I slid my hands forward along the tops of my legs until they were resting on my knees, just under the yoke. I figured that if the pilot made any sudden move forward with the yoke, I could grab it and pull it up so that we might climb instead of splash into the sea.

Finally, after what seemed like a very long time, but was probably no more than three or four minutes, the check pilot pulled back on the yoke gradually and we began to climb up to about fifteen hundred feet. I could feel the crew begin to relax. The loadmaster came in over the intercom to ask if anyone wanted something to drink. My throat was dry.

Little was said during the remainder of the short flight to Da Nang. I volunteered no information about flying the pattern, put down the gear and flaps when requested, and made the necessary radio calls. When the pilot tried to make some casual comment, I was abrupt and succinct in my answer. I had no desire to engage in discussion with him. I wanted him out of the seat as soon as possible.

After we landed at Da Nang I made some comment about how Major Crozier needed a little more time at the controls, since he was taking his check ride the next day (with one of the squadron check pilots), and the pilot said he'd done enough flying for the day. Major Crozier didn't really need any more time in the left seat, but that seemed like the best way to solve the problem. It must have been clear to the evaluator that not one soul on board had approved of what he had done.

When we got back to Cam Ranh and he had parted company with us, I apologized to the crew for what happened. If I had had the remotest idea he was going to do that, I said, I would never have let him in the seat. Was I scared? somebody asked. No, I said, I was more angry than scared. Why'd he do it? someone else asked. I didn't know, I said. Maybe it was time for him to go home.

The next day the crew flew while I sat around Cam Ranh. Major Crozier acted as aircraft commander while one of the squadron check pilots evaluated his performance. "Harry," I told him, "You'll do just fine. I guarantee the evaluator will complain about your approaches. He'll say you're waiting too long to descend. But don't worry about it."

When I saw Al and Harry in the club later that evening, I went over to see how the ride had gone.

"He complained about my approaches, just like you said he would," Harry said. "But otherwise, I did fine." Al nodded in agreement.

"Harry, you keep flying those high approaches," I said. "As long as you can land safely out of them, that's just what you want here in Vietnam—a high steep final. That way you'll keep exposure to enemy fire at a minimum."

Two days later we flew back to CCK. I had flown four in-country shuttles in a row. I had been flying in Vietnam, or to or from Vietnam, for sixty-seven of the previous seventy-four days. I felt tired.

David Vaughan, February 1968. After three months of airlift missions into South Vietnamese airfields, the eyes now have a more wary, if not quite weary, look.

Chapter 23

Bangkok Shuttle

It was the middle of the night when we passed through the squadron building on returning from Vietnam. I saw that we were not scheduled to fly for the next two or three days. That was a pleasant surprise. After I had taken a hot shower and slept for a few hours, I walked down to the squadron to learn what my next mission would be. Horse Pemberton was standing behind the ops counter when I came in. My name still wasn't up on the board.

"What's going on, Horse? When are you shipping my ass back to Vietnam?"

He raised an eyebrow. "I thought you might like a change of pace. How about the Bangkok shuttle?"

My eyes got big. Bangkok. My god. I had almost forgotten there was such a place.

"Wow," I said. "Who's flying with us?"

He gave me a look. "Me."

"Ah." I began to smile.

"If I go with you, I get to fly the airplane."

"Horse, if you send me to Bangkok, you're going to **have** to fly the airplane. I expect to do some serious relaxing. When do we leave?"

"In three days."

* * *

Karla was no longer associated with the China Nights. The Mama-san there had decided to open a new club on the road into Taichung from CCK, and Karla had made the move with her. The new club was not at all like the China Nights. The China Nights was a small, darkly lit club located in the middle of one of Taichung's downtown streets. The new club, the CCK Club, was large, gaudy, with lots of space and bright lights.

Karla was sitting at one of the tables at the back. She told me that the club had been open for only about a week. I looked around, impressed with the design and size of the club.

"You have busy time Vietnam?"

"Yes. Busy." She waited for me to say something, but I just shrugged. It was simpler that way.

"When do you leave?" One of her first questions to me, as always. How much time were we to have together?

"Three days. Going to Thailand this time."

She gave me a look. "How long you stay in Thailand?"

I shrugged. "Two, three weeks."

She sighed. "Of all my boy friends, you never around. I never see you. Ai-yo!"

She stood up. "We go. You buy me big dinner, spend lots of money, have a good time." She went over to talk with the Mama-san, who nodded. Karla walked back to me, her head high in the air, her gestures eloquent, graceful. She took my right arm in her left hand, squeezing it as we walked out to find a taxi.

* * *

We left for Thailand at a strangely reasonable hour, eleven in the morning, stopping along the way at Tainan, in the southern part of Taiwan, and then Clark Air Base. We landed at Clark just at sunset, the sun slipping down behind Mount Pinatubo. From Clark we flew to Udorn, crossing over Da Nang in the dark, where flares fell in a steady stream. At Udorn the air was warm and moist. The air always smelled better in Thailand. From Udorn we flew directly to Bangkok, arriving after midnight.

The van took us into town, to a new hotel, the University Hotel, where the transient aircrews were put up, one I had not been in before. Located near the soccer stadium, it had been recently built. When we drove in we saw a large animal scurrying across the driveway of the hotel in the dark.

"Cat?" I asked the driver.

"Rat."

The hotel was nice: large, air-conditioned rooms with small outside balconies, a large pool, and other pleasant diversions. But we didn't have much time to explore our surroundings, for we were scheduled to fly that evening.

We departed the airport just before midnight and flew cargo runs to Udorn, back to Takhli, and over to Ubon. From Ubon we carried cargo across the southern part of Laos into Tan Son Nhut, flying east into the rising sun, pinkish-red through the layered clouds between us and the South China Sea. As we descended into Tan Son Nhut, I could feel my stomach tightening. I relaxed only after we crossed the border on our return to Thailand. We flew directly back to Bangkok.

"Hey, Al," I said, as the van bounced into the city from the airport, "what are you planning to do tonight?"

"First, I'm going to get one of those massage girls from the hotel to come up to my room and give me a complete rubdown. Then, when I'm good and relaxed, I'm going to eat a thick, juicy steak. You know, one of those Kobe beef steaks. And then I'm going to pay a visit to this quiet little bar I know about down on the south side of town."

"Mind if I come along?"

"Not at all. Glad to have company."

Horse said he'd join us for the Kobe beef. The cab took us through the streets of Bangkok to Nick's Number One, the best Kobe beef restaurant in town. From the street the restaurant looked like a hodgepodge of buildings, as if it had been built one section at a time. The decor was strictly casual, candles on tables, Thai decorations on the walls, crowds of people eating at small tables, rooms filled with smoke and the aroma of food. We ate well, taking our time, enjoying our food. Then Al and I dropped Horse off at the hotel, and Al gave the driver the name of a bar.

The cab stopped in front of a nondescript building with a single neon sign above the awning. Inside, the lighting was dim, a small spotlight over a small dance floor, some lights over the bar in the back left. A few girls were sitting together at two of the

Chapter 23. Bangkok Shuttle

tables in the back. The bartender and another man at the bar gave us a quick look as we entered. A juke box against a side wall was playing some American music.

Al and I sat down at one of the tables. A man at the bar walked over and asked what we wanted to drink. Al and I both said scotch and water would taste good.

"Can you see if your friend is here?" I asked Al. He had been squinting, trying to discern a face he knew among those sitting at the tables against the back wall.

"No, can't say that I do. Of course, it's been a while since I was here. Ever since I got hooked up with you, I've been living in fucking Vee-yet Nam. She may not be working here anymore. Probably forgot all about me. When was the last time you were in Bangkok?" he asked me.

I had to think. "A long time ago. Ages ago. November. What's that, three, four months? And when I was here then, I wasn't especially excited about being in Bangkok. Can you imagine that?"

"Here they come," Al said, looking over my shoulder.

Two girls came up to our table, cautiously, warily, like cats approaching large mice. One was taller than the other. Both were slender. I couldn't tell at first which one was to be mine. Then the taller one stepped to Al, the shorter one to me.

They introduced themselves. Maryann and Helen. They told us their Thai names, but we agreed it would be easier to use their American names. Maryann was the shorter one, my companion. We ordered drinks. They were drinking tea, of course.

Maryann asked what I did. I told her we flew airplanes. What kind of aircraft did we fly? Where were we stationed? When I told her, she was a little impressed, possibly because we were from someplace besides Thailand. Most of the men she saw in the bar came from the air bases in Thailand, the F-4 boys from Udorn and Ubon, the F-105 boys from Korat and Takhli. How long had I been in Southeast Asia? How long had I been in Thailand? How long were we staying? Did Al fly with me? Was I married? Did I have any children?

Maryann had come to Bangkok from a little village halfway to Udorn. She was the youngest daughter in a large family. Her father and brothers worked as farmers, growing rice. She had left home because she was a girl and her father needed boys to work the farm. She had heard that with all the Americans in Bangkok there was lots of work. She could live in an apartment, a building where the wind and rain did not blow in. She could buy nice clothes. She could eat good food. She could live a good life, better than the life in her village.

She had had several boyfriends. She had known two American pilots from Takhli, one of whom had been killed over North Vietnam. Another American, a civilian, who had worked for an American construction company. Two Thai government officials. Her current boyfriend was an American pilot from Ubon, with a large red moustache, who could not come into the city often, who wanted to marry her and take her to America. She had a baby, a girl, three years old, fathered by a Thai who had been her boyfriend when she first came to Bangkok. She showed me a picture of the little girl, sitting on the floor, holding a book.

Maryann seemed unusually young. She said she was twenty-two, but I thought eighteen was more like it. She was shy, did not seem like the type of person who would be a bar girl in Bangkok. But then, not too long ago I didn't look for bar girls in Bangkok. She seemed to relax when she learned that Al and I were going to be around for several days. Yes, she would go back to the hotel with me, but not until the bar was ready to close, another two hours or so. Al was hitting it off with the girl he was with as well. Finally, the Mama-san decided the girls could go, and we left together in the same cab.

Maryann was shy in the elevator going up to the room, did not want to look up, kept looking at the floor. When we entered my room, she seemed uncomfortable. She undressed hurriedly and slid in under the sheet. She was so quiet I thought she was asleep. When I crawled into bed she seemed to pull away. I asked her if she was uncomfortable. I said she could go home if she was unhappy about being with me. She shook her head.

* * *

I and the crew left the hotel at 4:30 in the morning, an early start after a short night. When I climbed into the right seat, my breath smelled bad and my head felt fuzzy. Our mission was a passenger run, a series of short hops between Bangkok and the other bases in Thailand, hauling passengers and an occasional pallet or two of mail. Our first leg took us to Takhli, a thirty-minute hop. We departed as the sun broke through the high clouds. Once I raised the gear and flaps for Horse, I tilted my seat back to rest my eyes.

The next hop was from Takhli to Udorn, an hour-long leg. On this leg, I was able to sleep for twenty minutes. "Call me if you need me, Horse," I said, as I tilted my seat back once again.

From Udorn we flew over to Nakhon Phanom, a 45-minute leg which afforded me another fifteen minutes of sleep. I woke up in time to keep an eye on Horse as he shot the landing at Naked Fanny. The last time I had been over here, the runway was a little tricky. But when we rolled out on final, with the Mekong snaking under our left wing, a new, long, wide concrete runway appeared before us. Piece of cake.

Another 40-minute hop down to Ubon, and another 15 minutes of sleep. At Ubon there were rows of EC-121s, four-engine prop-driven Lockheed Constellations with large radar antennas mounted in them. They were clumsy-looking machines, with a large fin on top of the center part of the fuselage, and an even larger bulge beneath the belly. Their job was to fly in orbit over Laos and scan the skies for enemy aircraft. I had heard Bill Knipp, my old Dyess flying buddy, had ended up flying EC-121s, was perhaps at Ubon even then.

From Ubon we flew back to Bangkok, a little over an hour of flying time, a little over twenty minutes of rest. Flying in Thailand was pleasant: nobody shooting at you, few airplanes to watch out for, ground radar sites guiding you from base to base, nobody lobbing mortars onto the airfield every time you landed. The perfect cargo-hauling duty in the perfect war zone.

Our next series of hops was shorter: Bangkok to Udorn to Takhli and back to Bangkok. I was more alert by this time. We landed at Bangkok just as the sun was setting, a long day in the cockpit. Horse was beat. But I felt good. Al did, too. Navigating in Thailand was simple. I think he had slept as much as I had.

We changed out of our sweaty flying clothes, showered, and ate at the hotel. Horse turned down our offer of an evening out and said he needed to rest, as we had another mission scheduled the following day. But Al and I hopped in a cab to our bar. When we arrived, Maryann and Helen were occupied with other customers. After a while they came over to our table.

Chapter 23. Bangkok Shuttle

Maryann seemed to be more relaxed. Had she eaten breakfast before she left? No, she hadn't. Why not? Wasn't hungry. I looked at her. She was thin, couldn't have weighed more than ninety pounds. We danced for a while, and Al and I told lies to each other while the girls attended to other customers.

We went back to the hotel. Maryann was still reserved. I asked her why she had chosen me when we walked in? She said I reminded her of her first American boyfriend; he had not much hair either. But she had loved him and had cried when he had not come back to her. She was up and showered before I woke. She woke me up to say good-bye.

I went down to the restaurant and ordered the breakfast deluxe: eggs, steak, fresh orange juice, fresh rolls with fresh butter, fresh pineapple, fresh papaya, coffee. Then I went for a dip in the pool. A great life.

* * *

On our mission that day I was able to give Horse substantially more assistance than I had previously. We took off early in the afternoon. Only four hops, to Takhli, Udorn, then a long hop to Tan Son Nhut. We arrived at nine in the evening, avoiding the flares and ground fire to the west. The old tight-stomach feeling came as we descended into Tan Son Nhut. Back to Bangkok by eleven, to the hotel by midnight.

The following day I walked along Rama road, visiting the jewelry shops and the bronzeware shops. After working up a sweat walking in the Thai sun, I sat at a table outside a bar and ordered some cold Thai beer. I watched the traffic move past, the Thai men and women walking past on the street, inhaling the many aromas of Bangkok, enjoying it all, feeling my body relax. I hadn't realized how tense I had become, flying in Vietnam, and I was amazed to think of how different it was flying in Thailand instead of Vietnam. Two countries not that far apart, similar in climate, culture, and geography. I would never be able to relax flying in Vietnam.

Horse, Al, and I had agreed that we would eat at the Baan Thai restaurant, one of Bangkok's special places to eat. The Baan Thai featured authentic Thai food, served in several courses over an extended period of time, in a building that looked something like a Thai temple. While you ate your meals at a leisurely rate, musicians and dancers performed authentic Thai songs and dances. Al and Horse and I were seated at a low table, surrounded by silk hangings suspended from arches above. The Thai waitresses brought food and refilled our drinks. Two short weeks earlier Al and I had been eating cold C-rations on the steps of a C-130 on a dirt strip in the middle of a jungle. We looked at one another and smiled.

When we were finished eating, I asked Maryann to take me to the most popular dance hall in Bangkok. She led me on to the dance floor, with flashing lights and young bodies gyrating in syncopation. I ordered beer after beer while I danced. Maryann tried her best to look interested, to appear to be enjoying herself. But she was not an essential part of my entertainment, as I danced vigorously, only occasionally paying attention to her. She couldn't understand why dancing was important to me, why I was moving so frantically on the dance floor until my clothes were wringing wet. I knew she wasn't enjoying herself, but I disregarded her. I was trying to dance a dance of release, as I had that evening six months before in the Philippines. I wanted a vision of release to come to me then as it had before.

After we had danced for an hour or so, I was able to detach myself from my immediate surroundings and began to lose myself in the rhythm of the music. I wanted desperately to summon up a vision of a runway in my head. As I danced I recalled runways into which I had flown, and a vision began to take shape. But the vision was not of one runway, like the runway at Phan Thiet when I had danced at Angeles City. This vision consisted of many runways, one image blending into another. I couldn't distinguish among them. Bao Loc, Song Be, LZ English, Hue, Quang Tri. Dak To. Kham Duc. Khe Sanh. They merged and blurred and became nameless blank strips in the jungles and dark hills. I wanted to dance on each one—any one—in turn, but they wouldn't sort themselves out for me. They had all become a blur of runways, spinning before me, surrounded by trees and hills, dark clouds, rain and dust, mud and wind together. I couldn't float in slow motion as I had when I danced over the runway at Phan Thiet. There was too much pressure on me. A force was pushing me from behind, pushing me forward into a space that was too small, from which there was no escape. I had to land. There was no other option. But there was no runway before me. I felt the weight of the aircraft, the weight of the load it was carrying, the load I was carrying. I was always moving forward, forward, forward, towards the short runways with the trees and the hills surrounding them. And I couldn't resist that force. It wouldn't let me dance. I couldn't dance with that weight. I couldn't stand straight. There was no release. I couldn't dance.

Maryann pulled me off the dance floor. I fell into a chair, exhausted. When I focused on her face, her eyes were worried. She wiped my head with her hand. "You all right?"

I sat for several minutes, looking at her, hardly seeing her, looking at the dancers, looking at the lights suspended from the ceiling, listening to the sound of the music. I finished what was left of my warm beer. "We can go now," I said.

* * *

We were flying a pax run. Our first stop was Korat, a 45-minute hop. I had just tilted my chair back and was about to take a doze, when Virg Hill, the loadmaster, asked who wanted coffee and sweet rolls.

"Sweet rolls?" I said. "Where'd you find those, Virg?"

"I found this neat bakery not far from the hotel. They make great pastries!" I decided I could eat a little before I took a nap.

Virg handed me a sweet roll on a napkin and a cup of coffee. "Virg, you're beautiful!" It was so nice, sitting there with the aircraft on autopilot, Thailand moving past beneath, a hot roll and coffee in hand. On every one of our remaining morning takeoffs, Virg brought sweet rolls and coffee.

* * *

Maryann smiled when I came through the door of the bar. "I was worried about you," she said. "You want to go dancing again?"

"No," I said, "no more dancing."

"So what we do tonight?"

"We'll just sit and talk. I've got an early flight tomorrow morning. Tell me about this man from Ubon."

"He very nice man. Visit me all the time, give me money, want to marry me."

"So? What's the matter with that? Isn't he good-looking?"

Chapter 23. Bangkok Shuttle

"Oh, yes. Very good looking. Have bright red hair all over. But I no love him."

I looked at her. "Maybe you could fall in love later."

"I no love him."

And then I had to tell her about me. How did I like flying? I liked it. It was a lot of work, staying current, studying regulations and procedures, but it gave me experiences I wouldn't have had otherwise. Especially in the C-130. It showed me the world, America, yes, but also Europe, Africa, the Far East. The C-130 made it all possible, I said. It was the airplane that showed me the world.

And how did I like flying in Vietnam? I had done some of the best flying I had ever done, I said. I had not had any accidents, I had not broken an airplane, I had not hurt anyone with my airplane. Except for an Army guy at Qui Nhon. I had flown into and out of some difficult fields and situations. I had done the kind of flying I would not have believed I was capable of. I said I wished someone would have had a camera during some of my landings in Vietnam, because ten, twenty years from now I would never believe I had done these things myself. But now I was tired. I had been flying in Vietnam and Southeast Asia for thirteen months and I needed a rest. My time would be up soon and I would go back to America. No, I didn't know what America would be like. I was out of touch with events.

Would I be happy to see my wife? Probably, I said. But I wasn't sure how it would be between us. I had changed. And I was sure she had changed. Well, if you love one another, she said. Do you love your boyfriend from Ubon? I asked. She hesitated. He is thoughtful, steady. Maybe we don't need love, she said. It's a hard time for love, I said. A strange world, she said. Not like life in my village when I was young, she said. Nor in mine either, I said.

She woke me as usual when it was time to get up. Four o'clock; we had a seven o'clock block time. I ordered breakfast sent up for her, mostly fruit and bread, then I left, telling her to get some sleep.

* * *

We had another passenger run, going around the northern loop, Takhli, Udorn, Nakhon Phanom, Ubon, and back to Bangkok. Then a passenger run to Utapao, a new airfield southeast of Bangkok, built to accommodate our B-52 bombers, so they would not have to fly all the way from Guam to Vietnam and back to Guam every time they had a bombing mission. The new runway was long and wide, acres and acres of concrete designed to support B-52 operations. The field was so big it seemed like we taxied forever just to reach the passenger terminal. We offloaded some pallets and passengers, onloaded some pallets and passengers, and started to taxi out of the ramp area.

Then Virg came on the interphone. "Hey Captain Vaughan, one of the passengers has had too much to drink and he doesn't want to stay strapped in. He refuses to cooperate and is upsetting the other passengers."

I told Horse to stop the airplane where we were and got on the radio. "We've got a passenger who's had too much to drink," I said. "I want him off the aircraft." Within three minutes a blue Air Force vehicle had pulled up beside us and two security policemen got out.

"Open the crew entrance door," I told Virg. "The security police are outside. Make sure no one walks into a prop."

The security police soon removed our uncooperative passenger and we continued on our way to the active runway.

Then a short run up to Udorn again, and back down to Takhli. When we called in for landing instructions at Takhli, we were told to hold clear for an arriving flight of F-105s. There were four of them, and they flew down the middle of the runway at high speed, with a high-performance pitchout to the left. When we looked at the end of the runway, we could see the fire trucks, with their emergency beacons flashing. An emergency? None of the aircraft seemed to be having any problems. Something special was going on.

We were cleared to land after the last 105 touched down, and Horse brought us in smoothly. The 105s were preceded by the entourage of fire trucks, lights flashing. Somebody on one of the trucks popped some red smoke, and it drifted back through the taxiing aircraft. The 105s moved slowly, through the smoke, fire-breathing monsters moving through the fog of war. We followed at a respectful distance. The 105s pulled in front of the base operations building in a line and shut down their engines. Three of them were two-seaters, the missile hunters, whose job was to attack the North Vietnamese missile sites in advance of the attacking F-105s carrying bombs.

We were parked opposite them. There was a large crowd of men, some of them in colorful flying suits, gathered in front of base ops. We shut down and I walked across to watch. As the canopy lifted on the lead aircraft, the men gathered around let out a loud cheer. There was a wooden podium with the squadron insignia on it, and a big washtub full of ice and champagne. The lead pilot had flown his hundredth mission and was going home.

He stepped down out of his aircraft and slapped a goofy-looking yellow hat on his head as somebody poured champagne over him. He tilted his head back, trying to catch some of the brew in his mouth, but succeeded only in drenching his face. Somebody popped the top of another bottle and handed it to him. He took a long steady pull, then put his thumb over the opening, shook the bottle violently, and sprayed the contents over all those standing nearby. The party was still going on by the time we loaded up. We had to be careful not to taxi over any of the party-goers.

We were back at the hotel by ten in the evening. Time for a shower and one final trip to the bar. Neither Maryann nor I had much to say. In the morning I walked down to the lobby with Maryann and called a cab over. We walked awkwardly together, not saying anything. I opened the door of the taxi for her. She sat down in the back, looking straight ahead. She said something to the driver. I closed the door and they drove off. She did not look back.

We flew back to CCK by way of Clark, landing at eleven in the morning. When we walked into the squadron operations building to check our mail and the schedule, I was surprised to see the following notation by my name on the scheduling board: "local area only."

"Local area only? What does that mean, Horse?"

"Good news, guy. You're off the shuttle. You're going home."

Chapter 24

Old Head

Going home. The idea didn't want to sink in. Back to the States. America seemed far far away. During the last fourteen months I had been living in a world where normal time and tasks had altered significantly. I was used to seeing myself scheduled to fly. Or not to fly. Or to be scheduled for training. Or semiannual check flights. But not scheduled to leave the squadron.

Karla was working at the new club west of town, on the road into Taichung. "Go back to the States?" she asked. "When you leave?"

"Three weeks."

She sat back for a while. Then she moved forward, put her hand on mine. "Come on, we celebrate. I tell Mam-san I have to go." We caught a taxi to the MAAG Club for dinner. It seemed like a long time since we had eaten there. It felt strange to be able to spend so much time with Karla. But there wasn't much time, really.

* * *

Two days later we flew a local morning flight, five hours of pattern work, landings, drops, with new pilots, new navigators, new flight engineers, new loadmasters. Off the runway heading north, left turn towards the coast, another left turn down the coast for a low-level run into the practice drop zone. Drop a pallet of sandbags, back around for landings, coaching the new pilots. Remembering how I felt twelve months earlier, sweating around the pattern, watching altitude, airspeed, throttles, flight controls. I felt like I could do it in my sleep now. I briefly had the urge to show them how we had done it at Dak To, Bao Loc, Khe Sanh. But I couldn't get in the mood. This wasn't Dak To, this was a practice strip in the rice fields south of CCK. It wasn't the same thing. I found myself preoccupied, little caring whether the new pilots did it right or not.

A day later we flew our last mission as a crew. It was an easy flight, a Sunday drive across the South China Sea to Clark. We left at eleven in the morning and arrived at two in the afternoon, a three-hour flight, Far East Airlines. We carried the wing commander, Colonel Jones, down to the Philippines for a conference. He had awarded me my first Air Medal eight months before. He sat in the left seat, I in the right, an instructor pilot keeping an eye on the old man flying a milk run.

At Clark I spent the afternoon at the club. I had a good meal and spent a leisurely evening at the bar, enjoying the tropical breeze which blew in through the screened-in windows, saying good-bye to the pleasures of the Philippines. We flew back late the next day, carrying Colonel Lutton, the deputy wing commander. We left at seven in the evening, flying up the Luzon peninsula in the dark, the lights of the villages shining below us. Not a cloud in the sky. We flew across the Luzon Strait, the islands clearly visible in the clear moonlit night. The reverse course of my first trip outbound from CCK with Duke Williams. We shut down the engines at nine-thirty, a civilized, leisurely flying schedule.

I wasn't scheduled to fly for the next two days. "Why not?" I asked the duty officer.

"It's the weekend. We don't fly local flights on the weekend."

I went into Taichung early next afternoon. I had never before come into town at three o'clock in the afternoon. Karla was having her hair done. "Come with me while I have my hair done," she said. "Keep me company. I never see you much before now. Soon you go. Come with me."

I walked with her down the street where she lived, around a corner, down another street until we came to the hairdresser's shop. I went in with her and sat down in a chair. The Chinese girls in the shop chattered and laughed, looking at Karla and then at me. I looked out the shop window at a small park across the street, where small boys and dogs were chasing each other in the dust.

I felt strangely domestic, as if I had suddenly stepped out of a time warp, out of a world where events were determined by your takeoff time and the twelve-hour crew day. In that life night and day were equally important, equally unimportant. You flew when your turn came, and the demands were constant and predictable, even if the situations weren't. Get in and get out of the small runways without breaking something or getting shot. Land the airplane safely. Now I was sitting in a hairdresser's shop in Taichung on a sunny afternoon among a people whom I had lived with for a year but didn't really know.

Finally Karla was done. Her hair was swirled on top of her head, with strands of hair hanging down, framing her face. She looked lovely. We walked back to her room, stopping by a laundry where she collected some dresses which I carried for her. Karla was excited; she talked continually, explaining who the people were, what they were like, what her daily schedule was like, filling me in on details of her life of which I had little knowledge.

She dressed for the evening, more completely and more thoroughly than I had ever seen, and I realized she was dressing for a special occasion. We were going to eat at the best restaurant in Taichung. She had made reservations several days before. We were going to participate in a significant social event, something we had never done before. We were going to go out to eat as a result of planning, not spontaneously, at the last minute, on the spur of the moment, as we had always done. She was determined to demonstrate to herself, to her friends, and to me, that I was officially a part of her life, even if only for a few more days.

We ate at the Shanghai Restaurant. Karla looked elegant in a Chinese silk dress, dark red with a dragon pattern in the material, her hair high on her head, her face expertly accentuated with eyeliner and lipstick. I had never seen her look more beautiful. As we walked in, she moved royally, slowly and deliberately. I thought she would be nervous, appearing with me, one of the ubiquitous American airmen from the base. If she was, she never showed it. She seemed defiantly proud.

We ate at a booth set apart from the main dining area, and I realized how carefully she had seen to every detail of the evening. The décor was Chinese at its atmospheric best, red and black lacquer paint, templelike designs on the sides of the booths. She ordered for us. She knew what she wanted and we ate well. We began with soup. Sake, tea, rice, chicken and vegetables. She coached me when I attempted to use chopsticks. We sat and talked. I told her about Thailand, but she did most of the talking. She was determined to tell me about her life, and about how things were going at Mama-san's new club. She told me about her decision to join Mama-san and try their luck together, her determination to improve her situation and to make more money for herself and her son. She showed me the latest pictures she had taken of him. I could see he had grown and was changing from a baby to a boy.

I thought, my God, I've been here a long time. At first it was like a long trip to a strange country. The novelty of landing at new airfields, seeing new areas of the world, the challenges of landing on smaller and smaller runways. Since I had become an instructor pilot, since I had flown on the shuttle almost continuously for three straight months, this place had become home, and this woman had become a kind of wife. She was the first person I sought when I returned from Vietnam, the person who gave me solace from the pressures of those fearful runways. This woman and this environment were the realest things I had known for over a year in a world where there was no faking, no superficial routines to be followed, no artificial politeness, nothing done because it should be done but everything done because it had to be done. Living a hard, demanding life with no apologies because there was little time for apologies and none were required. You did what you did the best you could.

And now, just like that! I was moving into a different world, a world where we didn't fly on weekends. A world where social amenities were important. A world where regular daily routines were important. A world of rules, of decorum, and not a world of can you do it and not bust your ass. I wasn't sorry to be leaving Vietnam, away from the hard in-country runways. But I had a sense, even then, after only a month, that the kinds of awful, appalling experiences I had at Bao Loc, at Dak To, at Kham Duc, at Khe Sanh, were unique. They were visions of the strange world of an Air Force Oz, the capricious taskmaster, who gave you nearly impossible tasks to accomplish, who told an untruth when he said if you do them I will take you home again. Where the challenge of landing on an in-country runway surrounded by those difficult, menacing hills, was a raw, primitive experience unlike any other, where life was too intense to be lived safely for an extended length of time, where you were caught up in the exhilarating motions of duty, where you hoped the momentum of your actions would carry you through before you realized how frightening the experience was. Where what was written down on paper as a mission to be flown became a flight into another dimension, one which you flew maybe by the book, but mostly by intuition, by guess and by God, otherwise you might not return to the polite side of life.

After we finished our meal, we took a cab to the National Hotel, the nicest hotel in Taichung, where we danced and drank and talked. Karla drank scotch with me, not the tea she drank at the China Nights or CCK Club. She began to get just a little tipsy, as I was, and I realized she was enjoying an outing that was a legitimate social occasion, not fallout activity from bar girl duties. Finally we went back to her room and made love. Our lovemaking was easier, more relaxed than it had been before. I assumed the change was partly because this lovemaking was something she chose to do, not something that was expected of her. We fell asleep in each other's arms.

In the morning I bathed in Karla's tub while she brewed tea. "Come sit on the bed," she said. "I show you something." She had her photo album open in front of her. "I show you my family," she said. I sat down on the bed beside her while she pulled out some pictures, one by one, and laid them on the cover of the bed. I was surprised when I saw that they were pictures of the men she had known from CCK, not her family in Taipei. She handled each one gently as she held it up to tell me about each man smiling into the camera.

First picture. This my first boyfriend when I come to Taichung. He very nice boy who fly C-130. He like you, not here too much, but very nice to me when he come to see me. Next picture. This man fly airplane too, work on airplanes at CCK, want me to live with him all the time. Another picture. This man pilot too. He my boyfriend before you. This you. She held up a small picture of me, one of the spare pictures I had taken for my base identification photo. It was a very small photo, not a good picture. Why you not give me good picture? I shrugged. One final picture. This man pilot in your squadron. He my new boyfriend.

I recognized the face. I had seen him, a new guy, on the flight line. She arranged the pictures in a semicircle before her, a rainbow of faces. They all looked like me, part confident, stalwart aviator, part lost soul, wondering what happens next. It seemed a sad, touching thing she was doing.

"The pilot is dead," I said to myself, half aloud.

"What? My new boyfriend dead?" Karla looked at me with horror.

"Oh, no, no. He's not dead. He's fine. It's just something that came into my mind, a saying, sort of: The pilot is dead; long live the pilot."

Karla looked at me, puzzled, not following what I was saying.

She had to go to Taipei to see her son the following day. Would I see her when she returned? I said I would be flying for two or three days but would see her when I was through flying. I said I intended to take a few trips around Taiwan in the following days, to see parts of the island I had not been able to see because of my busy flying schedule.

She said I must go see Sun-Moon Lake. Yes, I said, I would like to see Sun-Moon Lake. It is very beautiful, she said. Chinese bride and groom go there. Did she want to go to Sun-Moon Lake with me, I asked. She was silent for a while before she answered, "Yes, I will go with you to Sun-Moon Lake."

I walked down the stairs to the street below. The smells of the street, food cooking, smoke from fires, all smelled familiar to me now. I walked to the train station where I knew I would find a cab.

* * *

I had two more flights that week, both local. The first flight was an instructor upgrade for two captains in the squadron, Davidson and Vickery. I sat in the left seat as first one and then the other flew the aircraft. They taxied the aircraft from the right seat, made the takeoff from the right seat, landed from the right seat. They were a little rough and uncoordinated, not used to operating the aircraft from the right seat. We stayed in the local pattern while they flew the aircraft and answered my questions about emergency procedures, adjusting the throttles and trim tabs accordingly when I retarded a throttle, simulating engine failure on one of the engines. Finally, after each one had worked up a decent sweat responding to emergency procedures while flying the aircraft safely in the traffic pattern, we landed. There I was, the old head, smiling at their confusion and awkwardness, when ten months earlier I had been exactly in their position.

The next day I sat in the right seat for another local flight while two new pilots took turns flying the low-level navigation route to the practice drop zone, where we dropped a couple of jump-rated men. Then a few times around the pattern in the auxiliary field, practicing regular and assault landings. Their flying techniques were typical of new guys: rough on the controls, hesitant at times, unpolished. "What's it like, flying in-country?" they wanted to know. "You'll find out soon enough," I said.

When I walked through the squadron I saw that my name had been removed from the scheduling board. "You're officially through flying missions for the 345th," the duty officer said. "Besides, we need the room on the board. Lots of new guys showing up." I recognized the names of some of the men I had known back at Dyess. "We'll get you on a flight in-country the first of April, so you can get your hazardous duty pay for the month, but you'll be riding all the way down and back."

I saw Al Williams in the navigator's section of the building. "Hey, Al, you going home too?"

"Nope, they're not letting me go home yet. I'm going up to a wing job, working in the planning office. No more busting my ass on in-country shuttles."

Ed Scholes and Virg Hill were being reassigned too, to supervisory positions on paper crews, where the primary function was to train and evaluate new members of the squadron, not fly as part of a regular in-country shuttle crew. My crew was being broken up, assigned to less strenuous duties. Our hard work was done. My roommate, Les Fredericks (with whom I had never flown in fifteen months) wasn't going home yet, but he assured me he would not be far behind.

* * *

Two days later I met Karla at her apartment. We drove up to the Sun-Moon Lake in a taxi in the afternoon, a forty-five-minute drive past rice fields, then up through hills and rocky washes until we came into rolling upland areas covered with lush growth. We drove past ox-drawn carts loaded with bananas and pineapples. The road kept rising gradually until suddenly we rounded a curve and there was the lake, stretching before us for several miles. Green hills rose on all sides, encircling it like a green setting around a blue jewel.

We stepped out at the hotel, an elegant structure that overlooked the lake. There was a golf course, a pool, and several patios for sitting and enjoying the view. There were few people around when we checked in, which surprised me, because the weather was perfect, not hot, not cold. Our room overlooked the lake. It was a large room with a luxurious bathroom, a large bed, tall drapes that hung from the ceiling to the floor over the window, pulled back to reveal the view.

We walked around the hotel grounds. A path led from the hotel down to a dock where several small boats were tied up. "We can take boat in morning," Karla said. "Boat will take us around lake. Many lovely temples around lake. Very pretty. Very nice to ride on lake. Very peaceful. Very smooth."

We walked back to the hotel and sat on an outdoor patio attached to the bar. "What you do when you go back?" she asked.

"I have to go to school for a while, and then I will be teaching at an Air Force school."

"You have children when you go back to States?"

"Probably. How about you?"

"Would like more children. But not possible."

"Why not?"

"Not find anyone who will marry me. I am dishonored woman among Chinese people. Not suitable for marriage."

The sun moved low in the sky and the air over the lake began to thicken. The far hills were fading from view. Down below, out on the lake, one of the little boats moved slowly across the lake, its wake expanding gradually behind it, twin lines of disturbance spreading farther and farther apart.

"Boats must go slow on lake," she said. "The lake holy place. Lake represent marriage of sun and moon. This valley so beautiful that sun and moon see it and want it for their own. At first they start to fight. Then they say, too pretty to fight here. So we share. Moon have one lake, sun have another. Later, two lakes become one. Waters from one lake mix with waters from other lake. They share waters, they married. So Chinese people say holy place. Build many temples. Chinese people come here on special occasions, pray to Buddha."

It was quiet. Sounds carried across the lake, and we could faintly hear the motors of the boats moving towards shore. The sun set behind the hills to the west, and it grew chilly. We went inside for one more drink in the bar, which was large, dark, quiet, and mostly deserted. Then we went to the room to change for dinner. The restaurant, like the bar, was large and ornate in the simple yet elegant Chinese style. We ordered a full course dinner, a diner's delight, but neither of us ate much, and we picked at our food.

Karla lay in bed, wearing a silk nightgown, lovely against the pillows. I reached for her. She watched me, her eyes wide open, unblinking. We made love, but I was restrained, uncomfortable. I felt clumsy, awkward. Finally we lay apart, staring at the ceiling far above us.

"When you leave Taichung," she asked.

"In ten days."

"You come see me before you go?"

"No," I said. "I have to think about going back."

She studied the ceiling. "How you leave Taichung?"

"I'll be taking the train to Taipei. In Taipei I catch a flight to Japan, then the States."

"What time train leave?"

I told her. She was silent for a long time. She was still awake when I fell asleep.

In the morning we dressed and walked down to the dock. The sun had risen above the hills to the east, and the early morning light filtered through the haze on the lake. The surface of the water was still. Several small wooden boats were tied up to the dock; each had a canopy with curtains to protect passengers from the wind and rain. But now the sun was shining, and the curtains were tied back.

"Do you want to ride with other people," Karla asked.

"No," I said. "let's have a boat to ourselves."

While we were deciding which boat we wanted, a man with a camera came up and said something to Karla. "He wants to know can take picture."

Karla and I stood together on the dock, our arms awkwardly around each other, like dates posing before a high school dance, while the man took pictures. Finally, he nodded. He was done.

Karla spoke to a man sitting at the wheel of one of the boats. We climbed in and sat at the back, an empty row of seats between us and the boatman in front. As we moved out into the lake, Karla reached out and trailed her right hand in the water.

The boat moved slowly across the lake. The sides of the hills, which were covered with trees and bushes, came down steeply to the edge of the lake. We headed east into the sun and morning haze. The water was dark and still. After ten minutes we reached the far shore, the site of a prehistoric village which had been restored to look something like its original appearance when the original inhabitants lived on the shore of the lake. A variety of animals were on display including monkeys and something like a squirrel with a beaver's tail. Lizards ran across the rocks. Vendors sold souvenirs and things to eat. We walked around the area, looking at the displays and then back to the boat.

"You want to see temples?" I nodded.

The boat moved out into the lake. By now the sun was well overhead and the haze had disappeared. Ahead of us I could see a small island in the middle of the lake. As we moved closer, I saw steps leading up to a temple surrounded by trees at the top.

"Chinese build many temples on lake. This temple most beautiful."

We pulled up to the small dock. Karla and I walked up the steps to the top. The temple was open on three sides, a small ornate roof supported by cement columns, colorfully painted. Incense was burning on the altar. No one was around. Karla stepped up to the altar and made a short prayer while I stood back and admired the view.

Later, in the boat, Karla asked if I wanted to see another temple. I said yes, any reason to stay on the lake. The boat headed toward a high hill that bordered the southeast side of the lake. When we tied up to the dock, I could see steps leading up to the left. "Where is the temple?" I asked.

"Temple up there," she said, pointing. "Not finished yet. Will be largest, highest temple on lake." She set off ahead of me, climbing the steps at a rapid pace. We climbed steadily for five minutes. Finally we reached a level area where I could catch my breath. We could see across the lake to the hotel. The white hotel buildings contrasted strongly with the green of the surrounding vegetation and the deep blue color of the lake.

"Beautiful," I said.

"Now you see why we say this holy place," she said. "Gods must live here." She looked at me. "You believe in God?"

"I believe in the idea of God," I said. "But that there is a God who pays attention to all of us, no, I don't believe it. I used to, but not anymore."

"What you believe?" she asked.

"The only meaning life has is the meaning humans give to it. The ways we shape our lives, the uses we make of them. The patterns of living we develop. The only universal pattern is motion, circular motion. Things go around, in cycles. Maybe God is a large, self-generating, whirling force," I said. She looked at me, confusion and some pain showing in her eyes.

"How about you?" I asked. "Do you believe in God?"

"Oh, yes, I believe there is a God," she said.

"How do you know?" I said.

Sun-Moon Lake, near Taichung, Taiwan, March 1968.

"I feel, here," she said, tapping her chest.

"Well," I said, looking at the lake, "if there is a God, he'd want to live here."

When I looked around, Karla was moving up the next set of steps. I was wondering how much farther these stairs extended, when we turned a corner to the right, and there, rising above the final flight of stairs, set in some trees, was the temple. It was built against the side of the hill. Like the other temple, it was open on three sides, but it was larger. Construction was still being completed around the rear and sides. The altar area was mostly complete, and incense was burning there. Karla walked forward and made another prayer while I stood to the side, enjoying the view of the lake far below. It was calm, peaceful, serene. I let my mind go blank.

I sensed her standing beside me. She looked out over the lake. "What were you praying for?" I asked.

"I pray for my boy. I pray for my family." She paused. "I pray for you."

"Thank you," I said. I reached for her. She came to me and we held each other.

When we stepped out of the boat at the hotel dock, the man held out the pictures he had taken. I paid him and gave them to Karla. "Now you have your picture of me," I said.

* * *

The next day I was scheduled for my last flight to Vietnam. I was riding down with one of the new squadron pilots. We were going to fly the usual route, over to Naha, then down to Tuy Hoa. At Tuy Hoa I would get off the airplane, wait a few hours, and board the next airplane returning to CCK. I was logging a few hours in-country so that I could receive my combat pay for the month.

Chapter 24. Old Head

The flight left after dark, eight in the evening. I sat on the crew bunk the entire flight. After we landed at Naha, I walked into the flight line snack bar for one last look around. We departed Naha after midnight. I sprawled out in the cargo compartment seats, trying to get a little sleep. It seemed strange to be logging flying time without having anything to do with the progress of the flight.

We landed at Tuy Hoa just as the sky in the east was starting to lighten. Tuy Hoa. A nondescript concrete runway on the coast of the South China Sea. A base from which I had flown many shuttle missions. The base where I drank beer with my brother and burned scrip. The base where I drank Cokes and watched the F-100s bomb Tuy Hoa village at the height of the Tet attacks. The first base I had landed at with Duke Williams when it was still under construction and the last Vietnam base I would see before returning to the States. I sat impatiently in the crew area near the duty desk, killing time until the crew that was returning to CCK finally walked in.

I moved onto the returning aircraft, settled myself in the uncomfortable red webbed seats, and listened to the sound of the engines starting. Bounce and sway out to the engine run-up area. Engines checked, taxi into position on the runway and hold. Lean to the rear of the aircraft as takeoff power is applied. Gear and flaps up, back to CCK. I stepped off the aircraft about two o'clock in the afternoon. Almost twenty-four hours, flying into Vietnam and back. My last time as a crewmember in a squadron C-130. My last time in a C-130.

For the next few days I alternated between checking out of the base and going on day trips around the island. I cleared through supply, arranged my finances, gathered medical records. I joined a group of base residents on a bus tour of the southern part of the island, where we toured the Buddha at Changua, the old Dutch fort near Tainan, and some Chinese temples.

Returning to the bus after one stop, I saw an airman holding a small radio to his ear. When I asked him what the news was, he said that there had been an assassination. "They got the uppity sumbitch," he said. "Who?" I asked, thinking Ho Chi Minh, General Giap. "Martin Luther King," he said. Oh, holy Jesus, I thought. What kind of a country am I going back to? I had been gone for fifteen months. What was America like now?

My departure routine continued with visits to the transportation office, to personnel, to the base library to return books. One last time I walked around the base, to the base exchange for souvenirs, to the O-Club for my last taste of chicken. I got a haircut, packed my things, pulled my map off the wall, removing the pins I had stuck in during the early days, when I knew only names of fields. Now, field names immediately created images in my mind, visions of airfields, hills, and runways.

Then, suddenly, it was time to leave. I walked down to the flight line one last time. When I approached the scheduling desk to sign out, Horse Pemberton came out. "Stay here a minute," he said. "We've got something for you." Soon all of the available squadron members gathered by the scheduling desk. Lieutenant Colonel John Zimmerman, who had replaced Colonel Craig as squadron commander, was there, as well as a number of crew members and operations staff. Colonel Zimmerman had a small cardboard box in his hand. He opened it and pulled out a bronze mug engraved with my name and details of my time in the squadron. "Something to remember us by," he said.

I thanked them all and shook hands. I thanked Horse especially for taking good care of me. He had been a good friend. When I walked out of the squadron building for the last time, I could hear the low growl of C-130 engines on the ramp as two C-130s moved slowly out of the parking area towards the taxiway. The smell of jet fuel came through the air, mixed with the aroma of food cooking in the flight line snack bar. As I walked away from the flight line, the noises faded.

By the time I had completed my final sign-out tasks and packed my bags, time was running short. I had to catch a cab to the Taichung train station. The squadron driver gave me a lift to the gate, where I signaled one of the red taxicabs parked in a line on the road leading to Taichung. "The train station," I said. "And hurry. I'm late for a train."

The cab raced into town down the familiar road. We drove by the area where new base housing for families was under construction. Past the new CCK club. Past the rice paddies, the graveyard, the market area, through town to the train station. When we arrived, the train was standing in the station, conductors were walking up and down, telling everyone to get on board, the train was about to depart. One of the porters came up to the cab. I showed him my ticket and said I had two bags that had to be loaded. He nodded and ran off with my bags.

I was looking up and down at the train, trying to identify the car that had my number on it, when I suddenly realized Karla was standing there looking at me. At first I didn't recognize her. She was without makeup, in a modest print dress, her hair hanging naturally down along her neck. She stood before me a plain Chinese girl. Her eyes, always her most expressive feature, were large and sad. I didn't know what to do. We looked at each other on the crowded platform.

I stood in confusion and discomfort, seeing her unhappy, hearing the porters urging me to board the train. As if to release me from my immobility, she stepped towards me, touched my arm, and kissed me on the cheek. She was carrying a brown paper bag, which she handed to me, saying, "Take this. I make for you. You go now."

She motioned me toward the train, which was about to leave. I looked at the train and saw one of the porters waving to me. I walked quickly toward the train, stepping on board as it started to leave. I handed the porter my ticket, and after he handed it back, I looked out the window to wave good-bye. But I could not see Karla's face in the crowd of people standing on the platform, and the train moved away from the station and the platform and the people on it were gone from view.

I walked uncertainly up the aisle until I found my seat number and sat down by the window. I looked out the window as we moved out of Taichung. I opened the package she had given me; inside was an item of clothing, rolled up, something made of wool. I pulled it out and unrolled it. It was a scarf, a yellow woolen scarf, long enough to wrap around my neck twice. I wondered how long she had been knitting it. I marveled at its intricate detail.

A man came down the aisle carrying a hot water kettle, a rack of glasses, and a container of tea leaves. He motioned. Tea? I nodded. He set his rack down, pulled out a glass, scooped some tea leaves into the glass, and poured hot water into the glass. He held the glass out to me, I thought, so I reached for it. No, no, he shook his head. Too hot. And he placed it in a wooden glass holder attached to the window. That's what he had been reaching for. He stepped back and smiled at me. Ah, money, I thought, and reached in my pocket. No, he shook his head. No money. He smiled at me again and walked down the aisle.

Chapter 24. Old Head

The tea leaves in the glass moved around, and as they moved, the color of the water darkened. Finally the glass cooled, and I held it in my hand. I held it up to the light, swirling the contents in my right hand, watching the tea leaves as they moved around within the glass, tumbling, spinning, caught in the movement of the water as it darkened. With my left hand I held the scarf Karla had knit against my cheek, feeling the rough warmth of the wool against my skin. I sat there for a long time, swirling the tea and watching the tea leaves, holding the scarf against my cheek as the train wound among the low hills and rice fields towards Taipei.

After

Six months later I was a graduate student on the University of Michigan campus in Ann Arbor. I walked across the quad, the sun shining through the leaves of the trees that bordered Angell Hall. I wasn't yet used to seeing the miniskirts worn by many of the girl students. Nor was I used to seeing antiwar protestors selling peace pins and antiwar buttons on every corner of the quad. The Air Force had instructed those of us attending school on civilian campuses to avoid drawing attention to ourselves. We did not have to wear our uniforms once a week as had been the practice in the old days.

President Johnson, who had shaken my hand when I graduated from the academy, had announced he was through with Vietnam. I agreed with his decision. After flying up and down the coast of South Vietnam, after landing at just about every field large enough to accommodate a C-130, I had come to the same conclusion. Winning or losing the war had never been more to me than an abstract concept while I was flying across the skies of South Vietnam; the only activity that had mattered to me was the challenge of trying to fly my aircraft safely and not break anything or anybody on board. Through luck and the remarkable resiliency of the aircraft, I had been more or less successful.

About five o'clock on a Wednesday afternoon in late September, fifteen or twenty of us Air Force students gathered for our monthly meeting. We were sitting in a room on the second floor of the building which housed the campus ROTC programs in wooden class chairs, the kind with a little bit of desk on the right side. Outside the sunlight slanted through the classroom windows. We were being given the usual advice about watching ourselves around the antiwar types, getting haircuts on a regular basis, and keeping up with our administrative paperwork.

I was about to return to the small apartment where my pregnant wife and I were living when the class leader, the senior Air Force student on campus, a major, walked down the aisle where I was sitting. "I think these are yours," he said, handing me a large manila envelope, and passed by. I sorted through the items and found, lying among other papers, two stiff paper certificates. One of them awarded me the second and third oak leaf clusters to my Air Medal. The second said I had been awarded the Distinguished Flying Cross.

A few days later I opened the *Air Force Times* to read that Captain David Risher had died in the line of duty. His C-130 had encountered a hill near Bao Loc in bad weather. Everyone on board had been killed.

Dave. Spunky, aggressive Dave. I had shown him how to land at Khe Sanh. He had teased me when I started singing "Rock of Ages" on short final. He had probably checked out as an instructor pilot in February. He had died on September 6, 1968, after spending over six months as an IP. How much of that time had he spent flying the in-country shuttle checking out new pilots, I wondered. And Bao Loc, where he had led Denny and me into the dense fog that shrouded the runway ends, had reached up and taken him.

Time passed, and I completed my Air Force education and Air Force career. During those years there were new assignments, new tasks to be undertaken, new information to be absorbed. Occasionally, in the process of looking for something else, personnel files, class notes, old tax forms, I would come across those stiff certificates mixed in with other pieces of paper collected during those amazing, improbable months when I flew the C-130 in Southeast Asia, and I would slip back in time, as through a narrow door into the past, and recall the experiences that had defined me more than any other in my life.

What I realized only vaguely then, but have come to realize more fully since, is that after flying into Bao Loc, Phan Thiet, An Khe Golf Course, An Hoa, Kham Duc, Dak To, and Khe Sanh, the world could never be the same for me again. Those experiences changed me in ways I did not understand then and do not fully appreciate yet. Those awful, terrible, wonderful weeks on the shuttle gave me enduring visions of runways that no one but those who flew to them could ever really know.

Incident at Tuy Hoa

Flying south to Cam Ranh down the coast
In the dark hours before dawn, I saw the light
Ahead. An aircraft, our speed, our level,
Heading towards us. Harry, Ed saw it, said
Yes, it's coming for us. A slow left turn,
It changed course too, red light against the night.
We turned harder left; it followed. Again
Left, it disappeared from view when we banked
our right wing up, rolled out, looked left, no light,
banked hard left, rolled out due south, original course,
no light. Gone. Stars blinking at us. Tuy Hoa
approach said no aircraft on their radar.
Nor did they see us until we squawked flash
on their black screen a green pulse that faded.

Postscript

When I wrote *Runway Visions*, I was primarily concerned to describe the challenges I faced as I evolved from co-pilot to aircraft commander to instructor pilot. When you are actively participating in flying activities in a combat zone, it is difficult, if not impossible, to develop a sense of the larger scheme of events of which you are, at the time, a small part. It is sufficient to mentally prepare yourself (and the others with whom you may be flying) for the task at hand: that day's flight itinerary, the condition of your aircraft, the fields you will be flying into, the loads you will be carrying, the weather conditions, the latest reports of hostile forces. You are a very small cog in a very large set of interlocking wheels. The primary sense you have of the significance of your work is the magnitude of the resistance you meet as you attempt to accomplish the mission: the ground fire you receive, the difficulty you face trying to get in and out of small fields in uncooperative terrain. It is only much later, after the passage of time and the maturation of your perception, that you are able to more completely situate yourself in the ebb and flow of world events.

In 2017 the Public Broadcasting Service (PBS) presented ten-episode series *The Vietnam War*, by Ken Burns and Lynn Novick. The program describes the history of American involvement in Vietnam from the earliest assistance in the late 1950s to the final pull-out from Vietnam in 1975. The series devotes as much time to the political situation in Vietnam and the United States as it does to ground combat in Vietnam. Viewing this series gave me the opportunity to visualize, at least in a limited sense, how my flying activities could be seen in the context of American involvement in the Vietnam conflict. Even though combat airlift activities were not featured in any of the episodes, I was more than a little surprised to discover the significance of the events that occurred in Vietnam during the time that I was involved in airlift activities in Southeast Asia.

Presented in chronological order, the ten episodes cover unequal time periods, depending on the significance of the events presented in each segment. The first segment, the introduction (titled "Déjà Vu"), reviews events in Vietnam that occurred over nearly a one-hundred-year period, from 1858 to 1961. The key event of this period is the French military defeat at Dien Bien Phu, near the border between northern Laos and Vietnam, where the French army had established an outpost. As a result of a lack of supplies and poor military planning, the French outpost at Dien Bien Phu was overrun by Vietnamese forces in May of 1954. The French government withdrew from Vietnam, and the country was divided into two halves at the Geneva Conference in July of 1954. The vote that was intended to create a unified government never occurred.

The second episode ("Riding the Tiger") covers the events that occurred during a three-year period, from 1961 to 1963, when President John Kennedy increased military support to the South Vietnamese government. The third episode ("The River Styx") covers events in a two-year period, 1964 and 1965; after the death of President Kennedy, President Lyndon Johnson significantly increased American aid to South Vietnam. Johnson used the Gulf of Tonkin incident (August 1964) to increase the number of American advisors present in the country to 23,000 by the end of 1964. The fourth episode ("Resolve") describes events during an eighteen-month period, from January of 1966 through June of 1967; during this period, the military action was increasingly transferred from the South Vietnamese to the American military forces. The fifth episode ("This Is What We Do") covers only a six-month period, from July of 1967 through December of 1967; this segment describes the increasing resistance of the Viet Cong and North Vietnamese to the American presence in Vietnam. The sixth episode ("Things Fall Apart") covers a seven-month period, from January through July of 1968; it describes the 1968 Tet Offensive and its effects.

The remaining episodes describe the decision to withdraw from Vietnam and its impacts. The seventh episode ("The Veneer of Civilization") covers a one-year period, from June of 1968 through May of 1969; the eighth episode ("The History of the World") covers an approximately one-year period, from April of 1969 through May of 1970; the ninth episode ("A Disrespectful Loyalty") covers events that occurred during nearly a three-year period, from May 1970 to March 1973; and the final episode ("The Weight of Memory") describes events after March of 1973. The emphasis of the Burns and Novick Vietnam War program is on the ground fighting in Vietnam and on the political decisions made by various American and South Vietnamese leaders from 1960 through 1975, so Air Force (and Navy) military activities in Vietnam and Southeast Asia are mostly ignored.

I flew into, around, and across South Vietnam for only a fifteen-month period, from February of 1967 through April of 1968, a relatively short period of time given the long (approximately twenty-year) span of American involvement in Vietnam. However, as a result of the way in which Burns and Novick divided the program into its various segments, I was in Vietnam during the time periods covered by three of the ten segments: episodes four ("Resolve"), five ("This Is What We Do"), and six ("Things Fall Apart"). Two of these three episodes (five and six) cover the smallest time frames each (6–7 months) and describe some of the most climactic events of the war, especially the 1968 Tet Offensive, during which I delivered supplies into the besieged field of Khe Sanh. I had the feeling at the time that I was involved in some of the most significant and intense military events of the war, and I was right.

In the first Burns and Novick segment during which I was in Vietnam (episode four, "Resolve," describing events from January 1966 through June of 1967; I was in Vietnam starting in February of 1967), I was flying as a C-130 co-pilot, learning the routes and techniques of flying in-country. During the entire fifth Burns and Novick segment ("This Is What We Do," July–December 1967), I was flying as an aircraft commander, developing my confidence in flying the C-130 and learning about the challenging flying conditions in South Vietnam. During the sixth Burns and Novick segment ("Things Fall Apart," January–July 1968; I left Vietnam in April of 1968), I was flying as an instructor pilot, teaching other C-130 pilots new to Vietnam how to fly into small fields in South Vietnam and survive. It was during this period, especially as a result of the February 1968 Tet Offensive, that "things" really did "fall apart," for that was the period of the siege of Khe Sanh, the intense ground fighting at the Citadel at Hue, and the fighting in Saigon, when the walls of the American Embassy were scaled by the Viet Cong. Although no C-130 activities were shown on the program, I was pleased to see how often the C-130 appeared in film clips, usually showing men in combat gear stepping off of or on to a C-130.

I greatly appreciated the information that Burns and Novick provided about the political decisions that were made in the United States from 1960 to 1975 and about the growth of the anti-war movements of the time. When I was in Vietnam, I had only a vague idea of what was occurring back in the United States. When I returned from Southeast Asia I went directly to graduate school at the University of Michigan and was only too happy to indulge in literary study and ignore the war, which I had decided was a very bad idea, especially after the 1968 Tet Offensive revealed the weaknesses and vulnerabilities of the U.S.-backed South Vietnamese infrastructure, the effects of which I could easily see as I flew my C-130 from Da Nang to Saigon.

Because I had been flying across much of South Vietnam during the hectic days leading up to the 1968 Tet offensive and the weeks that followed, I had a bird's-eye view of the impact of the Tet offensive on American operations. I had flown over or into fields whose runways and ramps had been torn up by mortar attacks. And even though those runways and ramps had been quickly repaired, it was clear to me that American and South Vietnamese control over the countryside was practically non-existent. I had seen for myself from the cockpit of a C-130 aircraft the visual evidence of a well-coordinated defensive plan executed by a force determined to resist our attempts to establish control over people and territory about which we understood so little. The Viet Cong and North Vietnamese forces may have lost the battle, but they were in the process of winning the war.

Pronunciation Guide

This is how I pronounced the names of the places where we landed. The pronunciations may not be the same as the pronunciations used by the people who lived in those places.

An Hoa: on wah
An Khe: on kay
Ban Me Thuot: ban mee too-it
Bao Loc: bay-o lock
Bien Hoa: ben wah
Bin Thuy: bin tooey
Cam Ranh Bay: kam rahn bay
Can Tho: kan tow
Chu Lai: chew lie
Cu Chi: koo chee
Dak To: dock tow
Dalat: da lot
Dong Ha: dong ha
Dong Xoi: dong soy
Duc Pho: dick foe
Hue Phu Bai: way foo buy
Kham Duc: kam duck
Khe Sanh: kay sahn
Kontum: kon toom
Korat: core aht
Minh Thanh: min tan
Nakhon Phanom: na khan fa nom
Nha Trang: nah trang
Phan Rang: fan rang
Phan Thiet: fan thyet
Phu Cat: foo kat
Pleiku: play koo
Quan Loi: kwan loy
Quang Ngai: kwahng nigh
Quang Tri: kwahng tree
Qui Nhon: kween yon
Song Be: song bey
Song Mao: song mah-o
Tan Son Nhut: tahn sun not
Takhli: tahk lee
Tuy Hoa: tooey wah
Ubon: oo bahn (alternate: you bahn)
Udorn: oo dorn (alternate: you dorn)
Vung Tau: vung tah-o

Military History of David K. Vaughan

David K. Vaughan graduated from the United States Air Force Academy in 1962 with a Bachelor of Science degree in engineering sciences. Commissioned a regular officer in the United States Air Force, he attended pilot training at Webb Air Force Base, Big Spring, Texas, from 1962 to 1963. While at Webb AFB, he flew T-37 and T-38 jet trainer aircraft. Upon completion of pilot training, he was assigned to fly the KC-97G, a four-engine, propeller-driven air refueling aircraft, flown by units of the Strategic Air Command. He was assigned first to the 44th Air Refueling Squadron and then the 307th Air Refueling Squadron, both units located at Selfridge AFB near Detroit, Michigan. While assigned to the 44th and 307th Air Refueling Squadrons, Vaughan often served on alert status at Selfridge AFB and at remote sites, including Harmon AB, Newfoundland; Goose Bay, Labrador; and Namao Air Field, near Edmonton, Alberta, Canada. When the KC-97 and B-47 aircraft were removed from active service, he transitioned into Tactical Air Command's C-130 aircraft, a four-engine, turbo-prop, tactical airlift aircraft.

Vaughan received his checkout in the C-130E at Sewart AFB, near Smyrna, Tennessee. In the spring of 1965, he was assigned to the 347th Tactical Airlift Squadron at Dyess AFB, Abilene, Texas; there he flew a variety of missions, including a 60-day temporary duty mission to Europe, where he flew out of Evreux AB, France, and Mildenhall AB, England. His cargo-hauling missions took him to Spain, Greece, Turkey, Libya, Senegal, and Liberia, in addition to the standard cargo runs to England, France, and Germany. At Dyess he also flew missions in support of the Military Airlift Command on fights to the Pacific, Japan, and Alaska.

In 1967 Vaughan volunteered to fly C-130E model aircraft in Southeast Asia and was assigned to the 345th Airlift Squadron, located at Ching Chuan Kang AB, near Taichung, Taiwan, where he was stationed from February of 1967 through April of 1968. Vaughan flew a variety of airlift missions to the Philippines, Japan, Korea, Guam, Thailand, and South Vietnam. As an instructor pilot, he flew almost continually on the in-country shuttle in South Vietnam from December 1967 through March 1968, during some of the most intense activities associated with the 1968 Tet Offensive. During this period he was involved in aerial re-supply efforts to numerous small forward operating airfields, including An Khe, An Hoa, Dak To, LZ English, Kham Duc, Hue, Bao Loc, Song Be, and Khe Sanh. He flew into Khe Sanh many times and was awarded the Distinguished Flying Cross for his last flight into Khe Sanh on 4 February 1968, when he and his crew delivered a load of ammunition in marginal weather conditions while the base was surrounded by hostile forces. During his fifteen months in Southeast Asia, he accumulated over 1000 hours of flying time, 500 of which were combat hours. In addition to the DFC, he was awarded the Air Medal with two oak leaf clusters.

After returning from Southeast Asia, Vaughan attended the University of Michigan, where, under Air Force sponsorship, he received a Master of Arts degree in English literature and language. He then taught English as a member of the English department faculty at the Air Force Academy. In addition to providing classroom instruction, he flew as an instructor pilot in the Academy's T-41 Flight Indoctrination Program, instructing ten cadets during his time at the Academy. In 1971 he attended the University of Washington, again under Air Force sponsorship, receiving his PhD in English in 1974. Following three more years of faculty duty at the Academy, he completed his Air Force career by serving as a liaison officer with the Maryland Wing of the Civil Air Patrol and then as training officer for the Middle East Region of the Civil Air Patrol at Andrews AFB, Maryland. He retired from the Air Force after twenty years of service in 1982, having accumulated over 3500 hours of flying time in training and cargo aircraft.

Index

A Shau Valley, SVN 58–61
Abilene, TX 9–11
Agent Orange (defoliant) 50
Airborne Command and Communications Capsule (ABCCC): Da Nang 55–61; Udorn 81–83, 102–103
aircraft: A-1E 53, 62; A-7 127; AT-37 23; B-52 9, 59–61, 63, 185; B-57 52; Beech Baron 53; Beech Model 18 53 (Turbo Porter 20; UH-1 ["Huey"] 56; C-7 140; C-45 90; C-46 41; C-47 20, 53, 165; C-121 20, 182; C-123 23, 36, 50; C-130A 9, 25, 111, 142; C-130B 9, 25; C-141 12; CH-53 ("Jolly Green") 62; CH-47 ("Chinook") 42, 64; F-4 39, 55, 81, 152; F-100 23, 50, 53, 154; F-105 20, 81; KC-97 9; KC-135 9, 63; O-1 53; RF-4 81; T-28 20
An Hoa AB, SVN 141–2
An Khe AB, SVN 23, 42–6, 63
Andersen AFB, Guam 62–3
Angeles City, PI 103–8
Armed Forces Network Radio Station 25

Ban Me Thuot, SVN 51, 176
Bangkok, Thailand 18, 20, 79, 180
Bao Loc AB, SVN 113, 123–5, 135–7
Behnke, Roland 159
Bien Hoa AB, SVN 22, 25, 49–51, 94, 171
Big Spring, TX 9
Binh Thuy AB, SVN 68
Brault, Charles 159
Brown, Michael ("Brownie") v, 38–54, 72–80
Butler, Tommy Lee v

Cam Ranh Bay AB, SVN 22, 39–41, 87, 110–13
Cambodia 19
Ching Chuan Kang AB (CCK), Taiwan 9–11, 190, 195
Chu Lai AB, SVN 96
Clark AB, PI 12, 100
Craig, Robert 11, 27–30
Crozier, Harry 165–178

Cu Chi AB, SVN 144
Cupp, Floyd 38–54, 72–80

Dak To, SVN 18, 116, 156–8
Dalat, SVN 52, 89
Dallman, Howard 159
Da Nang AB, SVN 18, 55, 97
Davidson, Captain 190
Detroit MI 9
Don Muang AB, Thailand 20
Dong Ha, SVN 77, 130, 134
Dong Xoai, SVN 165
Douglas, Jim 62
Duc Pho, SVN 72, 140
Dunn, Elaine 123
Dyess AFB, (Abilene) TX 9–12

50th Troop Carrier Squadron 2, 31, 116
Figgins, Jerry 134–143
Fordham, Larry v, 123–132
Formosa Strait 12
Fredericks, Les 12, 83, 191

Glenn, Joe 116
Gray, Giles 62
Green, Wade 162
Greenwade, Don v
Gulf of Thailand 19

Hartwig, Major 87–101
Hennessey, Captain 68
Hill, Virgis v, 154
Hiroshima, Japan 144
Ho Chi Minh Trail 18
Hope, Bob 123
Hue (Phu Bai), SVN 127

Iwakuni AB, Japan 119

Johnson, Gerald 159
Jones, Colonel 187
Jones, Michael ("Mike") v, 38–54, 72–80, 82–106

Kadena AB, Okinawa 36
Kham Duc, SVN 166–170
Khe Sanh SVN 18, 77, 128, 130, 135, 146, 159–62
King, Martin Luther 195
Klein, Karl v
Knipp, William ("Bill") v, 182
Korat AB, Thailand 19, 184

Korean Tiger unit 26
Kramer, Ross v, 139
Kricker, Frank v
Kurile Islands, Japan 144

Laos 18
Lewis, Gomer v
Lorson, Edgar ("Bill") v
Lutton, Colonel 187

Mack, Joe 116
Mactan AB, PI 9
McAdory, Louis 72
McChord AFB, WA 10
McNair, Barbara 123
McWilliams, Charles ("Chick") 123–132
Mekong River 20
Miller, Ernie 81
Milstead, Aubrey 52
Minh Thanh, SVN 47
Morris, Michael 134–143
Mount Pinatubo, PI 13

Naha AB, Okinawa 9, 36
Nakhon Phanom AB, Thailand 62, 185
Nha Trang, SVN 36–46, 165
Nhon Co, SVN 176

Passarello, Frank v, 38–54, 72–80, 83
Pemberton, Horace ("Horse") v, 179–186, 195
Phan Rang, SVN 52, 123
Phan Thiet, SVN 51, 89–92, 125
Phillips, Thomas 123
Phu Cat, SVN 72, 129
Plain of Jars, Laos 18
Pleiku AB, SVN 23
Potter, William 66–68
USS *Pueblo* 144

Quan Loi, SVN 47, 72
Quang Tri, SVN 172–5
Qui Nhon, SVN 23, 41, 92

Reece, Charles 115
Richardson, Sidney v
Risher, David ("Dave") v, 136, 144–49
Rodke, Phil 117
Royal Thai Air Force 20

Index

Saigon, SVN 20, 25
Scholes, Edwin ("Ed") 134–186
776th Tropp Carrier Squadron 2, 32
Smith, Edgar 114
Smith, Robert ("Bob") 116
Smith, Scott ("Press-On") 9
Song Be, SVN 139
squadrons: 50th Troop Carrier Squadron 2, 31, 116; 345th Troop Carrier Squadron 2, 11, 32; 347th Troop Carrier Squadron 11, 32; 776th Tropp Carrier Squadron 2, 32
Strategic Air Command 9
Sun-Moon Lake, Taiwan 191

Tachikawa AB, Japan 11
Taichung, Taiwan 31, 188

Taipei, Taiwan 11, 119
Takhli AB, Thailand 186
Tan Son Nhut AB, SVN 25, 96
Tet Offensive (1968) 144–163
345th Troop Carrier Squadron 2, 11, 32
347th Troop Carrier Squadron 11, 32
Torchinski, Irving ("Ski") v, 123–132
Troy, Richard ("Zero") 81
Tuy Hoa AB, SVN 22, 52, 123

Ubon AB, Thailand 19
Udorn AB, Thailand 81
University of Michigan 198
Utapao AB, Thailand 185

Vaughan, Lantry (brother) 149
Vickery, Charles 190
Vung Tao AB, SVN 51

Waldron, Kirk v, 110, 117
Walker, Gerald 123–132
Ward, Dennis 136
Watkins, Elmer ("Dusty") v
Webb AFB, TX 9
Welch, Raquel 123
Westmoreland, William 50
Williams, Al v, 134–186
Williams, "Duke" 12–26
Wilson, Glen 118
Wing, 314th Tactical Airlift 2
Wright, Roger v

Zimmerman, John 195

www.ingramcontent.com/pod-product-compliance
Lightning Source LLC
Chambersburg PA
CBHW060343010526
44117CB00017B/2942